the uncharted self

Published by LIBERTY IN PRINT
www.libertyinprint.com

First edition
Digest format

the uncharted self

Identity, war, and the limits of psychology

Talal Alali

Contents

Preface

The emperor is naked indeed

Psychology between art and science

Psychology has long lived in the shadow of the hard sciences, torn between striving for scientific rigour and grappling with the complexities of human behaviour. Many psychologists committed to a scientific approach strive to adhere to strict principles. They develop robust research methods and utilize mathematics – specifically statistics – to draw conclusions, aiming for findings that can be generalized beyond their often-biased samples. These biases frequently arise due to non-representative sampling methods or limited sample sizes that restrict the applicability of the results.

The aim of psychological researchers is to discover the laws that govern thought and behaviour (Maclin & Solso, 2008).

However, an increasing number of researchers have shifted away from pursuing psychology as a scientific discipline, arguing that its validity does not rely on, nor require, a commitment to scientific rigour. A similar trend has emerged among therapists, with several highly promoted new treatments lacking a substantial scientific basis.

Yet the truth is simple and stark: if psychology continues to drift away from science, it risks devolving into pseudoscience, potentially causing more harm than good. Addressing people's ideas, behaviours, and emotions is not art; it is a sensitive endeavour that must be governed by science and scientific principles.

Why does empirical science matter?

Imagine a woman hospitalized with multiple severe injuries. She claims that she was deliberately hit by a speeding car and accuses me, Talal, of being the driver. She is certain that I did it on purpose but doesn't know why. Can the police dismiss her claim simply because they know me and believe I wouldn't commit such an act? What if it's just her word against mine – should that be enough to close the case? Now, suppose I have several witnesses who attest that I was with them elsewhere during the accident, yet several other independent witnesses saw me hit her and flee the scene. What if there were video recordings from multiple cameras capturing the incident?

I asked several colleagues to consider this scenario and share their thoughts. One interesting response was that it all depends on the country's legal system. In a society where people are incapable of critical thinking, facts don't really matter, and it comes down to who has more connections. If I were well-connected, no one would care about the evidence even if I were guilty. In contrast, in a civilized society – one governed by scientific principles and not corruption – the evidence would be weighed objectively, with verifiable proof such as recordings carrying more weight than hearsay.

For centuries, humanity languished in the dark ages of myths, superstition, and chaotic laws, where truth was dictated by authority or the masses, regardless of observed reality. Authorities – whether religious, social, or political – and the masses caused irreversible harm time and again by instructing people to deny the evidence before their eyes and instead accept empty rhetoric. Millions perished from contagious diseases because they were assured that illness was a divine decree, something to be endured rather than prevented, or that one could treat a disease without understanding its biological basis. Famines were seen as a natural part of life rather than something that could be prevented.

The Scientific Revolution, driven by great minds, liberated us from the shackles of ignorance, deficiency, and knowledge monopoly. Galileo Galilei and Nicolaus Copernicus are perhaps the most famous figures, with Galileo's telescopic observations and Copernicus's heliocentric model radically altering our understanding of the cosmos and our place within it. They rejected what were considered divine facts and challenged authority, establishing a new way of reaching knowledge free from biases and open to everyone. They allowed humans to be equal when it comes to understanding reality. However, they were not alone. Johannes Kepler refined Copernican theory with his laws of planetary motion, and Isaac Newton unified these ideas with his laws of motion and universal gravitation, laying the groundwork for classical mechanics.

Thinkers like René Descartes and Francis Bacon transformed philosophy and methodology, advocating for rationalism and empirical research, which became the bedrock of modern science. In medicine, Andreas Vesalius revolutionized human anatomy, while William Harvey discovered the circulation of blood, fundamentally changing our understanding of the human body. Robert Boyle's work in chemistry and Christiaan Huygens's contributions to optics and timekeeping further exemplified the broad scope of the Scientific Revolution.

David Hume, though not a scientist in the traditional sense, played a critical role in shaping the philosophy of science. His work in empiricism and scepticism laid the intellectual groundwork for modern scientific inquiry, challenging assumptions about causality and the limits of human knowledge.

These scholars shattered the myth of human and Earth centrality, revealing that we are not the centre of the universe. Instead, we are fragile primates, left to fend for ourselves in a short, often harsh life. This sobering truth forced us to work diligently to prevent disease, create wealth, and sustain ourselves.

This unsettling yet empowering truth is what has enabled us to harness electricity, provide running water, establish modern healthcare systems, and build advanced educational institutions. It is this bitter reality that has allowed us to live longer, healthier, and more fulfilling lives.

In psychology, there is a substantial and well-established body of research that adheres to rigorous scientific methods, particularly in the fields of cognitive psychology and neuropsychology. Researchers have developed an impressive array of tools and methodologies to observe and document human behaviour, allowing for a deeper understanding of both the causal and probabilistic nature of various types of behaviour. This research has also led to the discovery of the biological, social, and personal foundations that underlie human actions and mental processes.

Cognitive psychology, for instance, has greatly advanced our understanding of mental functions such as perception, memory, and decision-making by applying experimental methods and statistical analysis. Neuropsychology has bridged the gap between psychology and neuroscience, using brain imaging and other technologies to explore how different brain regions contribute to cognitive functions and behaviour. Many studies in psychiatry have documented the effects of neurotransmitters and psychoactive drugs on our psyche.

These scientific advancements in psychology have not only improved our understanding of the human mind but have also led to practical applications in various fields, including mental health treatment and education.

However, despite these advancements, a tension remains within the field between those who advocate for psychology as a rigorous science and those who argue for a more interpretive or subjective approach. More importantly, some of the most critical concepts in psychology – such as the self and identity – remain challenging to study empirically and are still far from being fully understood. The complexity of these subjects, intertwined with subjective experience, cultural influences, and individual differences, presents significant challenges to researchers seeking to apply scientific methods to their study.

The limits of psychology

Self-report and the crisis in psychology

The vast majority of current psychological studies rely heavily on questionnaires as their primary data collection method. These questionnaires assume that participants fully understand the questions and respond with complete honesty. This assumption has proven to be highly problematic. Many participants may not fully grasp the questions, may choose responses that do not accurately reflect their true feelings, or may even provide dishonest answers. Most importantly, most people refuse to take part in psychological studies. To mitigate these issues, psychologists often use convenience samples, such as their students, which introduces additional biases and limits the generalizability of findings. While some questionnaires have proven to be more robust and reliable than others, the fundamental problem remains that self-report measures are inherently flawed.

The elephant in the room: Trust in psychology

The film *The Invention of Lying* by Ricky Gervais and others offers a poignant exploration of how deeply ingrained lying is in our lives. It underscores a reality that extends beyond the screen: lying is not merely a personal flaw but a societal norm, woven into the fabric of our professional and social interactions. Whether one is a physician, lawyer, judge, academic, journalist, husband, daughter, or friend, the act of lying often becomes an unavoidable part of both professional roles and personal relationships.

Society seems to operate on an unspoken understanding that lying is permissible, provided it falls within certain boundaries and/or is done by certain people. There is a tacit agreement that some lies are acceptable, even necessary, while others are deemed unacceptable. The line between these categories, however, is at times blurred, allowing deception to thrive under the guise of social or professional responsibility.

Consider, for instance, how both George W. Bush and Tony Blair remained popular and well-respected by many despite their roles in the invasion of Iraq and the lies about weapons of mass destruction (WMD). The same can be said about the pro-Brexit "Leave" campaign, which prominently featured the false claim that £350 million per week was being sent to the European Union and that this money could be redirected to the National Health Service (NHS) after leaving the EU.

During COVID-19 lockdowns, numerous government officials worldwide repeatedly misled the public about the facts and consequences of the policies imposed on them. Many also violated lockdown rules and restrictions while pretending to adhere to them.

A further case is Bill Clinton, who infamously lied about his relationship with Monica Lewinsky. This deception became a defining moment in his presidency. But that didn't stop him from being entrusted important and respectable roles throughout his life, such as serving as a keynote speaker in the Democratic Party Convention in 2024. He started his speech by asking the cheering audience: "Aren't you proud to be a Democrat?"

Another striking example is the letter signed by 51 former heads of American intelligence agencies, who falsely claimed that Hunter Biden's laptop was not genuine – a statement that misled the public at a critical moment, impacting perceptions and decisions at the highest levels.

These instances, among countless others, highlight a disturbing reality: not only do senior figures lie with ease but there also exists a certain tolerance, even expectation, for deception under specific circumstances. Society, it seems, is willing to accept being lied to and deceived when it aligns with particular narratives or serves the interests of certain individuals or groups. This creates an environment where truth becomes malleable, shaped by those in power and accepted by those who prefer the comfort of a lie to the discomfort of the truth.

This tolerance for deception poses a significant threat to scientific psychology, a field that relies on honesty, accuracy, and the integrity of the speakers' talk. When lying becomes normalized, it undermines the very foundation of scientific inquiry, making it increasingly difficult to discern reality from fabrication.

In the broader context, this issue raises critical questions about the role of truth in society. If lying is tolerated, even expected, in certain spheres, what does this mean for psychologist and scholars who depend on the truth to uncover the workings of the human mind? These are questions that must be addressed if psychology is to maintain its scientific integrity and continue to contribute valuable insights into human behaviour.

First-hand professional experience

This challenge is not just theoretical but has practical implications that I have experienced first-hand. For several years, I was part of a project aimed at studying aggression, resilience, and empathy using both quantitative and qualitative methods. My colleagues and I meticulously designed our research, employing various questionnaires and interviews to collect data and test our hypotheses. Initially, the results were promising. We had selected a sample of academics and educated individuals who approached the study with care, thoughtfully filling out the questionnaires and engaging earnestly in the interviews.

However, as we expanded our sample to include a broader demographic – students, inpatients, outpatients, and the general public – the situation changed drastically. It became increasingly evident that, to obtain any statistically significant results, we would need to apply stringent exclusion criteria to clean the data. The reality of working with a diverse population hit us hard. Unlike our initial sample, the broader group displayed inconsistencies and inaccuracies in their responses, making it clear that not everyone was engaging with the research honestly.

After extensive discussions, we ultimately decided against applying exclusion criteria that would have skewed the results. We work in a university where teaching takes precedence over research, and in such an environment, the pressure to publish is not as intense as in research-focused institutions. This allowed us the freedom to prioritize integrity over the number of publications. As individuals committed to scientific rigour, we did not feel comfortable publishing results that had little value or reliability.

Upon closer examination of the interview transcripts, the depth of the issue became even more apparent. Many participants were actively lying, fabricating information and ignoring facts. The data they provided was rife with contradictions, not only clashing with established evidence and logical reasoning but also with their own statements within the same exchange. This phenomenon of dishonesty on the part of the subjects within our study was a microcosm of the larger issue that plagues scientific psychology: the challenge of obtaining truthful, reliable, representative data in a world where lying has become second nature.

Academic pressures and research quality

The over-reliance on flawed self-report measures is further compounded by the immense pressure on researchers to publish continually within a narrow speciality, often at the expense of methodological rigour. In a reasonable scientific environment, a researcher might spend years developing a robust research plan, conducting thorough studies, and analysing data before publishing meaningful results. However, the current academic system rewards quantity over quality. Researchers are incentivised to produce simple, easily executable studies that often contribute little to the advancement of the field. These studies are frequently designed to be non-controversial and safe, avoiding challenges to established norms or topics that might provoke debate. As a result, it is not uncommon for researchers with extensive publication records to struggle to identify any significant or novel contributions to their discipline. The field becomes saturated with superficial research that hinders genuine progress and innovation in psychology.

Researchers, editors, and reviewers contribute substantial time and expertise to the scientific publishing process, yet receive little to no compensation for their efforts. Researchers must design studies, collect data, analyse results, and prepare manuscripts, often with significant financial and personal investment—all without direct remuneration (Larivière, Haustein & Mongeon, 2015). Editors and reviewers, essential gatekeepers of scientific quality and integrity, also remain unpaid, despite their critical role in upholding publication standards (Teixeira da Silva & Dobránszki, 2015).

Paradoxically, a small group of publishers monopolise the industry, reaping enormous profits from unpaid academic labour while charging exorbitant fees for access to published work (Larivière, Haustein & Mongeon, 2015). The costs of accessing journals and scientific databases have become increasingly prohibitive, creating substantial financial barriers for researchers and institutions alike (Van Noorden, 2013). This paywall not only restricts access to knowledge but also perpetuates inequalities, as only well-funded institutions and researchers can afford comprehensive access to current scientific literature (Schimmer, Geschuhn & Vogler, 2015).

In the competitive world of academia, the pressure to publish is immense, driven by the need to secure and maintain academic positions. The pursuit of a high h-index, a metric that measures both the productivity and citation impact of a researcher's publications, has become an obsession for many academics. This obsession often leads to the production of papers that are aimed more at boosting one's academic metrics than at contributing meaningful knowledge to the field. In some cases, this has resulted in a culture of reciprocal citations, where academics cite each other's work primarily to enhance citation counts rather than to engage meaningfully with the content.

This relentless pressure to publish has also contributed to more troubling trends within academia. The drive to increase one's h-index has, in some instances, led to the publication of fake papers and a rise in plagiarism – practices that are becoming alarmingly more common and, in some circles, more acceptable. Moreover, the manipulation of p-values, known as "p-hacking," has become a widespread practice, where researchers selectively report data or statistical results to achieve significant outcomes. This practice not only undermines the integrity of research but also contributes to the ongoing crisis of replicability in psychology and other scientific fields, where a significant number of studies fail to produce the same results when repeated.

Unscientific research and its impact

In 1973, David Rosenhan's study, "On Being Sane in Insane Places," was published in *Science*, becoming one of the most influential works in psychology. The study involved eight "pseudopatients," including Rosenhan himself, who feigned auditory hallucinations to gain admission to various mental institutions in the United States. All were diagnosed with psychiatric disorders despite behaving normally after their admission. This study claimed that mental hospitals were fundamentally flawed in diagnosing mental disorders, suggesting that even trained psychiatrists could not reliably distinguish between sanity and insanity.

Rosenhan's paper begins with the provocative question: "If sanity and insanity exist, how shall we know them?" He argued that there was no reliable way to distinguish between sanity and insanity and that the labels applied by psychiatry were arbitrary and often harmful. Despite being one of the most cited psychological studies in history – garnering over 5,000 citations – it was never replicated, raising significant concerns about its validity. In 2023, the historian of psychiatry Andrew Scull, drawing on the investigative work of journalist Susannah Cahalan, revealed that Rosenhan's study was a case of scientific fraud – a fabrication (Cahalan, 2019; Scull, 2023).

"On Being Sane in Insane Places" was not merely a flawed study; it was a fraudulent assault on psychiatry, empiricism, and the very principles of scientific inquiry. By claiming that even trained psychiatrists could not reliably distinguish between sanity and insanity, Rosenhan and those influenced by his work disregarded the substantial body of knowledge that had been built over millennia.

The repercussions of Rosenhan's study were profound and far-reaching, fostering antipathy towards psychiatric diagnoses and mental health professionals at a time when trust in institutions was already waning due to events like the Vietnam War and the Watergate scandal. This cultural backdrop made Rosenhan's findings particularly appealing to a public eager to challenge authority. The study significantly influenced revisions of the Diagnostic and Statistical Manual of Mental Disorders (DSM), leading to a more structured, symptom-focused approach in an attempt to restore credibility to psychiatry. Despite its eventual discrediting, the legacy of Rosenhan's work continues to shape public perception and institutional practices, contributing to the decline of trust in psychiatry. The real-world consequences for patients are stark, as the study potentially delayed or denied appropriate care to those genuinely in need. The ripple effects of this study continue to profoundly influence how mental illness is perceived and treated, shaping both public understanding and medical practices.

Similarly, the Stanford Prison Experiment (SPE), conducted by Philip Zimbardo in 1971, not only breached ethical standards in psychological research but also propagated a distorted and unsubstantiated view of human nature (Blum, 2018; Le Texier, 2019). Designed to explore the effects of perceived power in a simulated prison environment, the SPE suggested that ordinary individuals would commit extreme acts of cruelty when given authority. However, like Rosenhan's study, the SPE has faced heavy criticism for its lack of scientific rigour and ethical considerations. Serious concerns have been raised about the researcher's involvement in the experiment and allegations that participants were encouraged or pressured to act cruelly.

Both Rosenhan's study and the SPE present a deterministic and reductionist view that situational factors can heavily influence or dictate behaviour, undermining personal responsibility in moral decision-making. Moreover, both studies violated fundamental research methodologies, and their results contradict logic as well as observable realities. Historical examples, such as the resistance of many German soldiers and civilians during World War II who refused to join the Nazis, and the defiance shown by American soldiers during the Vietnam War against participating in atrocities, demonstrate that individuals can exercise moral agency even in coercive environments. The ongoing war in Ukraine further illustrates this point; it is unethical to claim that all Russians are complicit in the killing of Ukrainian civilians or that all Ukrainians uniformly oppose the Russian occupation. These examples challenge the notion that situations unilaterally determine behaviour and call into question the assumption that collective identity is self-evident.

These interconnected issues – ranging from questionable research practices to ethical lapses – compromise the integrity of psychological research and undermine public trust in the field. Addressing them is essential to restore rigour and foster genuine progress in psychology.

References

Blum, B. (2018). *The lifelong harm of the Stanford Prison Experiment*. Medium. Retrieved from https://medium.com

Brembs, B. (2019). Reliable novelty: New should not trump true. *PLOS Biology, 17*(2), e3000117.

Cahalan, S. (2019). *The Great Pretender: The Undercover Mission That Changed Our Understanding of Madness.* Grand Central Publishing.

Larivière, V., Haustein, S., & Mongeon, P. (2015). The oligopoly of academic publishers in the digital era. *PLOS ONE, 10*(6), e0127502.

Le Texier, T. (2019). Debunking the Stanford Prison Experiment. *American Psychologist, 74*(7), 823-839.

Maclin, K., & Solso, R. (2008). *Experimental Psychology*. Pearson.

Rosenhan, D.L. (1973). On being sane in insane places. *Science, 179* (4070), 250-258.

Schimmer, R., Geschuhn, K. K., & Vogler, A. (2015). *Disrupting the subscription journals' business model for the necessary large-scale transformation to open access*. Max Planck Digital Library.

Scull, A. (2023). Rosenhan Revisited: Successful Scientific Fraud. *Journal of the History of the Behavioral Sciences, 59*(2), 1-15.

Teixeira da Silva, J. A., & Dobránszki, J. (2015). Problems with traditional science publishing and finding a wider niche for post-publication peer review. *Accountability in Research, 22*(1), 22-40.

Van Noorden, R. (2013). Open access: The true cost of science publishing. *Nature, 495*(7442), 426-429.

Chapter 1

Who are we?

Our expectations, attitudes, social relationships, goals, psychological problems, and the way we live our lives are all intimately connected to our sense of who we are, according to a significant body of research. If understanding the function of each part of the brain is the ultimate goal for neurologists, and understanding the aging process is the grand ambition of medical researchers, then unravelling the complexities of the self is the pinnacle of achievement for psychologists in general and social psychologists in particular.

The way we perceive others is also largely based on our understanding of who we are and who they are. We see ourselves and others as independent humans and/or members of certain groups that have their own values and norms. Studying how we attempt to understand ourselves is a central question in psychology. We tend to understand ourselves through introspecting our values, beliefs, accomplishments, and self-image. We interpret our behaviour through the lens of how we see ourselves, how others see us, how we see them, and how we see this world. Hence, the concept of self is not just a theoretical construct; it actively shapes our reality and guides our interactions with the world.

A few years ago, I conducted open-ended interviews with individuals diagnosed with mood disorders. I asked them to speak about their experiences and what their goals, fears, and hopes were. My goal was to establish a connection between their expectations and the outcomes of the treatment, as well as how they evaluated medications versus talk therapy. I recorded these interviews, transcribed them, and then analysed the content. To my surprise, the main concern was not the outcome of the treatment or its efficacy.

Forty-two of the sixty-one interviewees discussed themselves as the central issue. Whether they indicated they could overcome their mental disorder or felt resigned, and whether they were satisfied with the medications or refusing to take them, their self-presentation consistently aligned with the stories they told about who they are. One of the most intriguing findings from this research was that individuals constructed complex, multifaceted narratives to present themselves in distinct ways. Each of these narratives of the self is a complex construction, characterized by its own internal logic and specific theme, and designed to achieve a final goal.

Phrases like "Being depressed is who I am," "I can't imagine living without anxiety," or "Being a drug addict is all I know" are common responses from patients in clinical settings when discussing their struggles. These statements reflect a deep connection between identity and psychological troubles, where individuals come to see their disorders not just as conditions they experience but as intrinsic parts of their identity.

Similarly, notions like "I see myself as a victim," "We are all victims," and "Everyone has a mental disorder" are prevalent and essential in psychotherapy. These beliefs underscore a fundamental tendency where people define themselves by their mental health challenges or perceived victimhood, often internalizing these roles as central aspects of their identity.

Understanding the self, therefore, is not about understanding who we are in a vacuum – it's about understanding how our identities are formed, how they influence our behaviour, and how they are shaped by our interactions with society. For psychologists, this pursuit of understanding the self is as much about exploring the internal processes that define individual identity as it is about recognizing the external forces that shape and reinforce it.

The importance of understanding the self extends beyond those who study psychology. Many people, even those with no formal background or interest in psychology, intuitively recognize the value of understanding themselves and others. Self-help books and coaching are based on the notion of reaching a true understanding of oneself to improve the quality of life.

I am an English gentleman!

A few years ago, I found myself in a pub in Edinburgh, intending to have a meal as quickly as possible and go back to work. The place was packed, and everyone was mesmerized by a football match being aired on a screen – it was part of the Euro tournament, with Scotland facing England. Despite my deep aversion to watching football (though I do enjoy playing it), I found myself caught up in the mass euphoria, watching and cheering along with everyone else.

At one point, a particularly skilful player took possession of the ball and made a dash toward the opponent's goal, bypassing several defenders. I cheered enthusiastically, only to realize that the pub had suddenly fallen dead silent, with many eyes gazing directly at me. I sat down instantly, and my eyes moved from the screen to focus on the horrible half-cooked burger. Luckily, the goalkeeper managed to catch the ball and gradually, the piercing eyes returned to the match, and the mass euphoria resurged. I was genuinely relieved that the player didn't score.

A few minutes later, a waitress brought me a plate of fries I hadn't ordered. She leaned in and whispered, "We're the minority here, so be careful. You don't want to end up on their bad side." The brunette waitress gave me a charming smile but there was a hint of concern in her eyes. It felt oddly comforting to know that she and I were now part of the same group. Soon, I realised that everyone else in the pub – all fifty-plus people – were passionately cheering for Scotland.

I couldn't help but notice that several of the loudest fans were foreign students. Some of them were donning Scottish hats and scarves and were shouting loudly for Scotland. In that moment, the question of identity resurfaced in my mind. Ruth, the waitress, assumed that she and I belonged to the same group: England fans, I presume. This was a pleasant change, as usually people would ask where I am from, and once I say Kuwait, many would assume that I am Arab, Muslim, and conservative. Some even imagine that I must have four wives and twenty children. When I try to explain that there are many Kuwaitis who are neither Arab nor Muslim, and that Kuwaitis come from different ethnicities, cultures, religions, and languages, the instant sceptical response is often, "But the majority?" Even when I clarify that there is no dominant majority, the conversation usually circles back to stereotypes about Arabs and Muslims – multiple wives, wealth, and a lack of meaningful occupation.

Different identity for different occasions

People tend to define themselves in various ways, but the question remains: Are we truly all of these things, some of them, or none? Are we members of a certain number of groups that shape our thoughts, actions, and feelings? Or are we autonomous individuals mainly concerned with our own personal interests? Can we be both at the same time?

Perhaps many people are simple animals driven primarily by the desire to fulfil the basic biological needs, by a rhetoric of "we against them" to satisfy these desires. Are we deep inside politicians who use our memberships in groups to satisfy our personal desires at the expense of the others, who are similar to us?

The complexities of identity and self-definition often come to the forefront in moments of crisis. When riots broke out in the UK in July of 2024, many of my academic friends found themselves confused and puzzled. Some were instructed by their superiors to adopt a specific stance. Once again, the basis for this directive was rooted in the idea of "us" as faculty members of a particular university and hence we should say x, y, and z.

During the Gaza conflict, which erupted after Hamas attacked Israel, killing and kidnapping civilians, several universities issued directives to their faculty members, advising them to remain compassionate and neutral, refraining from taking sides. Their administration assumed the role of the authority, dictating not only the identity of the academics but also how they should express that identity. In many cases the freedom of speech was stifled, and the society lost an important debate that could have informed them about what is going on.

These tension between individual autonomy and the collective identity imposed by institutions or groups resurfaced whenever there is a pressing question that needs to be addressed. When academic institutions, workplaces, or other organizations attempt to define who we are, they implicitly dictate how we should think, act, and feel. The expectation that we conform to a collective identity, especially in times of conflict or crisis, raises significant questions about the nature of self and the extent to which we can truly claim to be authentic.

Are we simply the sum of the groups we belong to, moulded by the expectations and norms of our environments? Or is there a core self that persists, regardless of the external pressures we face? The struggle to reconcile these aspects of identity is a fundamental challenge, one that becomes particularly acute in times of social upheaval and conflict.

The self and identity in social psychology

Does every human have a solid understanding of who he or she is? Can we have more than one self per body? The age-old question of the self is one of the most fascinating yet complex topics.

It is difficult to find an important philosopher or serious thinker who didn't discuss the self in general and identity in particular.

In social psychology, the concepts of "self" and "identity" are central to understanding human behaviour, emotions and cognition. Although these terms are closely related, they are distinct in their meanings and implications. The "self" generally refers to an individual's sense of who they are, encompassing their thoughts, feelings, and beliefs about themselves. This concept includes various elements such as self-concept, self-esteem, self-awareness, and self-perception. On the other hand, "identity" pertains to the social dimensions of an individual's self-concept. It involves how individuals define themselves in relation to others and the social groups to which they belong. Identity is a multifaceted construct that encompasses social identity and personal identity, each contributing to the way individuals perceive and understand themselves within a broader social context.

Identity

Identity is one of the most powerful components of human psychology.

During the Iraq-Iran War (1980-1988), millions of Shia Iraqis fought against Shia Iranians because they identified as Iraqis first. In stark contrast, thousands of Shia Iraqi soldiers defected to join the Iranian forces, fighting against their own country. Notably, the Badr Brigades, a Shia Iraqi force that fought for Iran, have been part of the Iraqi government since 2003. While many Iraqis view them as traitors and Iranian agents, their supporters see them as devout Shias.

In World War II, thousands of American soldiers of German descent fought under the American flag against their ancestral homeland. Similarly, in Ukraine, many citizens defended their nation against the Russian invasion, willing to sacrifice their lives for their identity. Yet, over a million Ukrainians moved to Russia, choosing a new life, language, and culture over their homeland.

The Rwandan genocide exemplifies how identity can drive people to extreme actions. Although sharing the same culture, ethnicity, and language, the Hutus and Tutsis slaughtered each other, driven by a fractured sense of identity.

While people often support their ingroup members, history is replete with examples of betrayal, from the kapos in concentration camps to politicians who harm their people for self-interest. Herodotus, in his *Histories*, distinguishes between "us," the civilized, and "them," the savage enemies.

Collective identity is central to human social life and a fundamental concept in social psychology (Hitlin, 2003; Tajfel, 1981; Tajfel & Turner, 1979, 1986). An individual's membership in a specific group plays a significant role in their interactions and understanding of the world. Identity provides a lens through which we understand ourselves and others, setting a standard against which we gauge our actions and beliefs.

Today, identity is studied across disciplines, including political science, history, sociology, and psychology. It attains its weight from its evident role in our daily life as individuals and groups. Many researchers argue that identity helps people find their position in relation to others and events (Schwartz, 2005). It shapes our understanding of who we are, who our group is, and how we differ from others. It provides us with a standard to gouge our feelings and acts against.

In traditional social psychology, identity is what defines us. It indicates who we are similar to, who we differ from. Moreover, it dictates expected, accepted, or discarded behaviours and beliefs that various groups of people have (Haslam & Reicher, 2006).

Psychology distinguishes between two types of identity: self-identity, the individual's understanding of themselves as a distinct human being (McCall & Simmons, 1978), and collective or social identity, based on affiliation with a group of other individuals sharing common traits that unite them as one group and differentiate them as individuals from non-group members (Edwards & Potter, 1992; Potter, 1996; Sacks, 1992; Wetherell & Mohanty, 2010; Widdicombe & Wooffitt, 1995). It is important to stress that the two identities are related. To establish themselves as unique, people tend to compare themselves to the ones close to them.

Collective identity and social psychology

The current study of identity in psychology evolved from the theories of Cooley (1902), Mead (1934), and Goffman (1959), which attempted to explain the self. Cooley (1902) argues that a person's understanding of his- or herself is based on the way other people see that person. This idea of the effect of other people's understanding of us on our understanding of our selves was further developed by Mead (1934). Mead attempted to explain the self through examining the relationship between the self and society. In his theory, he argues that the self could be described as having two parts, 'me' and 'I'. The 'me' is shaped by the society, while the 'I' alters our perception of the way the society views us. Mead constructs the relationship between the self and the society as a two-way relationship; on one side, the self plays several specific roles within society and on the other side, fulfilling these roles shapes the self. In these theories, the self is explained as a result of the roles a person plays within society. Widdicombe (1995) summarises this notion as:

> Identity produces particular kinds of action, or role performances which, in turn, are situated within a social milieu and presumably alter or shape the dynamic context. The image of self within role theory is a fluid, dynamic agentic one in which negotiation and "mutual shaping" between self and others who make up society are central. (p. 35)

Goffman drew on these understandings to create his dramaturgical theory. In this theory, he explains the relationship between the self and society through comparing them to theatrical acting.

He describes social rules as masks and each person has many different masks. Goffman (1959, p.9) summarises his theory as:

> On the stage one player presents himself in the guise of a character to characters projected by other players; the audience constitutes a third party to the interaction - one that is essential and yet, if the stage performance were real, one that would not be there. In real life, the three parties are compressed into two; the part one individual plays is tailored to the parts played by the others present, and yet these others also constitute the audience.

Moreover, Goffman maintains that there is a "distinctive moral character" which governs people's interaction with each other (1959, p. 24). This character is what gives universal meaning to people's interaction. Additionally, Goffman indicates that every society is governed by specific moral codes, and thus "any individual who possesses certain social characteristics has a moral right to expect that others will value and treat him in an appropriate way" (1959, p. 24).

The importance of the theories of self that were put forward by Cooley, Mead and Goffman to the current study of social identities is in their understanding of the relationship between the identities and the society. It is fair to say that these theorists have laid down the foundation of examining identities as part of the social interaction between the person and society. Nonetheless, until the 1970s social psychological studies approached human behaviour in general as individualistic behaviour. Collective or group behaviour was usually dismissed as "irrational" and "pernicious" (Herrera, 2003, p. 28). Consequently, collective identities were examined as an individualistic trait or predisposition rather than a product of interaction. Tajfel criticises the lack of adequate attention to the effect of human interaction on our behaviour, stating that:

> Experimental social psychology as we know it today is irrelevant only to the extent that it is a social science practised in a social vacuum... social psychology is a scientific study of hu-

> man behaviour; that the kind of behaviour it is concerned with is social behaviour (i.e. interaction between individuals, singly or in groups); and that this social behaviour is a function of or is determined by or is related to the social context in which it takes place. (1981, pp. 18-19)

There are two main theories that propose a comprehensive understanding of collective identity: Social Identity Theory and Self-Categorization Theory. Both remain significant and still function as basis for research in social psychology.

Social Identity Theory

One of the most influential theories that address collective identity in social psychology is Tajfel's (1971) Social Identity Theory (SIT). This theory originated in earlier studies of discrimination between groups (Tajfel, 1969, 1970, 1971). In several studies, Tajfel and later Turner (1975, 1978) found that when people are assigned to different groups, they develop social identities related to membership in these groups. As a result of developing these social identities, people start categorising themselves and others into in-group members or out-group members. Tajfel argues that social identities make people behave as members of the group rather than as independent individuals. He indicates that social identities function as a way of uniting in-group members and differentiating them from out-group members. Tajfel defines social identity as:

> ...that part of an individual's self-concept which derives from his knowledge of his membership of a social group (or groups) together with the value and emotional significance attached to that membership. (1978, p. 63)

Moreover, Tajfel (1978) argues that every society is composed of several self-evident social groups, and every individual is a member of different groups at the same time. Social groups stand in comparison to each other (e.g., gender, race, class). These groups provide us with salient social identities, which in turn influence our understanding of ourselves and others. SIT suggests that the various social identities people have are derived from their membership in various social groups at the same time. According to this theory, social identity is a functional and consequential objective designed to provide its members with a positive view of themselves. Tajfel (1978) further indicates that people tend to compare their group with other groups in a selective way that allows them to favour their in-group members over out-group members. Hence, one of the main notions of this theory is that identity is produced by a process of categorisation and comparison between groups. Tajfel (1981) maintains that "social categorisation can therefore be considered as a system of orientation which helps to create and define the individual's place in society" (p. 255). Moreover, every social identity is connected to the understanding of the group's norms and characteristics (Tajfel, 1981).

Social identity is understood in SIT as a salient but also flexible entity. Tajfel (1981) argues that if a specific collective identity stops providing its members with a positive evaluation of themselves, the members apply "social creativity strategies." These strategies allow the group members to maintain a positive social identity without leaving their group. One of these strategies is re-evaluating specific negative characteristics of their in-group in a way that makes these features more appealing and less negative. Another technique is bringing a historical characterisation or positive incident to the present so that the group seems more positive (Tajfel, 1981). Moreover, SIT suggests that members may leave their group for a new one once they become aware that it does not provide them with a positive identity. This indicates that individuals are capable of changing their collective identity when it can no longer serve the purpose it was created for.

To conclude, Social Identity Theory views social categories and social identities as mainly internal cognitive paradigms designed to provide us with self-satisfaction through affiliation with other individuals. In SIT, people's affiliation with various groups is a self-evident fact, although the way they view that affiliation is open to modification. It is important to note that SIT, along with Self-Categorization Theory (SCT) by Turner (1985), represents a breakthrough from the individualistic approach that dominated modern social psychology for a long time (Herrera, 2003).

Self-Categorization Theory

Self-Categorization Theory (SCT) originated in the work of John Turner (1982, 1984) and his colleagues. This theory is described by many researchers as a cognitively-oriented development of SIT. It is based on applying a cognitive approach to explain some of the critical ideas of SIT. SCT concentrates on how people identify with their social categories and the role of the process of comparison between different groups in creating collective identities. Turner argues that people have different social identities, and it is the various collective contexts that activate different social identities. Turner, Oakes, Haslam, and McGarty (1994) summarise the main ideas in SCT as:

> Self-categories are cognitive groupings of self and some class of stimuli as identical and different from some other class. Personal identity refers to self-categories that define the individual as a unique person by his or her individual differences from other (in-group) persons. Social identity refers to social categorizations of self and others, self-categories that define the individual in terms of his or her shared similarities with members of certain social categories in contrast to other social categories. (p. 454)

According to this theory, people have two forms of identity. The first is personal identity, which Turner describes as the identity that shapes our behaviour in the absence of a group context. The second identity is collective identity. The two identities result from "different levels of self-categorization" (Turner et al., 1994, p. 454). A social group is defined as "two or more individuals who share a common social identification of themselves" (Turner, 1982, p. 15).

One of the main bases of SCT is the notion that the world is very rich and complex, and people's cognitive abilities are limited. Consequently, we need to simplify the world by organising its components into categories. The categorisation process enables people to deal with the outside world effectively. Hence, categorising the components of the environment is done for cognitive reasons. People categorise themselves and others based on affiliation with specific categories such as gender, culture, and race. This implies that these categories are based on factual elements. The processes of categorisation and the formation of social identity take place within the brain. Thus, social identity is seen as "the cognitive mechanism that makes group behaviour possible" (Turner, 1984, p. 527). SCT explains the cognitive aspect of identity as:

> One aspect of the self is the cognitive aspect, the system of concepts of self a person uses to define him- or herself. Self-concepts can be thought of as self-categories or self-categorisations: cognitive groupings of the self as identical, similar or equivalent to some class of stimuli in contrast to some other class. (Turner, 1991, p. 78)

Turner (1991) explains how people affiliate themselves with specific groups at specific times through the idea of a meta-contrast ratio. In this paradigm, any "group of stimuli is more likely to be categorised as a single entity to the degree that the differences within that group (on relevant dimensions) are smaller than the differences between that group and some other stimuli" (Turner, 1991, p. 156). Furthermore, Turner (1991) argues that collective identities are based on real factors such as previous experience, goals, specific features, and so on. SCT also suggests that the collective identity activated must be appropriate to the situation. One of the most important ideas of SCT is the notion of depersonalisation – that is, as a social identity becomes salient, the personal identity that differentiates the person from other individuals diminishes.

This means that people behave as representatives of the characteristics of the group. In this case, group members behave in ways that confirm the stereotypical behaviour of the group. It is important to stress that SCT argues that the prototype of any group is not fixed; rather, it "varies as a function of the comparative context within which the group defines itself" (Turner, 1991, p. 169).

Common ground and differences between SIT and SCT

SIT and SCT share many fundamental similarities. In both theories, collective identity is explained as a product of comparison with relevant others. The "groups" in SIT or "categories" in SCT are taken as self-evident universal entities. For both theories, collective identity is seen as an internalised external reality. Social identity is a product of a cognitive system based on social comparison, which makes people perceive themselves as members of specific groups and not others. One of the main differences between SCT and SIT is the flexibility in the relationship between individual and social identities. Tajfel argues that the meaning of the group is open to reinterpretation and adjustment. According to SIT, people redefine the group or even leave their group if it stops providing them with a positive identity. In contrast, SCT views categories as universal and not open to reinterpretation, as Reicher (1996) notes:

> Thus, even if recent studies of stereotyping in the self-categorisation tradition insist that the group definition depends upon and varies with the social relations obtaining in context, they continue to operationalise (if not conceptualise) identity as a set of traits. (p. 329)

To sum up, Social Identity Theory and Self-Categorization Theory suggest that people perceive themselves and others either as in-group or out-group members. Group membership functions as a way of achieving a positive evaluation of the self. Each person is a member of various groups. People favour in-group members over individuals who do not belong to their group(s). People have various social identities at the same time, and each of these identities is activated by a specific stimulus in the absence of the other identities. Furthermore, conflicts between different social groups are an expected result of the existence of contradicting collective identities (Hogg, 1996, 2000, 2001a, b; Hogg & Abrams, 1988, 1999; Hogg, Terry & White, 1995). To date, most researchers who subscribe to SCT and SIT share the notion that social identity is a self-evident, independent factor (Herrera, 2003). Thus, the focus is on examining the effect of having this or that identity on people's interaction with each other. Moreover, most of these researchers treat the environment and people's perception of events as factual, and furthermore, they focus on examining people's behaviour individually. Despite being among the most influential and important theories, SIT and SCT are incapable of providing comprehensive explanations for group formation and collective behaviour, especially in relation to conflicts.

Critique of SIT and SCT

An increasing number of researchers influenced by Social Identity Theory and Self-Categorization Theory have started to examine how people present and argue over social identities in their talk-in-interaction and what their take on the event is (e.g., Hopkins & Reicher, 1996; Reicher & Hopkins, 2001). They report that social identities are not fixed or self-evident but are open to modification within the interaction. Huddy (2002) argues that:

> Self-categorization theory places an undue emphasis on the power of context to explain intergroup behaviour. This emphasis on situations ignores individual differences in identification, fails to consider the power of enduring cross-situational forces conveyed by history and culture to shape group boundaries and meaning, and neglects the frequently contested nature and meaning of group membership. (p. 826)

Similarly, Billig (1996) criticises a fundamental principle of SCT, which indicates that people do not have the capacity to process the complex components of the environment without categorising them into clusters such as race, gender, class, and so on. He argues that this understanding implies that people perceive and describe the different components of the world in one way. On the contrary, he maintains that people can and do describe subjects, objects, events, and people in many different ways. Carbaugh (1996) points out that there has been a shift in the view of identity from the "mentalist notion," which treats it as something that causes human behaviour, into something that is more of a "communication practice" among an increasing number of researchers in psychology. The recently developed discursive approaches have been employed by many researchers to examine various forms of collective identities. Antaki and Widdicombe (1998) summarise the discursive way of examining collective identities as follows:

> The identity category, the characteristics it affords, and what consequences follow, are all knowable to the analyst only through the understanding displayed by the interactants themselves. Membership of a category is ascribed (and rejected), avowed (and disavowed), displayed (and ignored) in local places and at certain times, and it does these things as part of the interactional work that constitutes people's lives. (p. 2)

Discursive understanding of social identity

A broad range of research conducted in many different disciplines, such as discourse analysis, conversational analysis, and ethnomethodology studies, offers an alternative understanding of collective identity to the traditional social and cognitive approaches (ten Have, 2004; Hepburn & Wiggins, 2005). For practical reasons, this approach can be described as a discursive approach. It shifts the focus from the individual to the interaction between people. Furthermore, it treats people's talk as a construction and interaction rather than as a reflection of the internal state (Edwards & Potter, 1992; Potter, 1996; Potter & Wetherell, 1987). Discursive studies of identity focus on the social actions accomplished by speakers through constructing this or that collective identity. By shifting the focus from the cognitive state to the linguistic construction of identities, discursive researchers can approach the issue of identity differently. Rather than asking what identities participants have and how they affect people's behaviour and perceptions, which is the main concern of SIT and SCT, discursive analysts investigate when, how, and why a specific identity is constructed and utilised. Although there is a debate among discursive and conversational researchers in relation to identifying and explaining collective identities, it is fair to say that most of these studies have been influenced by Sacks' (1992) ideas on conversation analysis (see Edwards, 1997, 1998, 1999; Hutchby & Wooffitt, 1998; Potter, 1996). Sacks indicates that for analysts to understand any examined collective identity, they need to see how the speakers themselves construct and affiliate with it. He states that (Sacks, 1992):

> Suppose you're an anthropologist or sociologist standing somewhere. You see somebody do some action, and you see it to be some activity. How can you go about formulating who is it that did it, for the purposes of your report? Can you use at least what you might take to be the most conservative formulation – his name? Knowing, of course, that any category you choose would have the [se] kinds of systematic problems: how would you go about selecting a given category from the set that would equally well characterise or identify that person at hand? (pp. 467-8)

Sacks maintains that researchers need to examine the categories and social identities that the speakers themselves invoke within their talk, rather than investigating categories that the researchers assume to be relevant. Widdicombe (1998) maintains that "a reference to a person's social identity is also a reference to their membership of a specific category" (p. 52-3).

Social identity is defined as the person's "display of, or ascription to, membership of some feature-rich category" (Antaki

& Widdicombe, 1998, p. 53). Thus, social identity is treated as something people construct within interaction, either as a goal itself or as a means to achieve further goals. As Edwards (1991) indicates, "Categorisation is something we do, in talk, to accomplish social actions" (p. 517).

Furthermore, based on this discursive approach, it is reasonable to claim that the events of a conflict and the groups involved should be examined as part of the social work that people conduct to achieve particular goals.

Hence, to address the questions of this thesis, we should examine how social identities and the defining events of the wars in Iraq and Lebanon are constituted, accepted, rejected, framed, and reconstituted through the utterances within interaction either as desired goals or as a means to achieve desired goals. This would allow us to gain a coherent understanding of how directly exposed individuals put together their experiences.

Discursive schools

Discourse analysis

> *consider language as a series of tools which acquire their purpose and function from the social and cultural milieux in which they are used*
>
> Ludwig Wittgenstein, 1953, p. 555

There are various definitions of discourse analysis (DA), some of which are very similar while others are contradictory. In fact, there are many different types of discourse analysis. This is because discourse analysis has been developed simultaneously by researchers who belong to different disciplines, such as psychology, sociology, media studies, and philosophy to answer questions related to these disciplines (Potter & Wetherell, 1987).

Thus, Potter and Wetherell (1987) argue that DA can be seen as a group of consistent and interrelated ideas that are bigger than a theory or a specific method. It is inclusive enough to contain different techniques and even different methods as long as they adhere to the central ideas that define DA. Discourse analysis focuses mainly on reformulating and reconstituting various social psychological topics such as attitude, attribution, and identity. Its most central idea, which is shared by discursive psychology, conversation analysis and ethnomethodology, is that talk should be examined "as a social practice in itself, with its own characteristic features and practical consequences" (Potter & Wetherell, p. 167). The most relevant type of DA to this book is the work that was developed by Gilbert and Mulkay (1984) and applied to examine social psychological topics by Potter and Wetherell (1987). These authors emphasise the importance of treating talk as a topic for investigation rather than a means that reflects what is going in within the people's psyches. They examine how people construct various types of accounts to attend to various social psychological topics, such as responsibility, credibility, identity, and so on. They also demonstrate that people's accounts are highly variable, indexical, and motivated. People can and do produce different and even contradictory opinions, attitudes, and descriptions of the same events, even within the course of a single conversation. For example, in a study that is both important and relevant to this book, Potter and Wetherell (1987) use discourse analysis to show how different New Zealanders accounted for the police and the protesters' conduct during conflicts that took place in relation to the Springbok rugby tour. Potter and Wetherell examine a riot which took place during the last game of the South African Springbok rugby team tour in New Zealand, when a group of New Zealanders who were against the Apartheid regime were trying to disrupt the game. The researchers conducted interviews with various New Zealanders asking them to talk about the event. They found that while some of the participants warranted the police actions through portraying them as natural human reactions, others denounced these actions, describing them as an unacceptable use of violence. Potter and Wetherell demonstrate that issues of accountability, responsibility, identity, and descriptions of the events are constructed by different speakers in order to warrant or denounce a specific side's (the police or the protesters') conduct within the conflict. Potter and Wetherell argue that the role of the analyst is not to search for the 'true' or accurate account, but rather to treat these accounts as rhetorical means constructed either as ends or to achieve desired ends within the interaction. In conclusion, DA considers people's constructions of self, others, or events as something that should be examined and viewed as rhetorical accomplishments and as a means to perform specific social actions.

Ethnomethodology

Ethnomethodology is one of the first and main contributors to discursive psychology via conversation analysis. The term ethnomethodology refers to the study of ordinary people's common sense. It can be explained as the study of common sense and its basis in interaction, and how this regulates our lives and gives meaning to our daily experiences (see Garfinkel, 1967). It focuses on the important role of discourse in people's construction and deployment of different components of their social world. One of the most important premises of ethnomethodology is that the researcher takes the role of an observer and a student rather than an expert and a teacher when conducting a study. As Agar explains:

> When you stand on the edge of a village and watch the noise and motion, you wonder, 'who are the people and what are they doing? 'when you read a news story about the discontent of young lawyers with their profession, you wonder, 'what is going on here?' Hypotheses, measurement samples, and instruments are the wrong guidelines. Instead, you need to learn about the world you understand by encountering it firsthand and making sense of it. (1986, p. 12)

Thus, ethnomethodology focuses on examining and explaining ordinary people's natural interactions. Furthermore, in ethnomethodology, researchers should not impose their understanding on the participants; rather, they need to view the interactions from the participants' understanding. As Goffman (1961, p. 283) points out, "the student of society can therefore use for his purposes the same models that members of society use for theirs". This means that researchers aim to identify the methods laypeople use to understand and explain various components of the environment. The ultimate goal is "to describe methods persons use in doing social life" (Sacks, 1984, p. 21). Furthermore, Edwards (1997) states that the main ethnomethodological contribution to DP is its idea that mundane descriptions and psychological topics perform discursive rhetorical functions.

Conversation analysis

Conversation analysis (CA) is a key contributor to discursive psychology and one of the most prominent qualitative analytical methods used to examine various social topics. It was developed soon after ethnomethodology was established. CA can be seen as an ethnomethodological enterprise that examines the interactional rules which regulate talk (ten Have, 2004). CA was initiated by Harvey Sacks in the form of lectures which he delivered at the University of California where he was teaching (Silverman, 1998). These lectures were published in 1992 by Gail Jefferson in cooperation with Emanuel Schegloff. Sacks was influenced by Erving Goffman's idea that talk is regulated by social sets of laws and that researchers should examine face to face interaction. Accordingly, talk should be viewed like other social institutions such as education or religion. Sacks was seeking to discover the social rules that regulate our daily interaction. In his paper "Everyone has to lie", Sacks (1975) developed a novel understanding of the nature of the rules that regulate our daily interaction. He indicated that verbal interaction is regulated by the sequence and the context of the interaction itself, rather than external social norms. He gave an example of how people respond to the mundane question of "how are you" by saying "fine". He suggested that this answer is the result of the conversational expectations, arguing that it is conventions that govern the interaction rather than the social system. In other words, he indicated that there is an expected answer for the question ('how are you?'). Hutchby and Wooffift (1998) provide a coherent account of the focus of CA:

> Conversation analysis is characterized by the view that how talk is produced and how the meanings of that talk are determined are the practical, social and interactional accomplishments of members of a culture. Talk is not seen simply as the product of two 'speakers-hearers' who attempt to exchange information or convey messages to each other. Rather, participants in conversation are seen as mutually orienting to, and collaborating in order to achieve, orderly and meaningful communication. The aim of CA is thus to reveal the tacit, organized reasoning procedures which inform the production of naturally occurring talk. The way in which utterances are designed is informed by the organized procedures, methods and resources which are tied to the contexts in why they are produced, and which are available to participants by virtue of their membership in a natural language community. (p.1)

One of the central premises of CA is the idea that talk is an interactive and well-structured activity. People do not talk accidentally; rather, utterances are "designed in their detail to be sensitive to their sequential context and to their role in the interaction" (Potter, 1996, p. 58). Consequently, the task of the researchers is to uncover these rules that organize people's interaction in order to reach a better understanding of our social world. Moreover, there is great emphasis on the sequence of utterances. Like discursive psychology, CA is concerned with understanding the action orientation of talk. An additional idea in conversation analysis that is relevant to DP and to this thesis is the notion that talk is indexical and reflexive. These ideas emerged initially in ethnomethodology. Indexicality refers to the understanding that the meaning of any segment of talk is related to the context in which it occurs. This notion is used in conversation analysis to emphasize the importance of examining the sequences of verbal interactions and how people orient to what is said earlier. It makes examining the surrounding conditions part of investigating the meaning of the words people uttered. This provides a clearer and more coherent picture of how people understand and respond to each other in the extract examined. The notion that talk is reflexive in nature refers to the idea that talk should be viewed as utilized to accomplish something. This notion is applied in CA and DP to examine the various discursive accomplishments of utterances (see Potter, 1996). Thus, when conversation analysts examine a transcript of a conversation, they need to transform their focus of "what happened, from a matter of a particular interaction done by specific people, to a matter of interactions as products of machinery" (Sacks, 1984, p. 26). Hence, one of the goals of CA is to discover those "machinery" that regulate people's interaction or "the tacit, organised reasoning procedures which inform the production of naturally occurring talk" (Hutchby & Wooffitt, 1998, p. 1). Another important idea shared by most discursive approaches is the notion that psychological and social topics do not arise in a void. Rather they are constructed as part of the social interaction which dominates humans' lives. An individual would not develop an identity if there were no comparable counterparts with whom the individual interacted and needed to relate, and a situation that allows the interaction and the comparison to take place is necessary as well. Hence, human behaviour is dominated by interaction, and to examine any psychological concept we need to pay attention to the situation in which the concept is brought to life.

The main difference between these approaches and traditional social and cognitive psychology lies in the characterization of what should be the subject of investigation. While discursive schools see the social interaction, which takes place in the form of words, as the central component of human social lives, they consider talk the subject of investigation. This contrasts with cognitive and social psychology, which view talk as reflective of what is going on within the speaker's mind. Thus, these researchers' task is to uncover these patterns in order to understand human behaviour. They investigate the way people perform specific actions and the goal behind these actions in order to understand the human social world. In contrast, researchers who belong to social and cognitive psychology treat talk as a form that reflects psychological states or processes.

Conversation analysis, discourse analysis, and discursive psychology view talk as action-oriented, and they have identified several rhetorical devices which people use to accomplish goals or to carry out particular actions. These include *active voicing* (Wooffitt, 1992), *extreme case formulations* (Pomerantz, 1986; Edwards, 2000), and *footing* (Clayman, 1992). I will highlight how these devices were constructed and deployed throughout my analysis. Although I do not adopt a CA approach in this book, it is treated as a useful resource, and I draw on some of its ideas and findings in the analysis. My focus on social psychological issues such as identities, rather than the interaction *per se*, makes discursive psychology a more appropriate approach for this study.

Discursive psychology, ideas and methods

> *discursive psychology is analytically focused on the way psychological phenomena are practical, accountable, situated, embodied and displayed.*
>
> Jonathan Potter, 2005, p. 739

Discursive psychology (DP) has been applied to examine various topics in psychology (Edwards & Potter, 2003; Hepburn & Wiggins, 2005). In particular, it has been effectively used to challenge the dominant cognitivist approaches and to expose their shortcomings. DP studies have re-examined some of the prominent social psychological topics such as attitudes (Potter & Wetherell, 1987), causal attributions (Edwards, 1991; Edwards & Potter, 1993), how people use psychological terms in their daily experiences (Edwards, 1999, 2005), cognitive scripts (Edwards, 1997), and collective identities (Potter & Wetherell, 1987; Antaki & Widdicombe, 1998). These psychological questions were re-investigated as discursive actions which take place within verbal interactions (Edwards & Potter, 2003; Hepburn & Wiggins, 2005). The focus was on how these psychological themes are constructed and deployed through talk as a part of the interaction and what their social functions are in this context. The results of these studies provide alternative explanations for various types of human behaviour. Potter (2005, p. 740) summarises DP's view of a non-cognitive psychology as:

> Psychology in DP is first and foremost something practical. Psychology in this sense is bound up with people's practices. Descriptions (of psychological, material or social objects) can be studied for the way they are invoked in activities such as blaming, complementing, inviting and so on (Potter, 1996).

Thus, in DP psychological concepts such as identity, attitude, memory, and feelings are examined as situated practices, or things we do *in situ*. Therefore, the meaning of any particular concept is based on the context, the way it was constructed, and the function it performed within the interaction. Hence, in DP researchers examine psychological concepts from the perspective of the people who are involved in the interaction by focusing on their utterances. Researchers do not assume the responsibility of deducing what a speaker meant in any segment of their utterances or what the desired goal was. They analyse how the speakers who are involved in the conversation orient to what was said and the meaning behind it. Consequently, the researcher's task is limited to understanding what the participants are doing in their talk-in-interaction (Edwards, 2006; Potter, 1996).

One of the invigorating features of DP is that researchers should not have a specific agenda; rather, they need to approach their questions with an open mind. As Sacks indicated, researchers "make a bunch of observations and see where they will go" (1984, p. 27). Thus, the researchers should be motivated by the intention of seeking to understand the examined interaction rather than confirming a pre-formulated hypothesis. This is in contrast to the majority of traditional studies in psychology, where researchers are motivated by the intention to confirm or reject the existence of a relationship between specific variables.

In discursive studies researchers do not seek to confirm specific hypotheses; rather, the way people construct, present, and describe their experiences is treated as the topic for investigation. Researchers highlight how the people involved in the interaction understand the action orientation of any segment of talk by examining next turns, rather than attempting to provide their explanation based on theories or pre-existing ideas. Discursive psychology is thoroughly empirical: its claims are based entirely on the actual data which is presented (Potter & Edwards, 2001).

In contrast to cognitive and social psychology, discursive psychology is not interested in gaining insights into the cognitive process that is presumed to be the foundation of all types of human behaviour including talk. It does not seek to understand or explain what is going on inside people's heads. It considers people's utterances the main arena for investigation, since this is where people interact and perform various forms of action, such as conforming, framing, accounting, promising, promoting, claiming, describing, and constituting specific events as realities.

One of the central ideas of DP is that people discursively construct their social lives through talk. Potter (1996) indicated that when people talk, they construct specific versions of the events and the environment. Different people may constitute the 'same' event in different ways. In fact, even the same person may provide different accounts of the same event within a single conversation. Different constructions are not random passive reflections. Rather, they are discursive accomplishments that perform specific social actions. Thus, examining different rhetorical accounts related to specific subjects would advance our understanding of how and why people discursively deal with this subject. For example, understanding why and how a specific group of people was portrayed within a specific account would add to our knowledge of discursive business done through invoking and making this group relevant within the social interaction. Discursive studies focus on what is presented, how it is presented, and why.

Constructing accounts as facts and realities

> *What we find in discourse is that participants describe the world in [particular] ways. Through naming and narrating them, people descriptively construct events as following, or as departing from, some normative or expected order.*
>
> Derek Edwards, 1997, p. 144

The term construction, which is a critical concept in discursive studies, refers to "the constructive nature of descriptions, rather than of the entities that (according to descriptions) exist beyond them" (Edwards, 1997, pp. 47-8). Discursive psychology studies focus on "how events are described and explained, how factual reports are constructed, how cognitive states are attributed" (Edwards & Potter, 1992, p. 2). Furthermore, DP argues that descriptions, like all other rhetorical actions, are indexical and reflexive. That means they cannot be examined in isolation from the context in which they occur. People construct descriptions and accounts to perform specific social actions, such as to blame, justify, or promise. These actions usually function as components of a bigger argument which the speaker is constructing. For example, in their discourse analytic study, Gilbert and Mulkay (1984) examined how a group of scientists managed the issue of accountability in their construction of their *empiricist repertoires*. They found that the scientists employed two different types of repertoires, the empiricist and the contingent repertoires. They used the empiricist repertoires to construct their beliefs and findings as factual, through presenting them as "following unproblematically and inescapably from the empirical characteristics of an impersonal natural world" (Gilbert & Mulkay, 1984, p. 56). In contrast, when the researchers were criticizing their opponents' findings, they constructed them as influenced by human factors rather than empirical procedures, which undermined the validity of the findings. Thus, this study demonstrates that rhetoric, as a social action, plays a central role in people's interaction, even in fields like the natural sciences, where one might expect rhetoric to be objective. Furthermore, it shows that people use rhetorical techniques to achieve tangible goals.

In summary, the issue of factuality in accounts is central to talk-in-interaction. Thus, people employ various techniques within their talk to address the factuality of their accounts. These techniques include *footing*, *the issue of stake*, *category entitlement*, *the construction of consensus* (see Potter, 1996). The use of these techniques is an important topic of investigation in DP, particularly for understanding how speakers handle sensitive issues within interaction. Nevertheless, producing accounts or descriptions is not as straightforward a process as it might seem; people often anticipate counterarguments for any account they provide. Therefore, DP studies emphasise the importance of examining how and why people address expected counterarguments. I will briefly review these techniques, as they are relevant to the analysis in this book.

Category construction, entitlement, and category membership in discursive psychology

Category construction within language is one of Sacks' (1992) most influential ideas adopted by discursive psychologists. In his "hotrodder" study, he examined how a group of youths discussed the issue of who they were and what they were doing in group therapy sessions. He argues that these individuals created a category for themselves, "hotrodders", through their talk-in-interaction. The label of the newly formed category was derived from the members' ownership of a specific type of customised cars, the hotrod. Sacks shows that these people used the descriptive term "hotrodder" as an effective way of constructing boundaries that define who belongs to the group and who does not (Edwards, 1998; Sacks, 1992). Furthermore, he argues that categories are "inference rich," which means they are associated with specific features, assumptions, and activities (known as category-bound attributes) (Sacks, 1992). Thus, the importance of categories stems out of the consequentiality attached to them. He argues that there are certain expectations and conventions associated with each category (Widdicombe & Wooffitt, 1995). A good example is this opening line of a story: "The baby cried. The mommy picked it up" (Sacks, 1992). Sacks (1992) reports that most people who come across this line would assume that the "mommy" is the mother of the child and that she picked up the child in response to the crying, which is an activity related to her identity as a mother. However, none of these details are mentioned and the story may be completely different. The assumptions are related to our understanding of the category-bound activities. This understanding makes us expect specific behaviour when a person is constructed through a specific identity.

Another influential feature of CA that was adopted by discursive psychologists is Sacks' central idea of *category entitlement* and the relationship between category membership and social identity (Potter, 1996). Sacks (1992) indicates that categories are constructed within interaction as rhetorical resources to perform specific social actions. In contrast to the majority of studies in social psychology, where researchers examine the categories that they think are important and relevant, Sacks argues that the relevant categories are those made relevant by the speakers themselves within interaction. Another important idea is the notion of *category entitlement*. This concept refers to the idea that being a member of a specific category incorporates having specific abilities, knowledge, rights, and duties. For example, being a police officer allows the person to ask certain questions in the event of a crime and entitles others to approach him or her with requests and information. Similarly, being a flight attendant carries the assumption that the person has knowledge about airplanes and airports. Being a doctor creates the expectation that the person will help in certain situations. However, the nature, boundaries, and implications of membership in any category, and the entitlements attached to the category itself, are not fixed. They can be constructed and deployed in many different ways (Potter, 1988). Each of the constructions is designed to perform specific social actions. For example, a doctor might justify his inability to help by explaining that he specialises in cancer and is not equipped to treat a broken leg. Hence, categories are flexible and negotiable.

Throughout this book, I will highlight how people construct category memberships and why.

Blame, accountability, and discursive psychology

> *A major element of the way psychology is woven into everyday practices is through the focus on accountability. How are individuals (or collectivities, organizations, or intra-individual entities) constructed as sites of responsibility?*
>
> Jonathan Potter, 2005, p. 740

Analysis in discursive psychology (DP) distinguishes between two types of accountability. The first type deals with how people construct blame and responsibility when discussing various issues, such as what happened, who is responsible, who is to be blamed, who should be praised, and so on. The second type concerns how people manage their own responsibility within their talk (Potter, 2005). Usually, these two types of accountability are interconnected; people address their own responsibility through highlighting the responsibility of others, and vice versa. As noted earlier, DP studies focus on the way people constitute various types of events in different ways and the intended goals of these constructions. Edwards and Potter (1992) indicate that issues of responsibility, accountability, and agency play an important role in people's discursive construction of events, items, and identities. As Edwards (1997) puts it:

> When people describe events, they attend to accountability. That is to say, they attend to events in terms of what is normal, expectable, and proper: they attend to their own responsibility in events and in the reporting of events. (p. 7)

Shotter (1989) defined social accountability as "the fact that we must talk only in certain already established ways, in order to meet the demands placed upon us by our need to sustain our status as responsible members of our society - where the "must" involved is a moral must" (p. 141). Thus, managing blame plays a central role in people's utterances. It is important to stress that, when examining descriptions, researchers do not treat them as facts, and their factual status is not even investigated in most discursive studies.

To summarise, discursive psychologists believe that accountability is strongly related to descriptions. In DP, when people talk, they attend to the issue of responsibility within their accounts and for producing the account. In this book, my main interest lies in understanding how people who have been in armed conflicts in Iraq, Lebanon, and Gaza construct and manage their experiences.

Critique of the discursive approach

Discursive schools assume that all people have a collective identity powerful enough to affect their perception of the world and, consequently, their behaviour. This generalisation, which serves as a premise for many studies, is not substantiated. Many people seem to care mainly about themselves and do not have any real attachment to a group, country, or collective identity unless it benefits them personally. In his book *Man's Search for Meaning*, Viktor Frankl highlights how many Jewish prisoners recruited by Nazi guards in concentration camps, known as kapos, enjoyed harming their in-group. He discussed how they were even more cruel than the German guards.

Moreover, discursive methods assumes that speakers are aware of the implicit as well as the explicit meaning of their talk and that taking a specific part of a conversation and analysing it as a primary form of interaction is sufficient to be considered as data. In reality, conversations do not take place in a void. People consider within their interaction the norms and the accepted rhetoric, as well as what is frowned-upon and even criminal. Hence, analysing specific discourse without discussing the identity of the speaker, their previous positions, the context in which they were speaking, and the targeted audience may affect the factuality and significance of the results obtained through discursive methods. Finally, it is essential to consider the identity of the speaker, their weight within their society, and the message their conveying when conducting discursive studies.

Representative discourse and collective identity

To truly understand the dominant identities within a group, one cannot rely on research conducted through questionnaires, or focus on any single segment of dialogue. Neither can we solely rely on the official and semi-official narratives conveyed through scripted speeches, media, and educational systems, as these are often designed to present ideal identities. The real insights lie in examining *representative discourse.*

Representative discourse is any account produced by an influential figure or layperson intended to be seen as factual and consequential portrayal of events and their real participants. These accounts discuss what is seen as sensitive topics as well as group characteristics and boundaries. Representative discourse reflects deep-rooted identities while actively shaping and reinforcing them. These powerful yet usually salient identities are presented as central to the conflict at hand.

For instance, the riots in Britain in August 2024 illustrate how official rhetoric presented the events and involved parties differently from the perspectives of the protesters/rioters and counter-rioters. The same can be said about the grooming gangs in the UK, which some influential figures described as motivated by ethnic and religious identity and linked to migration, while the official rhetoric rejected attributing these crimes to specific cultures, religions, or identities. Another example is how crimes committed by illegal immigrants in the United States, such as the murder of Laken Riley, were presented differently by Donald Trump and Kamala Harris during their 2024 presidential campaigns. Some media outlets attributed the crime to the collective identity of the perpetrator, while others saw it as an individualistic act. These varying presentations are used to sway public opinion to adapt specific policies and garner support for specific candidates.

The power of representative discourse

Focusing on representative discourse, in contrast to mundane talk, is an effective way to understand the collective identities that matter. It is not just about what is said, but also about who says it, in what context, based on what, and with what intent. For discourse to be representative, it must be:

1. **Significant**: It must relate to critical events or issues that are central to the group's identity. These are moments where identity is either affirmed or challenged, such as during national crises, religious events, or political upheavals.

2. **Mobilizing**: The discourse must aim to mobilize specific population towards specific actions. In conflict settings, leaders use such discourse to rally their base, justify aggression, or call for unity against a perceived enemy.

3. **Identity-related:** The discourse must explicitly and implicitly connect to the group's identity, particularly in the context of conflict. For example, in Iraq, Sunni and Shia identities are invoked not just in religious contexts but in political, geographical, and social ones as well, often with the intent of justifying actions or rallying support. Similarly, in the Ukraine wars, the Russian versus Ukrainian identities are invoked differently by Putin and Zelensky, yet in both cases they pertain to much more than just national identities.

Identity in conflict

Identity in conflict zones like the Middle East is not static; it is fluid, performative, and highly contextual. The same person might emphasize different aspects of their identity depending on the situation, the audience, and the desired outcome. During the Iraq-Iran War, for example, Iraqi identity was heavily emphasized in opposition to Persian identity, even though both groups shared significant cultural and religious commonalities.

In conflict, identity becomes a strategic performance. Individuals and groups adopt identities that align with the expectations and norms of their in-group, often in direct opposition to the out-group. This performative aspect of identity is crucial to understanding how conflicts are sustained and why peace processes so often fail.

In the Middle East, identity is deeply intertwined with historical grievances and religious narratives. The Sunni-Shia divide is not merely a religious difference; it is a deeply entrenched conflict with roots in historical events, political power struggles, and social inequalities. To understand these conflicts, one must examine how these identities are constructed, maintained, and weaponized through discourse.

References

Agar, M. (1986). *Speaking of ethnography*. London: Sage.

Antaki, C., & Widdicombe, S. (Eds.). (1998). *Identities in talk*. London: Sage.

Billig, M. (1996). *Arguing and thinking: a rhetorical approach to social psychology* (2nd ed.). Cambridge University Press.

Carbaugh, D. (1996). *Situating selves: The communication of social identities in American scenes*. Albany, NY: State University of New York Press.

Clayman, S. E. (1992). Footing in the achievement of neutrality: the case of news-interview discourse. In P. Drew & J. Heritage (Eds.), *Talk at work: Interaction in institutional settings* (pp. 163-198). Cambridge University Press.

Cooley, C. (1902). *Human Nature and the Social Order*. New York: Scribner's.

Edwards, D. (2006). Discourse, cognition and social practices: The rich surface of language and social interaction. *Discourse Studies, 8*(1), 41-49.

Edwards, D. (2005). Discursive psychology. In K. L. Fitch. & R. E. Sanders (Eds.), *Handbook of language and social interaction*. New York: Erlbaum.

Edwards, D. (2000). Extreme case formulations: Softeners, investment and doing non literal. *Research on language and social interaction, 33*(4), 347-373.

Edwards, D. (1998). The relevant thing about her: Social identity categories in use. In C. Antaki & S. Widdicombe (Eds.), *Identities in Talk* (pp. 15-33). London: Sage.

Edwards, D. (1997). *Discourse and cognition*. London: Sage.

Edwards, D. (1991). Categories are for talking: On the cognitive and discursive bases of categorization. *Theory and Psychology, 1*(4), 515-542.

Edwards, D., & Potter, J. (1992). *Discursive Psychology*. London: Sage.

Edwards, D., & Potter, J. (1993). Language and causation: A discursive action model of description and attribution. *Psychological Review, 100*(1), 23-41.

Edwards, D., & Potter, J. (2003). Discursive psychology and mental states. In H. Molder & J. Potter (Eds.), *Conversation and cognition*. Cambridge: University Press.

Frankl, V. E. (1984). *Man's search for meaning: An introduction to logotherapy*. New York, NY: Simon & Schuster.

Gilbert, N., Mulkay, M. (1984). *Opening Pandora's Box: A sociological analysis of scientists' discourse*. Cambridge University Press.

Goffman, E. (1959). *The Presentation of Self in Everyday Life*. London: Allen Lane.

Goffman, E. (1961). *Asylums: Essays on the social situation of mental patients and other inmates*. Harmondsworth: Penguin

Haslam, S. A., & Reicher, S. D. (2006). Stressing the group: Social identity and the unfolding dynamics of stress. *Journal of Applied Psychology, 91*(5), 1037–1052.

Hepburn, A., & Wiggins, S. (2005). Developments in discursive psychology. *Discourse & Society, 16*(5), 595-601.

Herrera, M. (2003). Constructing social categories and seeking collective influence: self-categorization and the discursive construction of a conflict. *International Journal of Psychology and Psychological Therapy, 3*(1), 27-57.

Hitlin, S. (2003). Values as the core of personal identity: Drawing links between two theories of self. *Social Psychology Quarterly 66*(2), 118–137.

Hogg, M. A. & Abrams, D. (1988). Social identifications: A social psychology of intergroup relations and group processes. London & New York: Routledge.

Hogg, M. A., & Abrams, D. (1999). Social identity and social cognition: Historical background and current trends. In D. Abrams& M. A. Hogg (Eds.), *Social identity and social cognition* (pp. 1-25). Oxford: Blackwell.

Hogg, M. A. (1996). Intragroup processes, group structure and social identity. In W. P. Robinson (Ed.), *Social groups and identities: Developing the legacy of Henri Tajfel* (pp. 65-93). Oxford, UK: Butterworth-Heinemann.

Hogg, M. A. (2000). Social identity and social comparison. In J. Suls & L. Wheeler (Eds.), *Handbook of social comparison: Theory and research* (pp. 401-421). New York: Kluwer/Plenum.

Hogg, M. A. (2001a). Social categorization, depersonalization and group behavior. In M. A. Hogg & R. S. Tindale (Eds.), *Blackwell handbook of social psychology: Group processes* (pp. 56-85). Oxford, UK: Blackwell.

Hogg, M. A. (2001b). Social identity and the sovereignty of the group: A psychology of belonging. In C. Sedikides & M. B. Brewer (Eds.), *Individual self, relational self, collective self* (pp. 123-143). Philadelphia, PA: Psychology Press.

Hogg, M.A., Terry, D.J. and White, K.M. (1995). A tale of two theories: A critical comparison of identity theory with social identity theory. *Social Psychology Quarterly, 58* (4), 255-269.

Hopkins, N. & Reicher, S. D. (1996). The construction of social categories and processes of social change: Arguing about national identities. In G. M. Breakwell & E. Lyons (Eds.), *Changing European identities: Social psychological analyses of social change* (pp. 69-93). Oxford, Butterworth-Heinemann.

Huddy, L. (2002). Context and meaning in social identity theory: A response to Oakes. *Political Psychology, 23*(4): 825-838.

Hutchby, I., & Wooffitt, R. (1998). *Conversation analysis.* Cambridge: Polity Press.

McCall, G.J. and Simmons, J.L. (1978). *Identities and interactions: an examination of human associations in everyday life.* Revised edition. New York: Free Press.

Mead, G. H. (1934). *Mind, self and society.* University of Chicago Press.

Pomerantz, A. (1986). Agreeing and disagreeing with assessments: Some features of preferred/dispreferred turn-shapes. In J. M. Atkinson & J. Heritage (Eds.), *Structures of social action: Studies in conversation analysis.* Cambridge University Press.

Potter, J. (1996). *Representing reality: Discourse, rhetoric and social construction.* London: Sage.

Potter, J. (2005). Making psychology relevant. *Discourse & Society, 16*(5), 739-747.

Potter, J. & Edwards, E. (2001). Discursive social psychology. In W.P. Robinson & H. Giles (Eds.), *Handbook of Language and Social Psychology* (pp. 103-118). London: Whey.

Potter, J., & Wetherell, M. (1987). *Discourse and social psychology: Beyond attitudes and behaviour.* London: Sage.

Reicher, S. (1996). 'The battle of Westminster': Developing the social identity model of crowd behaviour in order to explain the initiation and development of collective conflict. *European Journal of Social Psychology, 26*, 115-134.

Reicher, S. & Hopkins, N. (2001). *Self and nation.* London: Sage.

Sacks, H. (1975). Everyone has to lie. In M. Sanchez & B. Blount (Eds.), *Sociocultural dimensions of language use* (pp. 57-80). NY, Academic Press.

Sacks, H. (1984). On doing 'being ordinary'. In M. Atkinson & J. Heritage (Eds.), *Structures of social action.* Cambridge University Press.

Sacks, H. (1992). *Lectures on conversation.* Oxford: Basil Blackwell.

Schwartz, S. J. (2005). A new identity for identity research: Recommendations for expanding and refocusing the identity literature. *Journal of Adolescent Research, 20*(3), 293–308.

Shotter, J. (1989). Social accountability and the social construction of "You". In J. Shotter & K. J. Gergen (Eds.), *Texts of identity* (pp. 133-151). London: Sage.

Silverman, D. (1998). *Harvey Sacks and conversation analysis: key contemporary thinkers.* Cambridge: Polity Press Silverman.

Tajfel, H. (1969). Cognitive aspects of prejudice. *Journal of Social Issues, 25*(4), 79-97.

Tajfel, H. (1970). Experiments in intergroup discrimination. *Scientific American, 223*(5), 96-102.

Tajfel, H. (1971). Social psychology of intergroup relations. *Annual Review of Psychology, 33*, 1-30.

Tajfel, H. (1978). *Differentiation between social groups: Studies in the social psychology of intergroup relations.* London: Academic Press.

Tajfel, H. (1981). *Human groups and social categories.* Cambridge University Press.

Tajfel, H. & Turner, J.C. (1979). An integrative theory of intergroup conflict. In W. G. Austin & S. Worchel (Eds.), *The social psychology of intergroup relations.* California: Wadsworth Inc.

Tajfel, H. & Turner, J.C. (1986). The social identity theory of intergroup behavior. In S. Worchel & L. W. Austin (Eds.), *Psychology of intergroup relations.* Chicago: Nelson-Hall.

ten Have, P. (2004). Understanding qualitative research and ethnomethodology. London, England: Sage Publications.

Terry, D. J., Carey, C. J., & Callan, V. J. (2001). Employee adjustment to an organisational merger: An intergroup perspective. *Personality and Social Psychology Bulletin, 27*(3), 267-280.

Turner, J. C. (1975). Social comparison and social identity: Some prospects for intergroup behaviour. *European Journal of Social Psychology, 5*(1), 5-34.

Turner, J.C. (1978). Social comparisons, similarity and ingroup favouritism. In: Tajfel, H. (Ed.), *Differentiation between social groups* (pp. 101-140). London: Academic Press.

Turner, J.C. (1982). Towards a cognitive redefinition of the social group. In H. Tajfel (Ed.), *Social identity and intergroup relations* (pp. 15-40). Cambridge University Press.

Turner, J.C. (1984). Social identification and psychological group formation. In: H. Tajfel (Ed.), *The social dimension: European studies in social psychology* (Vol. 2, pp. 518-538). Cambridge University Press.

Turner, J.C. (1985). Social categorization and the self-concept: A social cognitive theory of group behavior. In E. J. Lawler (Ed.), *Advances in group processes: Theory and research* (Vol. 2, pp. 77-122). Greenwich, CT: JAI Press.

Turner, J.C. (1991). Social influence. Milton Keynes: Open University Press.

Turner, J.C., Hogg, M., Oakes, P., Reicher, S., & Wetherell, M. (1987). *Rediscovering the social group: A self-categorization theory.* Oxford: Blackwell.

Turner, J.C., Oakes, P. J., Haslam, S. A., & McGarty, C. A. (1994). Self and collective: cognition and social context. *Personality and Social Psychology Bulletin, 20*(5), 454-463.

Wetherell, M. & Mohanty, C. T. (2010). *The SAGE handbook of identities.* London: Sage.

Wetherell, M., Taylor, S. & Yates, S. (Eds.) (2001). *Discourse theory and practice: A reader.* London; Sage.

Widdicombe, S., (1995). Identity, politics and talk: a case for the mundane and the everyday. In: S. Wilkinson & C. Kitzinger (Eds.), *Feminism and discourse*, pp. 106-127. London: Sage.

Widdicombe, S., & Wooffitt, R. (1995). *The language of youth subcultures: Social identity in action.* Hertfordshire: Harvester Wheatsheaf.

Wittgenstein, L. (1953). *Philosophical Investigations* (G.E.M. Anscombe, Trans.). Oxford: Blackwell.

Wooffitt, R. (1992). *Telling tales of the unexpected: the organization of factual discourse.* Hempstead: Harvester Wheatsheaf.

Chapter 2

Wars and identity

I can't bear the thought of many hundreds of millions of people dying in agony only and solely because the rulers of the world are stupid and wicked and I can't bear it.

Bertrand Russell, *Face to Face* (BBC), 1959

Wars are fought with words as much as with force. Since the time of Cicero, philosophers, theorists, and decision-makers have debated and rationalised war in various ways (see Bell, 2009; Burke, 2004; Oddo, 2011; Regan, 1996). *The Histories* of Herodotus begins by discussing wars, the different nations involved in them, and how each one defined themselves and their enemies.

The existence of an armed conflict devoid of conflicting narratives is simply unimaginable. War is a collective human institution that is described, explained, and rationalised chiefly through rhetoric. Rhetorical accounts play an essential role in setting the ground for, instigating, continuing, and extinguishing armed conflicts (see Des Forges, 2007; Glenny, 1992; Regan, 1996; Thompson, 2007). Discursive schools argue that people construct rhetorical accounts as a way to perform specific social actions such as blaming, accusing, and warranting (see Antaki & Widdicombe, 1998; Billig, 1995; Edwards & Potter, 1992, 2003; Edwards, 2005; Potter, 1996, 2005; Potter & Wetherell, 1987; Sacks, 1992; Schegloff, 1999; Widdicombe & Wooffitt, 1995).

This book examines lay and political discursive accounts of the armed conflicts that took place in Iraq from 18th March 2003 to August 2008, in Lebanon from 12th July to 14th August 2006, and in the aftermath of the attacks inside Israel on 7th October 2023. I investigate how influential Iraqi, Lebanese, Palestinian, and Israeli politicians convey these conflicts in their own words and the discursive goals behind their narratives. I also analyse the discourse of laypeople who were directly affected by these wars, focusing on how they present themselves, their experiences, and the conflicts. By examining these important accounts, the book sheds light on these conflicts and on the people's views of them. It also allows us to understand the relationship between identity, trauma, and conflicts.

Through analysing several lay and political accounts of the wars in Iraq, Lebanon, and the Israeli-Arab conflict, I discuss two influential and profound presuppositions in psychology and several other disciplines. The first presupposition is the conventional characterisation of war as an idiosyncratically negative experience that is expected to cause lasting effects on people's psychological, mental, behavioural, and social capabilities. This precise understanding has influenced the perception and handling of war across a range of various scientific fields, particularly in health studies, sociology, political science, and psychology. Based on this characterisation, a significant number of researchers have been focusing on detecting and projecting pathological effects of wars. For example, Muldoon and Downes conducted their study on post-traumatic stress symptoms (PTSD) under the hypothesis that "war and political conflict have grave consequences" (1997, p. 146). This notion was treated as an established, self-evident fact and functions as the very premise of the study. Moreover, they describe the targeted population of the study as "post-conflict Northern Ireland". The use of the description "post-conflict" to portray Northern Ireland is an indicator of the way these researchers perceive the war and its implications.

Since the Second World War, an enormous body of studies has been dedicated to examining various negative effects of wars on people. Researchers have focused on examining civilians, children, females, and soldiers, with one of the main goals being to establish what pathological reactions are associated with war and which groups within the population are more vulnerable (e.g., Albertyn, Bicker, Millar & Rode, 2003; Ajdukovic, 1998; Begic & McDonald, 2006; Miller et al., 2002; Thabet, Tawahina, Sarraj& Vostanis, 2008; Thulesius & Håkansson, 1999; Weine et al., 1995, 1998; Witmer & Culver, 2001). This approach has been extended to study experiences considered analogous to the experience of war in terms of containing traumatic events, in particular terrorist attacks, violent crime, car accidents, and natural disasters (North et al., 1999; Orth et al., 2008; Schlenger et al., 2002; Ursano, Fullerton, Vance & Kao, 1999). The findings of such studies are inconsistent and even contrasting (cf. Beiser & Fleming, 1986; Chung & Singer, 1995; Gan and Solomon, 1987). On one hand, a large number of studies indicate that there is a positive correlation between the experience of war and the development of specific pathological disorders (see for example, Ajdukovic, 1998; Dybdahl, 2001; Smith, Perrin, Yule & Rabe-Hesketh, 2001). On the other hand, the results of several studies did not show any significant differences between people who have been in war and others who have not. For instance, Hotopf et al. (2006) conducted a comprehensive study that compared 4,722 British soldiers who served in Iraq to 5,550 soldiers who did not serve. The researchers examined symptoms of post-traumatic stress disorder, common mental disorders, general well-being, physical symptoms, fatigue, and alcohol consumption in the two samples. The results showed a slight increase in negative symptoms, but no major differences between the two groups of soldiers were detected. Currently, there is universal agreement among psychologists that the majority of people who experience war will not develop major psychological or mental disorders. Nonetheless, thus far there is no conclusive theory that explains the significant differences in people's reactions toward armed conflict. Within the book, I examine in more detail the results of some of the psychological studies already mentioned. Hence, it is worth taking a step back and questioning the long taken-for-granted presupposition of **war as solely a negative experience.** I do not presuppose a specific nature of war. I do not assume that it is negative or positive; rather, I collect and analyse accounts that individuals built to portray their experiences of the wars.

The second profound presupposition I discuss through analysing accounts of war is the understanding of the relationship between collective identity and war. This understanding is based on the traditional social psychology conceptualisation of collective identity, which crystallised in Henri Tajfel's social identity theory (SIT) (1978, 1981) and its cognitive extension, self-categorisation theory (SCT) (Turner, 1991). In these theories, collective identity is established as a universal, self-evident, and stable entity that retains a significant influence on people's perception and behaviour. Moreover, according to this understanding, collective identity is a salient internal entity that is activated by external situations in which people interact as groups rather than individuals. This understanding has been drawn upon to inform studies in political science, sociology and social psychology that examine armed conflicts and the role of collective identity (e.g., Crnobrnja, 1996; Finney, 2002; Hammack, 2006).

A significant number of studies in different fields are based on the idea that in most conflicts, the fighting sides have salient collective identities that differ from each other. The collective identity plays a dual role within conflicts. On one hand, it unites the in-group's members. On the other hand, it differentiates the in-group's members from members of the other group (e.g. Gartzke & Gleditsch, 2006; Wendt, 1994). Researchers influenced by this understanding assume that the collective identities of the sides of any war are a self-evident fact that affect people's interactions with each other. Collective identity is treated as one of the main causes of conflicts between people.

Several researchers have shown that this understanding of collective identity and its applications that examine collective identities within armed conflicts have several significant practical and theoretical shortcomings. On the theoretical side, Potter and Wetherell (1987) criticised the traditional social psychology's understanding of identity, indicating that it treats the process of categorisation as inflexible and mechanistic. A significant number of researchers argue that collective identity should be treated in research as something that we produce rather than what we are (see Billig, 1995; Edwards & Potter, 1992, 2003; Edwards, 2005; Potter, 1996; Sacks, 1992). According to this understanding, collective identity is a discursive means which we build and use to reach desired ends, rather than being an end in itself. Thus, people construct, modify, assume, negotiate, and deploy collective identities as part of their daily social interaction with each other. Accordingly, Herrera indicates that "the categories involved in a conflict should not be taken for granted, since different parties to the conflict may have different ideas of what the sides in the conflict actually are" (2003, p. 28). Furthermore, studies conducted by Edwards and Potter (1993), Herrera (2003), Lomsky-Feder (1995), and Leudar, Marsland, and Nekvapil (2004) have demonstrated that different people produce different accounts of the same war, particularly in terms of the collective identities of the groups involved. Moreover, they showed that these accounts perform a specific discursive function within the social interaction.

On the practical side, several studies that analysed armed conflicts have shown that the meaning and implications of social identity within armed conflicts are complex and important issues that should be a topic of study. For example, Sokolovic (1995) reports that during the Bosnian War, which is predominantly described as an ethnic war, a number of Serbian soldiers were throwing un-activated grenades at their enemies, Bosnian Muslims, with messages saying: "This is all I can do for you" or "We are not all the same" or "I wish to come back on your side". Moreover, he indicates that thousands of Serbs deserted and refused to fight, and hundreds of thousands of Serbs left the areas that were under their "own" authority and "went all over the world" (1995, p. 119).

On conflicts and social identities

War is arguably one of the oldest and most imperative human institutions. It has played a central role in nations', groups', and individuals' lives throughout history (see Bell, 2009). Almost every state in the world has been established as a result of a war and has taken part in an armed conflict for one reason or another. Currently, war represents one of the most serious and persistent challenges to mankind. Currently, over 2 billion people are affected by ongoing wars. There are several different definitions of war, and there is viable intellectual debate within various disciplines, seeking to define and differentiate between the various types of conflicts or wars (see Hynes, 2004). I do not intend to discuss the different definitions of war or to distinguish between the different types of conflicts, for practical reasons. Rather, I accept the Cambridge Academic Content Dictionary's definition of war as "armed fighting between two or more countries or groups" (2009, p. 1073).

Within mainstream psychology, armed conflicts have been mostly approached via their associations with negative effects on the psychological, emotional, and mental well-being of the exposed population (e.g., Albertyn, Bicker, Millar & Rode, 2003; Ajdukovic, 1998; Begic & Mcdonald, 2006; Miller et al., 2002; Thabet, Tawahina, Sarraj & Vostanis, 2008; Thulesius & Håkansson, 1999; Weine et al., 1995, 1998; Witmer & Culver, 2001). Nonetheless, in the last twenty years, a limited but increasing number of studies have attempted to examine the subtle yet influential presupposition: an armed conflict is viewed in the same way by different people and sides (e.g., Graham, Keenan & Dowd, 2004; Herrera, 2003; Leudar, Marsland & Nekvapil, 2004, Oddo, 2011). These studies have indicated that different speakers construct different accounts for the same war, and they have shown that the involved parties are constructed differently by different speakers. This argument is influenced by the discursive understanding of human interaction. Discursive and conversation analysts argue that subjects, objects, and events do not have a unified nature. Rather, through rhetoric, people construct and present different accounts for every component of the world as part of their talk-in-interaction. This position is the starting point for this book.

In this chapter, I review several topics that are related to the question of this study, divided into five sections. Each section briefly covers a specific topic. In the first section, I discuss war, focusing on studies that seek to explain the practices, dynamics, and implications of modern wars. In the second section, I discuss a number of psychological investigations of war, reviewing studies that examined psychological disorders associated with armed conflicts. The third section discusses a number of studies, cases, and theories that explain the relationship between collective identity and war. In the fourth section, I present an overview of the theoretical understanding of collective identity. In the fifth and final section, I highlight the rationale for the role of rhetorical accounts in relation to armed conflicts from the perspective of discursive schools and non-discursive researchers.

Modern armed conflict

Modern wars differ in many essential aspects from the wars that took place prior to the Second World War (Goldson, 1996). Currently, the course of modern wars is not limited to decision-makers' and high-ranking army officers' rationales.

Statesmen across the world pay close attention to public opinion, knowing that they can no longer take their countries to war without securing adequate public support (see Woodward, 2004). The Gaza War (2008-2009) is a clear example of how international public opinion can play a key role in relation to armed conflicts. This war was extinguished – prematurely, from the point of view of the Israeli generals – as a result of the pressure exerted upon them by various international and local civic organisations. Intellectuals, journalists, and laypeople who took to the streets of Europe, the US, and other parts of the world brought that war to its conclusion. Bertrand Russell (2004) indicated that military power is ineffective without public support.

At the same time, modern war has an extremely deleterious face in terms of its effects on the general population. Civilian fatalities in wartime have increased from five percent of the total casualties at the dawn of the past century, to fifteen per cent during the First World War, to sixty-five per cent by the end of the Second World War, to more than ninety per cent in present-day wars (United Nations, 1996). Several countries have been defeated due to civilian casualties. The best example is Japan's surrender in the Second World War after two of its civilian cities were attacked with nuclear bombs, an attack that resulted in hundreds of thousands of innocent people losing their lives and injuring many more. Nowadays, this attack functions as an example of the effectiveness of targeting civilians to achieve a quick and decisive victory from the point of view of military planners.

According to Hynes (2004), by the 1990s, nine out of every ten people who lost their lives due to conflicts were civilians. He indicates that modern weapons are a major reason for the dramatic increase in civilian casualties. Millions of children have lost their lives as a result of modern wars. In 1992, five hundred thousand children under five years old died as a result of armed conflicts worldwide (United Nations, 1996). In the Chechen war, between February and May of 1995, 40 per cent of all civilian casualties were children. Red Cross workers reported discovering children's bodies that were systematically executed with bullets in the temple. In Sarajevo, almost one child in four has been wounded as a result of the armed conflict. In the last ten years, between four and five million children have been wounded or disabled. The number of refugees from armed conflicts worldwide increased from 2.4 million in 1974 to more than 114 million by the end of September 2023. Moreover, there are another 30 million people displaced within their own countries. Children and women make up an estimated 80 per cent of displaced populations (United Nations reports, 2023).

The majority of current wars take place within states rather than between states and for the most part civilians are directly affected (Gartzke & Gleditsch, 2006; Atlas, Licklider, 1999). The ongoing armed conflict in Iraq is a clear example of the volatile nature of modern wars. It started with the 2003 American-led invasion which was aiming at toppling Saddam's regime – a war that was supported by several Western and Arab countries, implicitly or explicitly – as well as considerable segment of the Iraqi society (Allawi, 2007; Coburn, 2008). The military campaign succeeded in overthrowing Saddam's regime swiftly and with limited losses. However, shortly afterwards an armed and violent insurgency movement emerged. It was led by Arab Sunni Iraqis who were the governing group and held most of the important positions during Saddam's reign (Allawi, 2007; Chehab, 2005; Coburn, 2008). They were supported by various external organisations and states in their effort to evict the foreign troops and re-establish their control over other Iraqi groups. The insurgency targeted foreign troops as well as Iraqi people who were considered pro the new situation or against the old regime. Subsequently, Iraq descended into bloody conflict which claimed the lives of tens of thousands of people and divided the Iraqis into conflicting groups, mainly, along the well-established sectarian and ethnic lines (Allawi, 2007; Chehab, 2005; Coburn, 2008). A significant number of researchers and politicians attribute the ongoing conflict in Iraq to the American military intervention. In contrast, other scholars contend that the existence of conflicting collective identities which divide the Iraqis is the underpinning cause of the ongoing conflict. In January 2005, the Iraqi Ministry of Health released a report for the previous six months, which was based on hospital records. The report showed that 3,274 people were killed and 12,657 injured in violence related to the war. Of these, 2,041 died as the result of military action, whereas 1,233 were killed due to terrorist attacks (BBC News, Jan 2005). In the last six months of 2014, the reported number of civilians killed was 10,895, with many thousands more injured. According to a group of academics in the United States and the United Kingdom known as the Iraq Body Count, around 188,000 Iraqi civilians were killed in the period from May 2003 until the end of 2016 (Iraq Body Count, 2024). Although the number of deaths has drastically decreased in recent years, the sectarian war is far from over.

In sum, war is a continuing human institution that has complex and significant effects on people's lives. In modern conflicts, civilian populations are both a central player and the main victim. This justifies dedicating significant psychological studies to examining the various aspects of wars.

Psychological studies of armed conflicts

Psychology, due to its goals, the current dominance of cognitive approaches, and the obvious detrimental nature of war, has been focusing on the negative psychological implications of war. The vast majority of psychological studies that have examined armed conflicts start from the dominant understanding of war as a cluster of solely negative experiences. Thus, it is rational for psychological researchers to expect and examine the development of pathological reactions among people who have been exposed to wars. As a result, a large number of studies have focused on uncovering the negative effects of the experience of war. These studies have also focused on identifying who is at risk of developing psychological disorders as a result of conflicts.

Studies that examined the negative effects of the experience of war

A large number of studies have examined the relationship between exposure to combat-related stress and developing specific psychopathological symptoms. These symptoms are characterised by re-experiencing traumatic war events (e.g., having flashbacks, nightmares, or intrusive thoughts), emotional numbing, and avoidance of circumstances reminiscent of war experiences, and hyper-arousal. These symptoms together form post-traumatic stress disorder (PTSD) (American Psychiatric Association, 1994). To date, in psychology, PTSD is the most investigated topic in relation to war.

The findings of these types of studies show that a significant but limited percentage of individuals exposed to war will develop PTSD (Kulka, 1990; Sutker & Allain, 1996). In an attempt to examine the lasting effects of wars on people, a team of 22 researchers surveyed 2,091 Rwandan individuals, eight years after the end of Rwandan genocide. The aim was to determine the nature of the experiences the Rwandan society had been exposed to and the lasting psychological effects of these experiences. The results indicated that the majority of the examined individuals reported being exposed to what can be described as a traumatic experience in relation to the war, with 75.4 percent of the sample reporting that they were forced to flee their homes, 73 percent lost a member of their family, and 70.9 percent had property destroyed or lost. In addition, 2,074 out of the 2,091 participants indicated that they were exposed to some form of violence. However, only 518 participants (24.8%) out of the 2,091 total participants reported symptoms meeting PTSD criteria (Pham, Weinstein & Longman, 2004).

Similarly, Hotopf and others (2006) compared a random sample of 4,722 British soldiers who served in Iraq to a sample of 5,550 soldiers who did not serve. The participants in the two samples were asked to fill in a questionnaire that covered PTSD, mental disorders, general well-being, alcohol consumption, physical symptoms, and fatigue. The results did not show a significant difference between the two samples in any of the examined criteria. Accordingly, Kellezi, Reicher, and Cassidy (2009) indicated most people who have been exposed to armed conflicts do survive without developing any mental, psychological, or emotional disorder. A significant body of research indicates that people are capable of overcoming various negative events related to armed conflicts. Whether we are examining civilians amid armed conflicts, people displaced as a result of armed conflicts (Gorst-Unsworth, Van Velsen & Turner, 1993), victims of torture (Holtz, 1998; Van Velsen, Gorst-Unsworth & Turner, 1996), indeed, several studies have shown that even Holocaust survivors and victims of the Rwandan genocide have overcome that adverse experience without developing any significant pathological reaction (see Antonovsky, Maoz, Dowty & Wijsenbeek, 1971; Pham, Weinstein & Longman, 2004; Yehuda, McFarlane & Shalev, 1998).

This suggests that it is important to examine other aspects related to war alongside the negative psychological consequences. The question of how and why people who have been in war construct such experiences in their own words is of great importance to understanding war. Currently, a limited but growing number of researchers are examining different aspects related to armed conflicts. The role of social identity in relation to war is one of the growing areas in psychological research (e.g., Herrera, 2003; Leudar, Marsland & Nekvapil, 2004). As Pham, Weinstein and Longman (2004) indicated, "one of the tragedies of war is that individuals suffer not for anything they have done but simply because of the category they happen to belong to" (p. 74).

The relationship between armed conflicts and collective identity

Thompson (1980) argues that people can kill fellow human beings if they label them as an enemy. The relationship between collective identity and war is usually taken as profound and self-evident. It is almost a universal presumption in the social sciences that people may kill (or warrant the killing of) others if they view these "others" as members of a different group (cf. Graham, Keenan & Dowd, 2004; Herrera, 2003; Leudar, Marsland & Nekvapil, 2004). This is proposed to be especially prevailing when the other group is depicted as constituting a serious threat to themselves or their own group (see Gartzke & Gleditsch, 2006; Glenny, 1992; Robinson, 2005; Thompson, 1980). This presumption functions as the underlying basis for a significant proportion of social research studies that discuss war. A substantial number of researchers have argued that social identities play a vital role in instigating and sustaining wars (see Glenny, 1992; Sokolovic, 2005). They also indicate that social identities influence people's positions toward conflicts. Differences between collective identities are widely blamed for many armed conflicts (cf. Broch-due, 2005; DeRouen, 2007; Mamdani, 2001).

Various armed conflicts have been attributed to and associated with differences in the salient collective identities among the fighting parties. Many researchers chronicling modern wars have hinted at the role of conflicting identities in the course and nature of the armed conflicts they address (Castano & Slawuta, 2008, Gartzke & Gleditsch, 2006; Atlas, Licklider, 1999). For instance, the differences in sectarian identities are seen as a principal cause of the civil conflicts in Iraq (Fearon, 2008), Lebanon (O'Balance, 1998), and Northern Ireland (Tonge, 2006). Equally, ethnic identity is widely described as one of the defining origins of the Rwandan civil war, which resulted in the loss of hundreds of thousands of lives (Mamdani, 2001). The Iraqi army's attacks against the northern part of Iraq in the 1980s are yet another example of what is described as the role of collective identities in facilitating armed conflicts. In these attacks, more than 180,000 Iraqi Kurds lost their lives (Makiya, 1993). Thousands of people were murdered with nerve and mustard gas. Thousands of Iraqi Kurdish women were raped, and more than three hundred towns and villages were completely or partly destroyed

(Hiltermann, 2008; Makiya, 1993). The Iraqi government described these campaigns as a war of self-defence. One of the justifications given was the description of Kurds as foreigners and traitors who had backstabbed Iraqis. Another example of what is portrayed as evidence of the relationship between conflicting identities and armed conflicts is the Pakistani army's attack against Bangladesh after its declaration of independence in 1972. Pakistani soldiers killed thousands of Bengali civilians. It is estimated that between two hundred and four hundred thousand Bengali women were raped (Makiya, 1993).

Additionally, when thinking of Al-Qaeda, it is hard to overlook its radical religious identity, which functions as a rhetorical catalyst for justifying its criminal attacks against different groups of people. In almost all of his speeches, Bin Laden constructs himself as speaking on behalf of true Muslims, who he argues are being oppressed by Christians, Jews, and their proxies.

At the same time, "group fragmentation" and the "resurrection of sub-identities" among fighting groups is an endemic, self-evident phenomenon in modern wars. Indeed, in most civil conflicts that have taken place in the past forty years, the fighting sides which were perceived as having unambiguous salient collective identities have since fragmented into smaller groups along the lines of newly elevated collective identities. A prime example is the Lebanese civil war (1976-1991), which started as a war between Christians and Palestinian Muslims who had conflicting goals. Throughout the course of this war, the Christian party fragmented into several competing groups. Each of these groups developed a new salient identity that replaced the previous one. The same thing happened on the Lebanese and Palestinian Muslim side, which also fragmented into several groups, with each one of these groups further splintering into even smaller groups. The group fragmentation process is usually accompanied by two striking phenomena. Firstly, with every fragmentation a sub-identity is invoked, which provides a new definition of the conflict for the fighting sides. Secondly, almost every fragmentation is accompanied by a confrontation between the new group and its mother group (see Atlas & Licklider, 1999; Gartzke & Gleditsch, 2006).

Sudan offers another compelling example, having witnessed civil wars from 1955-72, 1983-2005, and again from 2023 to the present. The initial conflict began as a struggle between the Muslim north and the non-Muslim south, where the southern population felt suppressed. As the wars continued, new groups kept emerging with new identities and demands. Factions within both the north and south began fighting amongst themselves. In 2023, yet another civil war broke out between the state army and a militia that had been affiliated and allied with it for many years.

In Zimbabwe, the rebels that toppled the white government fragmented into several factions and fought against each other viciously (Atlas & Licklider, 1999). In Afghanistan, once the Mujahideen reached Kabul in 1992, they started attacking each other, starting a bloody war that lasted for many years and has not ended yet (see Wahab & Youngerman, 2007). Moreover, many civil conflicts have taken place in countries that were in inter-state conflicts. Another important example is Iraq, which descended into a civil conflict in 1992 and in 2004, shortly after it was defeated in inter-state wars. Right after the two wars ended, Iraqis started fighting against each other on a sectarian and ethnic basis. This indicates that collective identities need to be considered as a topic for investigation when discussing wars, rather than approaching them as an independent factor. It is important to pay attention to how and why people who are in conflicts convey collective identity.

In the following sections, I briefly review some of the theories and understandings of collective identity in social psychology.

Discursive understandings of war through rhetorical accounts

The argument that considers rhetoric to be an important aspect of armed conflicts is by no means exclusive to discursive or rhetorical studies. Indeed, a substantial number of researchers who have explained and chronicled various armed conflicts have paid considerable attention to the narratives of the examined conflict (e.g., Codevilla & Seabury, 2006; Glenny, 1992; Huppauf, 1997; Schnabel & Carment, 2003). These researchers have indicated that the accounts of wars produced by different sides function as effective tools to create specific realities. Hence, examining the discourse of any war is considered an instrumental means of understanding the course of armed conflicts.

It is argued that when people describe a war, they mainly concentrate on specific incidents which they see as the defining events (cf. Glenny, 1992). These events are not the whole conflict but they are usually presented as the most relevant and important events or motives of the conflict. In particular, these include: the trigger incident that caused the conflict, the motive behind the conflict, the final result of the conflict, and the definition of the fighting sides. These issues are not neutral testimonies of the war; rather, they are discursive formulations that are designed to convince the audience to take a specific position in relation to the conflict. Consequently, in almost all conflicts, defining these incidents is a highly controversial and sensitive issue due to their evaluative nature. Lomsky-Feder (1995) criticises the lack of attention in research to the way people understand and present their experiences of armed conflicts. She blames this lack of attention on the dominant presupposition that presents the experience of war as solely a traumatic experience. She maintains that "the prevailing research does not ask whether and how war experience is integrated into the world of the individual, or whether the experience necessarily distorts and disturbs his life" (Lomsky-Feder, 1995, p. 464).

Potter (1996) demonstrated that the same event could be constituted differently by different people or even by the same person. These accounts and constructions of events are either for desired ends or as a means to achieve further goals. In modern armed conflicts which are covered by various types of media outlets, politicians and media personnel play an important role in constituting the events of the conflict, identifying and defining the groups involved and forming general public opinion toward the conflict (Billig, 1995; Reicher, 1996; Hutchby, 2006; Herrera, 2003). Accounts of individuals who are in such positions are considered elite opinions (van Dijk, 1993). Elite opinion plays a significant role in justifying, promoting, warranting, or rejecting a specific side or position (Kuusisto, 1998; Campbell, 1993; Herrera, 2003). It is also designed to mobilise people to behave in a specific way. For example, Leudar et al. (2004) analysed public speeches delivered soon after the September 11th attacks by US President, George W. Bush, the British Prime Minister, Tony Blair, and the head of Al-Qaeda, Osama bin Laden. They found that the three different speakers constructed different accounts of the exact same event. However, all these accounts are motivated accounts that are designed to accomplish a specific social action. These accounts were constructed as discursive means to warrant the speaker's position at the expense of the opponent's argument. For instance, Bush's accounts were designed to portray the attacks as an aggression and consequently to prepare the ground for retaliation. Blair's accounts functioned as a way of condemning the attacks and affiliating with the Americans against Al-Qaeda. Bin Laden's accounts were designed to warrant the attacks and condemned the American retaliation. It is important to stress that the three different speakers constructed the involved groups in a way that served their own interests.

Moreover, several studies have indicated that in wartime, people who are directly involved in the war can provide different accounts of the events of war. Issues such as who was involved, the causes, and who is responsible for the conflict are controversial and sensitive questions (Herrera, 2003; Reicher, 1996). For example, Lomsky-Feder, (1995) reported that Israeli soldiers who participated in the same conflicts provided very different accounts of their personal experiences of the conflict. They responded to issues such as who was involved, whether they were affected or not, why, and how the war started and finished in significantly different ways.

References

Allawi, A. A. (2007). *The occupation of Iraq: Winning the war, losing the peace.* New Haven, CT: Yale University Press.

American Psychiatric Association. (1994). *Diagnostic and Statistical Manual* (Vol. IV, 4th ed.). Washington: APA.

Antaki, C., & Widdicombe, S. (Eds.). (1998). *Identities in talk.* London: Sage.

Antonovsky, A., Maoz, B., Dowty, N., & Wijsenbeek, H. (1971). Twenty-five years later: A limited study of sequelae of the concentration camp experience. *Social Psychiatry, 6*(4), 186–193.

Atlas, P. & Licklider, R. (1999). Conflict among former allies after civil war settlement: Sudan, Zimbabwe, Chad, and Lebanon. *Journal of Peace Research, 36*(1), 35-54.

BBC News (2005, 30 January). Iraq Health Ministry Figures. [online]

Begic, S. & McDonald, T. W. (2006). The psychological effects of exposure to wartime trauma in Bosnian residents and refugees: implications for treatment and service provision. *International Journal of Mental Health and Addiction, 4*(3), 319-329.

Beiser, M. & Fleming, J. A. E. (1986). Measuring psychiatric disorder among Southeast Asian refugees. *Psychological Medicine 16*(3), 627–639.

Bell, D. (2009). *The first total war: Napoleon's Europe and the birth of modern warfare.* Boston, MA: Houghton Mifflin Harcourt.

Billig, M. (1995). *Banal Nationalism.* London: Sage Publications.

Broch-Due, V. (2005). *Violence and belonging: the quest for identity in post-colonial Africa.* London: Routledge.

Burke, E. (2004). *Reflections on the revolution in France* (edited by L. G. Mitchell). Oxford University Press. (Original work published 1790)

Cambridge University Press. (2009). *Cambridge academic content dictionary* (p. 1073, "war").

Campbell, D. (1993). Cold wars: Securing identity, identifying danger. In: F. M. Dolan & T. L. Dumm (Eds.), *Rhetorical republic: Governing representations in American politics*, 39-60. Amherst: University of Massachusetts Press.

Castano, E., Slawuta, P. & Leidner, B. (2008). Social Identification Processes, Group Dynamics and the Behavior of Combatants. *International Review of the Red Cross, 90*(870), 259-271.

Chehab, Z. (2005). *Iraq ablaze: Inside the insurgency.* London: I.B. Tauris.

Chung, R. C., & Singer, M. K. (1995). Interpretation of symptom presentation and distress: A Southeast Asian refugee example. *Journal of Nervous and Mental Disease, 183*(10), 639-648.

Coburn, P. (2008). *Muqtada al-Sadr and the battle for the future of Iraq.* New York, NY: Scribner.

Codevilla, A. & Seabury, P. (2006). *War: ends and means* (2nd ed.). Washington: Potomac Books.

Crnobrnja, M. (1996). *The Yugoslav drama* (2nd ed.). London/New York: I.B. Tauris Publishers.

DeRouen, K. (2007). *Enduring internal rivalries: A new framework for the study of civil war.* Paper presented at the annual meeting of the Southern Political Science Association, New Orleans, LA, Jan 03, 2007.

Des Forges, A. (2007). A call to genocide: radio in Rwanda, 1994. In: A. Thomson (Ed.), *Media and the Rwanda genocide* (pp. 41-54). Pluto Press.

Dybdahl, R. (2001). A psychosocial support programme for children and mothers in war. *Clinical Child Psychology and Psychiatry, 69*(6), 425-436.

Edwards, D. (2005). Discursive psychology. In K. L. Fitch. & R. E. Sanders (Eds.), *Handbook of language and social interaction.* New York: Erlbaum.

Edwards, D., & Potter, J. (1992). *Discursive Psychology.* London: Sage.

Edwards, D., & Potter, J. (1993). Language and causation: A discursive action model of description and attribution. *Psychological Review, 100*(1), 23-41.

Edwards, D., & Potter, J. (2003). Discursive psychology and mental states. In H. Molder & J. Potter (Eds.), *Conversation and cognition.* Cambridge: University Press.

Fearon, J. (2008). Economic development, insurgency, and civil war. In E. Helpman (Ed.), *Institutions and economic performance* (pp. 292-238). Cambridge: Harvard University Press.

Finney, P. (2002). On memory, identity and war. *Rethinking History, 6*(1), pp. 1-13.

Gan, S., & Solomon, Z. (1987). *Combat stress reactions: The enduring toll of war.* New York, NY: Plenum Press.

Gartzke, E. & Gleditsch, K. S. (2006). Identity and Conflict: Ties That Bind and Differences That Divide. *European Journal of International Relations, 12*(1): 53–87.

Glenny, M. (1992). *The fall of Yugoslavia: the third Balkan War.* London: Penguin.

Goldson, E. (1996). The effect of war on children. *Child Abuse & Neglect: The International Journal, 20*(9), 809-819.

Gorst-Unsworth, C., Van Velsen, C. & Turner, S. W. (1993). Prospective study of survivors of torture and organised violence: Examining the existential dilemma. *Journal of Nervous and Mental Disease, 181*(4), 263-264.

Graham, P., Keenan, T., & Dowd, A. (2004). A call to arms at the end of history: a discourse-historical analysis of George W. Bush's declaration of war on terror. *Discourse and Society 15*(2-3), 199-221.

Hammack, P. L. (2006). Identity, conflict, and coexistence: Life stories of Israeli and Palestinian adolescents. *Journal of Adolescent Research, 21*(4), 323-369.

Herodotus. *The Histories.* (Various ed. Original work published c. 440 BCE.)

Herrera, M. (2003). Constructing social categories and seeking collective influence: self-categorization and the discursive construction of a conflict.

International Journal of Psychology and Psychological Therapy, 3(1), 27-57.

Hiltermann, J. 2008. Failed responsibility: Iraqi refugees in Syria, Jordan and Lebanon. *International Crisis Group Middle East Report, 77*, p.iii, 1-42.

Holtz, T. H. (1998). Refugee trauma versus torture trauma: A retrospective controlled cohort study of Tibetan refugees. *Journal of Nervous and Mental Disease, 186*(1), 24-34.

Hotopf, M., Hull, L., Fear, N. T., Browne, T., Horn, O., Iversen, A. , Jones, M. , Murphy, D., Bland, D., Earnshaw, M., Greenberg, N., Hacker Hughes, J., Tate, A. R., Dandeker, C., Rona, R. & Wessely, S. (2006). The health of UK military personnel who deployed to the 2003 Iraq war: a cohort study. *Lancet, 367*(9524), 1731 –1741.

Huppauf, B. (1997). Modernity and violence: observations concerning a contradictory relationship. In B. Huppauf (Ed.), *War, violence and the modern condition* (pp. 1-29). Berlin/New York: de Gruyter.

Hutchby, I. (2006). *Media talk: Conversation analysis and the study of broadcasting.* Maidenhead: Open University Press.

Hynes, H. P. (2004). On the battlefield of women's bodies: An overview of the harm of war to women, *Women's International Studies Forum, 27*(5-6): 431-445.

Iraq Body Count. (2024). *Documented civilian deaths from violence.* Retrieved from https://www.iraqbodycount.org/

Kellezi, B., Reicher. D. & Cassidy, C. (2009). Surviving the Kosovo conflict: A study of social identity, appraisal of extreme events, and mental well-being. Applied Psychology; An international Review. Special issue: *Social Identity, Health and Well-being, 58*(1), 59-83.

Kulka, R. A. (1990). *Trauma and the Vietnam War generation: report of findings from the National Vietnam Veterans Readjustment Study.* New York: Brunner/Mazel.

Kuusisto, R. (1998). Framing the wars in the Gulf and in Bosnia: The rhetorical definitions of the Western Power Leaders in Action. *Journal of Peace Research, 35*(5), 603-620.

Leudar, I., Marsland, V. & Nekvapil, J. (2004). On membership categorization: 'Us,' 'them' and 'doing violence' in political discourse. *Discourse & Society, 15*(2-3), 243-266.

Leudar, I. & Nekvapil, J. (2007). The war on terror and Muslim Briton's safety: A week in the life of a dialogical network. *Ethnographic Studies 9*, 44-62.

Lomsky-Feder, E. (1995). The meaning of war through veterans' eyes: A phenomenological analysis of life stories." *International Sociology, 10*(4), 463-482.

Makiya, K. (1993). *Cruelty and silence: War, tyranny, uprising, and the Arab world.* New York, NY: W.W. Norton & Company.

Mamdani, M. (2001). *When victims become killers: Colonialism, nativism, and the genocide in Rwanda.* Princeton: Princeton University Press.

Miller, K. E., Weine, S. M., Ramic, A., Brkic, N., Djuric Bjedic, Z., Smajkic, A., Boskailo, E. & Worthington, G. (2002). The relative contribution of war experiences and exile-related stressors to levels of psychological distress among Bosnian refugees. *Journal of Traumatic Stress, 15*(5), 377-387.

Muldoon, O. T. & Downes, C. (2007). Social identification and post-traumatic stress symptoms in post-conflict Northern Ireland. British *Journal of Psychiatry, 191*(8), 146–149.

North, C.S., Nixon, S.J., Shariat, S., Mallonee, S., McMillen, J.C., Spitznagel, E.L., & Smith, E.M., (1999). Psychiatric disorders among survivors of the Oklahoma City bombing. *Journal of the American Medical Association, 282*(8), 755-762.

O'Balance, E. (1998). *Civil War in Lebanon, 1975-92.* London: St. Martin's Press Inc.

Oddo, J. (2011). War legitimation discourse: Representing 'Us' and 'Them' in four US presidential addresses. *Discourse & Society, 22*(3), 287-314.

Orth, U., Cahill, S. P., Foa, E. B. & Maercker, A. (2008). Anger and posttraumatic stress disorder symptoms in crime victims: A longitudinal analysis. *Journal of Consulting and Clinical Psychology, 76*(2), 208–218.

Potter, J. (1996). *Representing reality: Discourse, rhetoric and social construction.* London: Sage.

Potter, J. (2005). Making psychology relevant. *Discourse & Society, 16*(5), 739-747.

Potter, J., & Wetherell, M. (1987). *Discourse and social psychology: Beyond attitudes and behaviour.* London: Sage.

Regan, R. J. (1996). *Just war: Principles and cases.* Washington, DC: Catholic University of America Press.

Reicher, S. (1996). 'The battle of Westminster': Developing the social identity model of crowd behaviour in order to explain the initiation and development of collective conflict. *European Journal of Social Psychology, 26,* 115-134.

Robinson, A. (2005). The mythology of war. *Peace Review, 17*(1), 33 – 38.

Russell, B. (2004). *Power: A new social analysis.* London, UK: Routledge. (Original work published 1938.)

Sacks, H. (1992). *Lectures on conversation.* Oxford: Basil Blackwell.

Schegloff, E.A. (1999). Discourse, pragmatics, conversation analysis. *Discourse Studies, 1*(4), 405 – 435.

Schlenger, W. E., Caddell, J. M., Ebert, L., Jordan, B. K., Rouke, K. M., Wilson, D., Thalji, L., Dennis, J. M., Fairbank, J. A. & Kulka, R. A. (2002). Psychological reactions to terrorist attacks: findings from the national study of American's reactions to September 11. *JAMA 288*(5), 581–588.

Schnabel, A., & Carment, D. (Eds.). (2003). *Conflict prevention: Path to peace or grand illusion?* Tokyo, Japan: United Nations University Press.

Smith, P., Perrin, S., Yule, W. & Rabe-Hesketh, S. (2001). War exposure and maternal reactions in the psychological adjustment of children from Bosnia-Hercegovina. *Journal of Child Psychology and Psychiatry, 42*(3), 395-404.

Sokolovic, D. (1995). Is there an ethnic problem? *Balkan Forum, 4*(13), 61-95.

Sokolovic, D. (2005). How to conceptualize the tragedy of Bosnia: Civil, ethnic, religious war or...? *War Crimes, Genocide & Crimes against Humanity 1*(1), 115-130.

Sutker, P. & Allain, A. (1996). Assessment of PTSD and other mental disorders in World War II and Korean Conflict POW survivors and combat veterans. *Psychological Assessment, 8*(1), 18-25.

Tajfel, H. (1978). *Differentiation between social groups: Studies in the social psychology of intergroup relations.* London: Academic Press.

Tajfel, H. (1981). *Human groups and social categories.* Cambridge University Press.

Thabet, A. A., Abu Tawahina, A., El Sarraj, E., & Vostanis, P. (2008). Exposure to war trauma and PTSD among parents and children in the Gaza strip. *European Child & Adolescent Psychiatry, 17*(4), 191-199.

Thompson, A. S. (1980). Counseling psychology in the year 2000. *The Counseling Psychologist, 8*(4), 21–22.

Thompson, A. (2007). *The media and the Rwanda genocide.* London: Pluto Press.

Thulesius, H. & Hakansson, A. (1999). Screening for posttraumatic stress disorder symptoms among Bosnian refugees. *Journal of Traumatic Stress, 12*(1), 167–174.

Tonge, J. (2006). *Northern Ireland.* Cambridge: Polity Press.

Turner, J.C. (1991). *Social influence.* Milton Keynes: Open University Press.

United Nations. (2023). *Children and women among displaced populations.* Retrieved from https://www.un.org

United Nations (1996, 26 August). *Promotion and protection of the rights of children: Impact of armed conflict on children.* Retrieved from http://www.unicef.org/

Ursano, R. J., Fullerton, C.S., Vance, K., Kao, T.C. (1999). Posttraumatic stress disorder and identification in disaster workers. *The American Journal of Psychiatry, 156*(3), 353-9.

Van Velsen, C., Gorst-Unsworth, C. & Turner, S. (1996). Survivors of torture and organized violence: Demography and diagnosis. *Journal of Traumatic Stress, 9*(2), 181-193.

Wahab, S. & Youngerman, B. (2007). *A brief history of Afghanistan.* New York: Facts On File.

Weine, S.M., Becker, D.F., McGlashan, T.H., Laub, D., Lazrove, S., Vojvoda, D. & Hyman, L. (1995). Psychiatric consequences of "ethnic cleansing": Clinical assessments and trauma testimonies of newly resettled Bosnian refugees. *American Journal of Psychiatry, 152*(4), 536-542.

Weine, S.M., Vojvoda, D., Becker, D.F., McGlashan, T.H., Hodzic, E., Laub, D., Hyman, L., Sawyer, M. & Lazrove, S. (1998). PTSD symptoms in Bosnian refugees one year after resettlement in the United States. *American Journal of Psychiatry, 155*(4), 562–64.

Wendt, A. (1994). Collective identity formation and the international state. *American Political Science Review, 88*(2), 384-396.

Widdicombe, S., & Wooffitt, R. (1995). The language of youth subcultures: Social identity in action. Hertfordshire: Harvester Wheatsheaf.

Witmer, T. A. & Culver, S. M. (2001). Trauma and resilience among Bosnian refugee families: A critical review of the literature. *Journal of Social Work Research and Evaluation, 2*(2), 173-187.

Woodward, K. (2004). Questions of Identity. In: K. Woodward (Ed.), *Questioning identity: Gender, class, ethnicity* (pp. 5 – 41). London: Routledge.

Yehuda, R., McFarlane, A. C. & Shalev, A. Y. (1998). Predicting the development of posttraumatic stress disorder from the acute response to a traumatic event. *Biological Psychiatry, 44*(12), 1305-1313.

Chapter 3

Tales of wars: Voices of the people

Establishment of Iraq, Lebanon, and Israel

The Middle East is a region of old and deep-rooted identities

Bernard Lewis, 1998, p. 9

The current states of Iraq, Lebanon, and Israel, like many other countries in the Middle East, were established as a result of agreements between European powers and local leaders following the defeat of the Ottoman Empire in the First World War. The Sykes-Picot Agreement of 1916 and subsequent treaties, such as the Treaty of Sèvres in 1920, were instrumental in delineating the borders of contemporary Middle Eastern states. While the French and British attempted to consider ethnic and sectarian divisions in their border-drawing efforts, the complex intermingling of different groups across the region made it nearly impossible to create entirely homogeneous nation-states. As a result, many of the new borders cut across ethnic and sectarian lines, laying the groundwork for future conflicts.

Before the Second World War, most of the region was nominally under the control of the Ottoman Caliphate, though many areas were governed by regional rulers with their own political systems. The Ottoman Empire, particularly in the later years of its rule, increasingly repressed minorities and non-Muslim populations, often treating them as second-class citizens. The Turkish elite, which dominated the Ottoman administration, acted as the ruling class, maintaining control over various ethnic and religious groups through a combination of coercion and the administrative autonomy granted under the Millet system.

The Millet system allowed different religious communities, such as Christians and Jews, to manage some of their own affairs in matters such as marriage, education, and religious practices. However, this system also reinforced the secondary status of non-Muslims within the empire, as they were subject to various restrictions and higher taxes. The Syrians and Lebanese, particularly the Christian communities, suffered greatly under Ottoman rule, paying a heavy price for their aspirations for self-determination.

In major cities and towns, diverse communities coexisted, each governed by their own religious councils as recognised by the Ottomans. However, with the fall of the Ottoman Empire, Western powers felt compelled to establish new borders and national institutions to regulate the movement of people and goods and to establish national states.

In the case of Iraq, Israel, and Lebanon, the borders have juxtaposed groups of people who have different religious, ethnic, and racial identities. Looking at the modern history of the region, one can argue that Iraq – predominantly Kurdish in the north, Sunni in the west, and Shiite in the centre and the south – is an artificial state in terms of its national identity. Iraqis have hardly acted freely as a unified nation in the past thousand years. The same applies to Lebanon, which was initially a French idea to protect the Syrian Christians, as they were called then, through creating a state in which they could be the majority. Jews have been suppressed in the Middle East for centuries. The British administration helped establish the state of Israel to protect the Jews who were living as minorities in the Middle East as well as Europe and to give them a state. Eight hundred thousand Jews had been banished from their homelands in Iraq, Syria, Egypt, Iran, and Morocco by the national governments that took control of these countries after the end of the British and French mandates.

The three countries have witnessed and participated in numerous civil and inter-state conflicts. Given their diverse ethnic, religious, and sectarian makeup, these conflicts are often deeply rooted in the interplay among these various groups that make up the populations. Thus, the issue of collective identity in Lebanon, Iraq, and Israel is an essential and consequential one. It is deeply associated with the discourse of the armed conflicts through which these countries have been living. Studying the inter-group relationships in these three countries might provide useful information for other countries in the region that are experiencing similar situations. It also may provide useful ideas for countries that are, or expect to become, ethnically or religiously diverse communities either due to immigration or other factors.

The war in Iraq

On 19th March 2003, American, British, and other coalition forces launched the Iraq War, marking the beginning of the Second Gulf War, with the primary objective of toppling Saddam Hussein's regime. The invasion was justified by the US and UK governments based on several key arguments. Chief among them was the belief that Saddam's regime possessed weapons of mass destruction (WMDs), which posed a significant threat to regional and global security. Despite extensive international debate, these claims were later discredited as no WMDs were found in Iraq. Additionally, the coalition alleged links between Saddam Hussein's government and terrorist organisations, including al-Qaeda, though these connections were also later disproven.

Beyond the security threats, the coalition highlighted the humanitarian aspect of removing a dictator responsible for gross human rights violations. Saddam Hussein's regime was notorious for its brutal repression of internal dissent, particularly against Iraq's Kurdish and Shia Muslim populations. During the late 1980s, Saddam's government launched the Anfal campaign against the Kurdish population in northern Iraq, a systematic military operation that included mass killings, destruction of villages, and the use of chemical weapons, most infamously in the town of Halabja in 1988, where approximately 5,000 civilians were killed. This campaign has been widely recognized as an act of genocide.

The Shia population, primarily in southern Iraq, also suffered severe persecution under Saddam's rule. Following the 1991 Gulf War, when a Shia uprising erupted in the south, Saddam's forces brutally suppressed the rebellion, resulting in the deaths of tens of thousands. The repression included mass executions, torture, and the destruction of entire communities. After the fall of Saddam Hussein's regime in 2003, numerous mass graves were uncovered across Iraq, providing concrete evidence of these atrocities. Estimates suggest that these mass graves contain the remains of hundreds of thousands of Kurds, Shia, and other victims of Saddam's regime.

The discovery of these graves revealed the extent of the regime's crimes, with the total number of victims estimated to be in the hundreds of thousands. These graves, often located in remote areas, were left undisclosed for years, further compounding the suffering of the victims' families, who were often left without knowledge of their loved ones' fates.

Several Arab states supported the Western coalition's invasion of Iraq, either covertly or explicitly, particularly Egypt, Saudi Arabia, Kuwait, and Qatar, which provided essential logistical support to the coalition forces. By 8th April 2003, the former Iraqi regime had collapsed, and the Iraqi army was nowhere to be seen. The Americans established the Coalition Provisional Authority (CPA) to administer Iraq. On 13 July 2003, the Iraqi Governing Council (IGC) was established as a provisional government of Iraq. In January 2005, the first elections in post-Saddam Iraq took place. As a result of this election, the Shiites and the Kurds gained a significant share in the Iraqi government for the first time since the establishment of Iraq. At the same time, the Sunnis in Iraq saw the American invasion and the formation of the IGC as undermining their long-standing monopoly of power over Iraq (see Sifry & Cerf, 2007; Woodward, 2004). Thus, soon after the fall of the regime, various Sunni organisations, such as Al-Qaeda, started an insurgency movement aimed at forcing the Americans to leave and at the same regaining power. These organisations enjoyed significant support from the Arab countries that advocated for toppling Saddam but feared the Shiites' and Kurds' rise to power (see Ajami, 2006). Tens of thousands of Iraqis, mainly Shiites, were massacred in suicide attacks carried out by the Sunni insurgents. By 2006, Iraq was literally in a state of civil war between Iraqi Shiites and Sunnis, which claimed the lives of thousands of people and displaced many more Iraqis. The war lasted for over ten years. The different reactions to Gaza war of 2023 and Israeli attacks against Hezbollah show that Iraq remains in a volatile situation, where open civil war could erupt at any time.

Lebanon amid armed conflicts

Lebanon, although currently less violent, remains largely in a similar situation to Iraq. Lebanese people have been in several civil conflicts and wars with Israel since 1948.

The July 2006 war was a major open confrontation between Lebanese Hezbollah and Israel and a precursor of the 2024 conflict. To date, the name of this war is still disputed in Lebanon.

Hezbollah refers to it as the July War; in contrast, several other Lebanese media outlets describe it as the Israel-Hezbollah War (see Achcar & Warschawski, 2007). Since this war, Lebanese society has been divided into two main competing factions: the opposition party and the government party. The opposition party is composed of all the significant Shiite organisations, i.e., Hezbollah and AMAL, in addition to the Free Patriotic Movement, which has the biggest Christian bloc in the Lebanese parliament, and other smaller political parties. The government group, in contrast, is composed of the biggest Sunni organisation, the Future Movement, and other smaller Christian and Druze parties. It is important to note that the opposition parties gained more than 55 per cent of the overall votes in the 2009 parliamentary election, but due to the biased geographic distribution of the seats, they won 57 out of 128 seats. From 2006 to 2008, the opposition parties staged several protests and a sit-in in the heart of Beirut City in an effort to sack the government, and this is where I conducted most of my interviews in Lebanon. In May 2008, militiamen loyal to the opposition clashed with armed militia loyal to the Lebanese government. The opposition fighters took over several important sites in Beirut and other cities and forced the government to negotiate with them. On 21 May 2008, the rival Lebanese factions signed what is known as the Doha Agreement. This agreement resulted in the formation of a national unity government and banned resorting to violence to resolve domestic disputes.

I have shown that there is a dominant presupposition underlying most, if not all, prior psychological studies: war is essentially and principally a negative experience with long-lasting effects on people's psychological, behavioural, and mental states. Thus, a significant number of psychological studies have been dedicated to uncovering the exact psychological and mental consequences of the war experience or the mechanisms that protect people from the effects of war. However, the findings of these sorts of studies are often inconsistent or contradictory (cf. Kellezi, Reicher & Cassidy, 2009; Lifton, 1973; Milgram, 1986; Muldoon & Downes, 2007). Furthermore, the majority of people who have experienced major wars, such as the Second World War, have overcome most of the psychological and mental implications of that experience. Indeed, several studies have demonstrated that most of the countries that participated in the Second World War enjoyed their longest and strongest economic and cultural boom shortly after the end of that war.

In her study of the ways in which veterans describe their experiences of war, Lomsky-Feder (1995) found that different soldiers present different understandings and evaluations of the same war. Similarly, Sokolovic (2005) argues that war is a complex issue and the accurate way to understand any war is to examine the views of the people who experienced that war. The persistence of war, whether it occurs in the form of civil conflicts or inter-state wars, suggests that the ways in which armed conflicts are described and justified need to be examined thoroughly. Examining how people who are in war rhetorically construct, warrant, reject, and describe the events of the war is an important way to understand war from a discursive perspective (cf. Billig, 1995; Edwards & Potter, 1992; Hammack, 2006; Leudar & Nekvapil, 2007; Potter, 1996).

In this chapter, I do not start from the view of war as self-evidently a negative experience; instead, I adhere to a discursive psychology approach. The starting point for this book in general, and this chapter in particular, is what Harvey Sacks (1984) describes as examining people's utterances without having a pre-established agenda. I analyse a number of lay accounts that discuss armed conflicts that took place in Iraq and Lebanon. The goal is to understand how people who have been in war portray their experiences of the war in their own words.

Here, I show that the participants, both Iraqi and Lebanese laypeople, convey their experiences of war through building coherent accounts in the form of complete tales. Different speakers employ various discursive strategies to create different versions of the war. In these accounts, when asked to talk about their experiences of the war, participants do not merely present descriptions of their experiences; rather, their accounts contain both characterisations and explanations of the war's events, which are interwoven.

Furthermore, each one of these accounts comprises positive and negative portrayals of specific aspects of war. These contrasting portrayals are integrated into coherent stories of the war. These stories are designed to perform various discursive functions.

Data and analysis

This chapter draws its data from semi-structured interviews which were conducted and recorded in Iraq in 2005 and in Lebanon in 2006. The participants are all civilians who had been living in their countries during the conflicts. The subjects were approached at Basra University as well as in the streets or coffeehouses in Basra city (2005) and were asked to participate. The Lebanese participants were approached in coffeehouses, as well as a sit-in protest which was organised primarily by Shiite and Christian parties in Beirut (2006) to demand the removal of the Lebanese government. The analysis process began with listening to the tape recordings several times. As Hutchby and Wooffitt (1998) indicated, listening and understanding the data during the transcription process is an important part of the analysis.

The incorporation of noble principles

In the following three extracts, the participants convey coherent tales of the war. In the analysis, I focus on examining how, in each of these tales, the speakers incorporate positive evaluations into descriptions of the effects of the war.

EXTRACT 3.1. PARTICIPANT NUMBER 1, AROUND 60 YEARS OLD, MALE, TAXI DRIVER; BEIRUT, LEBANON.

I: can you tell me something about yourself?
P: I'm from the South
south of Lebanon (.) my name is H.M.M.
I: can you tell me about the events that took place in July

and August?
P: thank God it was not that bad (.)
no dignity without sacrifices (.2)
we can't preserve our dignity
and honour without giving up blood (.)
if we want to have dignity then we have to sacrifice (.)
you didn't go to the south to see the attacks? (2)
ohhh they have destroyed so many buildings, many many
buildings
were entirely destroyed (.) a whole complex was erased
nothing remained from those huge new buildings
almost nothing, many many people have lost their lives
the attacks were savage and brutal
they didn't spare civilians or the elderly (.)
or women not even the children

In this extract, the interviewee introduces himself as being "from the South". The general account reported by various media outlets and the participant's account (see lines 11-19) portray the south of Lebanon as the region most affected by the war. It is a predominantly Shiite area and is typically described as the base of Hezbollah. Thus, through describing himself as a person who belongs to that Lebanese area, the participant is building what Sacks (1992) describes as *category entitlement* for himself. He is presenting himself as someone with direct knowledge of the war, entitled to speak about the war, and capable of presenting a factual account of the events (cf. Potter, 1996).

In line 3, he presents his full name, which can be seen as a way of taking responsibility for the argument he will present (see Edwards, 1997). The participant here is attending to the issue of accountability in a way that is designed to make his account seem factual (Potter, 1996). In line 6, he constructs a concise assessment of the war, saying "thank God it was not that bad". Genette (1980) indicates that speakers can convey their accounts of the same subjects, objects, and people in many different ways. At the same time, Potter (1996) maintains that people's accounts are driven by their interests, are constructed with consideration for expected counter-arguments, and are designed to make the person's position seem acceptable. The participant here is constructing what can be described as an unexpected, short appraisal of the war which seems positive and performs several discursive actions (cf. Billig, 1995; Edwards & Potter, 1992, 2003; Edwards, 2005; Potter, 1996; Sacks, 1992). This formulation implies that the war, although "bad", did not break the people. Thus, it implies that Lebanese people are capable of surviving despite the losses. Through this account the participant is subtly portraying himself, and consequently his group, as resilient people who did not accept defeat. The participant does not present complaints and does not attempt to support his evaluation, which makes his assessment seem factual (see Potter, 1996).

In lines 7-10, the interviewee invokes the concepts of "dignity and honour" as part of the rationale of the war. He builds these two notions as essential objectives that "cannot be preserved" "without giving up blood". In this formulation, the speaker is constructing and utilising the notions of "dignity and honour" in a manner similar to how William of Normandy invoked the notion of noble blood to warrant his war (as cited in Billig, 1995, p. 1). This account reifies the two concepts, "dignity and honour", into existential objectives that deserve "sacrifices". This is designed to discursively portray the speaker and his group in an appealing light, as people with principles who make sacrifices to uphold these principles (cf. Billig, 1995; Potter, 1996). This is analogous to Graham, Keenan, and Dowd's (2004) point that "Throughout history, political leaders have convinced millions of people to sacrifice their lives and the lives of others in warfare for some greater good or other" (p. 200). Most importantly, through invoking these concepts, the speaker establishes them as the standard for evaluating the war. This enables him to avoid discussing aspects of the war that do not support his argument, such as comparing the losses on both sides. Hence, the participant here is framing the war in a way that warrants Hezbollah's activities and prepares the ground for supporting its rationale.

In lines 12-17, the interviewee illustrates the negative consequences of the war. He focuses explicitly on describing the physical consequences of the Israeli attacks. In lines 12-15, he uses *extreme case formulations* to describe the effects of the attacks, saying "many many buildings were entirely destroyed" and "nothing remained from those huge new buildings". Pomerantz (1986) argues that people tend to use extreme case formulations when they are discussing moral activities, such as warranting, rejecting, and criticising, and that these formulations are effective rhetorical devices designed to invoke the maximum or the minimum state of the subject, object, or event discussed. Here, the participant deploys these formulations to emphasise the harmful consequences of the war, with the extent of damage implying that the act of destruction was deliberate. It is important to note here that the speaker is talking only about civilians and civilian infrastructure that have been attacked. This frames the Israeli attacks as erroneous and difficult to warrant, since civilians should not be targeted according to international laws and common sense. In lines 18 to 19, the participant constructs the attacks as intentional and evil, saying that the Israeli Army "didn't spare civilians or elderly". In line 17, he describes "the attacks" as "savage and brutal". It is also important to highlight that the negative descriptions of the war in lines 12 to 19 only discuss the attacks that were carried out by Israel, and without providing any explanations for why such acts were carried out. Through indicating that the Israeli Army "did not spare civilians or the elderly", the participant depicts Israel as the aggressor that deliberately targeted the vulnerable masses. Thus, this account assigns the blame solely to Israel. It portrays Israel as responsible for destroying the civilian Lebanese infrastructure and killing "many many people".

It might seem as if this detailed account of the war, which is organised around words such as "destruction", "brutal", "savage", and "attacks", contradicts the initial general assessment of the war as "not that bad". To fully understand the discourse of this account, it is important to go back to lines 7-10. In these lines, the speaker invokes and deploys notions of "sacrifices", "dignity", "blood", and "honour". In effect, this allows the participant explicitly to illustrate the negative events of the war without being seen as accepting defeat, and to re-frame them in relation to more positive aspects.

In line 10, the speaker deals with what could be one of the key psychological questions related to modern armed conflicts, namely, how civilians view the destructive effects of armed conflicts. He constructs a deductive argument: "if we want to have dignity, then we have to sacrifice". Through this formula, the participant reconstitutes killing, destruction, and other losses that were inflicted on him and his people as a result of this war (cf. Billig, 1995). Such reconstitutions are a principal part of every armed conflict and a necessary price for the preservation of more important objectives: honour and dignity. Here, he is converting concrete negative consequences of war, which usually function as generic evidence in opposition to war, into amorphous objectives. It is important to stress that the speaker does not deny, underestimate, or minimise the deleterious effects of the war or the devastation inflicted on the Lebanese as a result of this war. Nonetheless, he brings in "dignity and honour" as notions that attenuate the negative psychological effects of the war's events and draws a moderate overall assessment of the war ("not that bad"). The idea of preserving dignity and honour allows the speaker to claim that they have accomplished something important in the war, and that the losses the Lebanese people sustained can be viewed as sacrifices which the Lebanese people did not make in vain. Through building up the importance of dignity, which the participant states cannot be maintained without blood, he subtly prepares the ground to warrant support for the rationale of the resistance. Importantly, the speaker's repeated use of the words "we" and "our" implies that he speaks as a group member. However, the speaker does not identify his group. This allows him to avoid entering into the controversy attached to discussing collective identities in Lebanon, which makes the argument more coherent.

To sum up, in this account, the speaker discusses his experience of the war in ways that present an overall positive evaluation. Though it begins by playing down the negative aspects of the war, and then goes on to stress its harmful effects, it is nevertheless a coherent account. By stressing the negative effects, it portrays Israel as the evil side in the war, to which blame is solely attributed and acquitting Hezbollah of any responsibility. By depicting the war as one that his group can endure, he portrays his own side as resilient. By framing the war as about abstract principles, this endurance is transformed from suffering and loss into noble sacrifice.

In the following extract, the same speaker presents a sad personal experience related to the war.

EXTRACT 3.2. PARTICIPANT NUMBER 1, AROUND 60 YEARS OLD, MALE, TAXI DRIVER; BEIRUT, LEBANON.

P: let me tell you something (1)
I have lost a young man in the war with Israel in 2000
I'm proud that I have a martyr
we raise our children to be martyrs
and they raise theirs to be traitors
this is the difference between us and them.
I: may I ask you what your feeling was when that happened?
P: believe me I was very patient (.8)
very patient
it was as if it happened to someone else

In the above extract, the participant discusses the death of his young son due to the war. He reformulates losing his son, which is generically a sad event, into having a martyr. This reformulation allows the speaker to build a different account that entails different features and characteristics of losing his son. He portrays "having a martyr" as something of which he is "proud". In line 4, he continues building up the significance of having a martyr; he states that "we raise our children to be martyrs". This formulation implies that having a martyr is a reason for satisfaction rather than sadness. Thus, the speaker uses the notion of a martyr, which he builds in a specific way, to re-characterise the death of his son. Here, he is presenting a personal experience; this makes his account appear factual (Potter, 1996). Through the use of the word "we", the speaker implies that he is talking as a member of a group rather than as an individual, yet in line 8, he describes his personal feelings when he lost his son as being "patient" and, in line 9, as "very patient". This patience is hearable as a form of individual endurance, for the greater good of his group. Thus, the speaker manages to present concrete representations of the negative consequences of the war while at the same time portraying a positive message. Through invoking notions of martyrdom and patience the participant reformulates the implications of war. By reifying these ideas, the participant reformulates losing a son into gaining a martyr.

In the following extract, another participant also deals with the war through discussing his personal experience.

EXTRACT 3.3. PARTICIPANT NUMBER 2, 40 YEARS OLD, MALE, PARTICIPANT IN THE PROTEST; BEIRUT, LEBANON.

I: first though can you tell me something about yourself?
P: my name is Y.M.
several people were yelling "his brother is a martyr"
P: (1) I have lost my brother
he was killed, it was an accident he was just passing one of the bridges
he was going to his work (.) he was not fighting (.2)
he was not in the battlefield when he was killed
I consider him a martyr
because he died as a result of aggression from another country that was attacking Lebanon on its territory
Lebanon wasn't attacking them (.)
I felt the loss I have lost my brother
I have overcome my feelings through my belief
and the support from friends and family
mostly through the belief
in the end the one who kills is killing a body
not the values, or the rights, not the cause

all the killing
the brutal killing that has taken place during the war
did not accomplish anything
despite thousands of people who have been killed (.)
the Israelis couldn't achieve any victory
that is also due to the belief
maybe my brother's destiny was to die at that moment
many people wanted to die instead of him (.)
since he died for a cause
a cause that is just and right

In this extract, the speaker presents what could be considered a testimony of his personal experience of the war. The participant chooses to make his brother's death the focus of the interview, a topic that makes the account more factual and harder to counter (cf. Edwards & Potter, 1992; Potter, 1996). He builds up what happened to his brother gradually, starting with neutral terms, saying that the brother was "killed" in an "accident" while he was "going to his work". This conveys the ordinariness of the circumstances in which his brother was killed. The interviewee further emphasises that his brother was a non-combatant, stating that he "was not fighting, he was not in the battlefield when he was killed" (lines 7-8), cementing the notion that this was not a part of the formal war. Nevertheless, in line 9, the speaker describes his brother as a "martyr".

In lines 10 to 11, the speaker explains why he considers his brother a martyr, implying that the notion may be heard as problematic. He indicates that his brother "died because of aggression from another country that was attacking Lebanon on its territory". Hence, the speaker describes the war as an "aggression on Lebanon". This formulation is commonly used in the discourse of wars to attribute the blame to just one of the two fighting sides (Herrera, 2003). By framing the war as an aggression on Lebanon, he presents Lebanon as a passive victim, implying that the Lebanese, like his brother, are innocent victims.

The literal translation of the Arabic word *shahīd* means "witness". It is culturally used to describe people who lose their lives while fighting for their religion or country. In Islamic mythology, martyrs do not die; they just move from one state to another and stay alive as God's witnesses. Thus, one of the main implications of being a martyr is that a person is not dead. Hence, his family and friends should not be sad. Moreover, families that have martyrs are expected to show pride. Through this formulation, the participant manages to shift the feelings associated with the event from sadness to pride through employing a cultural concept (cf. Billig, 1995; Edwards & Potter, 1992, 2003; Edwards, 2005; Potter, 1996, 2005; Sacks, 1992; Schegloff, 1999).

In lines 17 to 23, the speaker discusses the result of the war. He frames what Israel has done as killing the "body" but "not the values, or the rights, not the cause". The use of the three-part list functions as a way to emphasise the notion that the enemy did not win (Atkinson, 1984). Through invoking the concepts of "values" and "belief", the speaker brings in more positive features relating to the war, as it counters any argument that Israel has won the war. The notions of "values" and "belief" also shift the focus away from more concrete data, such as the number of casualties and the scale of destruction on both sides. In other words, in this case, the speaker invokes relative concepts that are hard to completely discard to counter an expected argument that might be based on more tangible evidence.

In lines 19 to 20, the speaker constitutes a discursive formulation on the basis of actions and results of the attacks. He constructs what Israel was doing in the war as "killing" and "brutal killing". This consequently prepares the ground for denouncing Israel, not just its activities. Nevertheless, the result of this killing is not the expected victory but, rather, failure: "they did not accomplish anything" (line 21), and right prevailed. This formulation constitutes one of the sides in the war, Israel, in a very negative way, and therefore its opponent more positively, and resembles the classic narrative of the conflict between good and evil, where evil is stronger in the beginning and inflicts a significant damage but for one reason or another, good eventually wins. By referring to criteria that are relative and amorphous (such as beliefs, values, and causes) rather than more concrete data (such as casualties, including the speaker's brother), the concrete negative aspects of war are transformed into a more abstract positive portrayal: the evil aggressor has been defeated.

In line 23, he introduces the final result of the war, stating that "the Israelis couldn't achieve any victory", attributing that to the Lebanese people's "belief" in their just cause. The speaker uses the notion of "belief" twice: in lines 14 and 16, as the reason that helped him overcome his loss; and in line 24, as the object that prevented Israel from achieving victory. This formulation links the notion of belief in personal loss to political reality, and frames the death of his brother as related to the victory over Israel.

To summarise, the speaker constitutes the accidental death of his brother, a non-combatant, as an act of martyrdom, and the war as an aggression of another country against his country. By stressing the negative aspects of the war, the wrongness of the aggressor is built up, while the appeal to abstract concepts allows him to portray the war as a victory, in which his brother played a role after all.

In the next section, the participants organise their accounts of the war around emotional experiences.

Invoking the role of feeling in constructions of resilience

In the next two extracts participants discuss the war through describing and explaining their feelings during the war.

EXTRACT 3.4. PARTICIPANT NUMBER 3, 24 YEARS OLD, MALE, PROTESTER; BEIRUT, LEBANON.

I: how did you feel in the beginning of the war and later on?
P: without a doubt we were scared, we felt fear
because the war was (.2) if I may say barbaric

especially the air raids with the smart weapons and the missiles
which could get us wherever we were (.5)
what increased our fear was the attacks on the infrastructure
if you are near a bridge or you need to pass through a bridge
to go to your work you would be afraid
this thing happened with me (.)
there was an air bombing in front of me
I was going to my work and just in front of me
five seconds away from me my friend died (martyred)
and I survived
this increased my fear and what made it even worse
is that they did not spare any important area or bridge (.2)
so yes we were afraid
but the resistance withstanding surprised us
frankly we knew that Hezbollah is strong and organised
but not up to this degree (.)
maybe the whole world was surprised
not just the Lebanese
this is why we calmed psychologically
we knew after a week that with their resistance
we would survive
and this is what happened
and we have contributed with some things
and they resisted and defended Lebanon
this is what took away our fear
especially after we had seen that
the Israelis are incapable of advancing

In the above extract, the speaker describes his emotional experience. Discursive theorists argue that presentations of "feelings" add authenticity to accounts and make them seem factual (Edwards, 1997). Like the previous extracts, this account contains two different pictures. In lines 2 to 16, the speaker illustrates the negative feelings and the factors that generated these feelings. In line 2, he presents "fear" as the dominant feeling. In line 3, he justifies why they were frightened by describing the war as "barbaric". Further on, in lines 4 and 5, he precisely identifies an aspect that caused fear: "the air raids with the smart weapons and the missiles which could get us wherever we were". It is important to stress that he uses the words "we" and "ours" throughout his talk, especially when discussing the feelings and general experiences of the war. The use of the words "we" and "our" implies that he is not exceptional in this experience; rather, it is a collective experience and he is speaking as a member of a group of people who share this understanding.

In lines 10 to 14, he presents a personal life-threatening experience in which there was "bombing in front of" him. He states that his "friend died" while he "survived". In line 15, he frames the attacks as intentional, stating that the Israeli Army "did not spare any important area or bridge". This functions as a justification for being "afraid". Overall, this account of the events and of feelings of the people characterises the war based on fear, attacks, and death.

However, in line 17, he presents a positive experience, that of the "resistance". He explains in lines 18-19, how the "resistance withstanding" was surprising, indicating that "we knew that Hezbollah is strong and organised but not up to this degree". Here, he describes the strength of Hezbollah as a pleasant surprise that made the speaker and his group "calm psychologically". He attributes the change of feelings from "fear" to being psychologically calm to the understanding that they "would survive", "and this is what happened". Thus, though the speaker describes the negative face of the war, he simultaneously constitutes a favourable aspect: the ability of the resistance to withstand the attacks, which led to a redeeming ending.

In the next extract, the participant deals with emotional experience in a different way.

EXTRACT 3.5. PARTICIPANT NUMBER 4, 30 YEARS OLD, MALE, BUSINESSMAN; BEIRUT, LEBANON.

1 I: Have you been affected by the war and how?
2 P: yes we have been affected financially but not emotionally (.)

why not emotionally?
because for the first time
we felt that the Arabs' dignity came back
for the first time we felt that the Arabs
and I do not want to talk just about the Lebanese
I want to talk about the Arabs who have been silent
for long, long periods while the petrol was being stolen
they were stealing the petrol
while the Palestinians' lands were being stolen
while the head of the Palestinian Authority Yasser Arafat
was being assassinated (.) while they were carrying out
attacks against Lebanon
with the massacres that took place and everything
our rights were despoiled and we were silent
this time we felt something different
we felt happy we had our dignity back
they ran away defeated
the effect was very positive emotionally
and when the emotional effect is positive no one speaks
about material losses

In the above extract, the interviewee also builds an account that contains two distinct sides. The first one, in lines 9 to 16, is a sad story of Israeli aggressions against Arabs over a long period prior to the 2006 war. The second story (lines 2 to 8, 17 to 22) is a story of resilience that is organised around specific implications of the last war. In line 2, the speaker uses the word "we" to answer the question, which again implies that he is talking on behalf of a group. As an effect, this presents the argument as reflecting the opinions of a group of people, thereby strengthening the power of the opinion. He states that they "have been affected financially but not emotionally". In line 3, the participant assumes the role of the interviewer by asking a question, which he answers in the following lines. Changing the setting of the interview allows the participant to talk more freely and take more time to build up his argument. Furthermore, it allows him to choose the topic of the conversation. He forms a complete tale to answer his question rather than a concise response, one that is similar to the previous accounts of the war.

In lines 4 to 5, the participant explains why he has not been hurt emotionally. He attributes that to the idea that this war brought the Arabs' dignity back. He portrays restoring Arab dignity as an important objective that mitigated the negative emotional effects of the war. The speaker continues using the word "we", which implies that he is speaking on behalf of a group, and identifies his group as "Arab, not just Lebanese". This extends the group portrayed by the speaker as his group in relation to the war, which is a technique used by speakers to make their arguments more appealing (see Hopkins & Reicher, 1997; Reicher & Hopkins, 2001). In lines 9 to 16, the interviewee paints a negative picture of the Arabs' situation caused by Israel's attacks. He points to specific incidents such as the assassination of "Yasser Arafat" and the "attacks against Lebanon". Highlighting these well-known incidents is designed to portray Israelis as inherently aggressive and, consequently, the side that bears the blame. In line 15, he describes the attacks carried out by Israel against the Arabs as "massacres".

In line 16, the speaker shifts the attention, indicating that in this war they "felt something different" in contrast to what used to happen in the previous conflicts. In lines 18 to 19 he describes their feelings as being "happy" because Israel was "defeated". This characterises the Israeli as craven in contrast to the Lebanese who were presented as gained their dignity back. He states that the "positive" feelings alleviate any negative effects of the financial loss. This discursive formulation does not deny the occurrence of financial losses rather it attenuates it influence on the overall rational of the war. In conclusion, through invoking the history of the Arab-Israeli conflict the speaker presents the 2006 war as a moral triumphant for the Arab, without denying the losses that resulted from it.

In the following extract, the participant discusses the war through focusing on the involved sides.

EXTRACT 3.6. PARTICIPANT NUMBER 5, MALE, 35 YEARS OLD, PROTESTER; BEIRUT, LEBANON.

I: can you tell me about the events that took place in July
and August?
P: what happened is that ohh the last war was agreed upon
between the current government and Israel
to eradicate a specific group from Lebanon
and the proof is that what has been attacked is just
one group in Lebanon
and its houses have been destroyed and
on top of all that they didn't give us any aid or anything
we are here protesting to achieve our right
and to form a clean government cleaner than the current one

In the above extract, the participant reformulates what the interviewer presents as "events" (line 1) into "war" (line 3). He frames this description as general knowledge, thus he does not provide any further information to support it. In lines 4 to 5, he describes the "war" as something that was coordinated between "the current government and Israel" "to eradicate a specific group from Lebanon". Here, the speaker presents the Lebanese government as an accomplice of Israel against a group of Lebanese citizens. Furthermore, describing the war as a result of an agreement between two countries formulates the two countries as responsible for the "war". This formulation portrays Israel and the Lebanese government as being united against a group of Lebanese. Hence, the national identity is not relevant in this constitution of the conflict. The conflict is not between the Israelis and the Lebanese or between Israel and a part of Lebanon; it is a war in which the Lebanese government cooperates with another state against some of its own citizens. It is important to note here that the speaker identifies the responsible side explicitly, while he is vague when identifying the targeted Lebanese group that has suffered from the war and was not aided by the government. In lines 10 to 11, the participant shifts the issue from what happened in the war into what he is doing at the time of the interview and what he wants to accomplish in the future. The goal is to "form a clean government" and this is to be achieved through protesting. He does not present it as a personal stand; rather, through the repeated use of the words "we" and "our", he implies that he is speaking as a member of the aforementioned group, which will replace the current government and create a better situation.

To conclude, the speaker draws a picture of the war and then uses it as a premise to justify his current behaviour, which is participating in a protest against his government. The way the speaker accounts for the war is designed to address his present behaviour as much as the previous experience. However, the way the speaker describes the war implies that he and his group have overcome it, despite the losses they sustained, and now look forward to better times.

In the next extract, the speaker reaches a similar conclusion to the previous ones by focusing on different aspects.

EXTRACT 3.7. PARTICIPANT NUMBER 6, AROUND 40 YEARS OLD, MALE, TEACHER; BEIRUT, LEBANON .

I: how would you describe the events that took place
in July and August?
P: I think it was necessary that Hezbollah attacked the Israelis
because we have prisoners there and these prisoners
were captured
while defending the country (.) they are people like us
so we should bring them back to their country
so they could live in peace and freedom (.)
we did not expect that the Zionist reaction
would be this way and with this brutality
but thank god we were tough and we triumphed

In the above extract, the speaker discusses the war through attending to the trigger incident. He reformulates the trigger incident of the war in a way that absolves Hezbollah from the blame for causing the war (cf. Edwards & Potter, 1992; Potter, 1996). He does not deny that Hezbollah is the side that carried out the first attack in the war, but he counters the blame attached to the initial armed attack through describing the attack as "necessary". To further justify that attack, he avoids discussing whether the attack was the trigger of the war or whether it was right or wrong. Instead, in lines 4 to 7, he creates an account that explains and justifies the "necessary" Hezbollah attack by highlighting its motive: rescuing Lebanese "prisoners" in Israel who "were captured while defending the country". In line 4, the speaker aligns himself with Hezbollah through the use of the term "we". He also uses the term "we" repeatedly later to imply that he is representing the opinion of the Lebanese. In line 8, the participant describes the goal of Hezbollah's attack as allowing the prisoners to "live in peace and freedom". This formulation justifies the attack and constitutes it as an act of benevolence.

In lines 9-10, the participant describes the Israeli reaction as unexpected and brutal. This absolves Hezbollah of responsibility for the war and designates Israel as culpable instead. As noted previously, the deleterious aspects of the war are emphasised, yet are made subordinate to the resilience of his people, which, in turn, led to a "triumph" (line 11). Thus, the speaker is able to describe the war suffering in a way that portrays the enemy as evil and his own side not only as righteous but also as victorious.

The incorporation of other moral evaluations

In the following two extracts, the participants organise their accounts of war around various positive aspects.

EXTRACT 3.8. PARTICIPANT NUMBER 7, 20 YEARS OLD, MALE, A PROTESTER; BEIRUT, LEBANON .

I: Have you been affected by the war and how?
P: the thing that affected me the most
was the fact that the Lebanese nation was united
and the way the Lebanese people supported the resistance
and the Southern people

EXTRACT 3.9. PARTICIPANT NUMBER 8, 22 YEARS OLD, FEMALE, STUDENT; BEIRUT, LEBANON .

P: I consider the aggression (.)
the war the event that happened in July
with all its ugliness with all its cruelty
and all the adverse scenes that were there (.)
that war ended the idea that the Israeli Army is invincible
it gave a bright face to Lebanon and what is going on
within Lebanon
and to the resistance
it made the whole world see that Lebanon is the one
being attacked

In the first extract, the speaker presents a positive picture of the war by highlighting what could be described as a positive side effect of the war. He identifies the aspect that affected him the most as "the fact that the Lebanese nation was united and the way the Lebanese people supported the resistance and the Southern people". Unlike the previous extracts, the speaker does not refer to negative aspects but speaks as an individual by using the construction "I consider…", thus avoiding potential criticism (e.g., that there were more significant negative effects) by providing only a personal opinion.

In Extract 3.9, the speaker uses several powerful terms to build a negative account of war. He describes what happened in July as "cruel", "ugly", "aggression", and a "war" that involved "adverse scenes". Nonetheless, these negative direct characteristics of the events do not lead to a bleak final assessment of the war. Rather, they contribute to a surprising positive outcome of the war, which is "ending the idea that the Israeli Army is invincible" (line 5). In lines 6 to 8, he continues to build up the positive effects of the war, indicating that "the war gave a bright face to Lebanon and to what is going on within Lebanon and to the resistance". In lines 9-10, the participant produces a closing positive assessment of the effects of war, saying that "it made the whole world see that Lebanon is the one being attacked". Thus, in this extract, the participant manages to transform a negative account of the war into one that is positive, while attributing ugliness, aggression, and cruelty to the Israeli Army.

In the next extract, the speaker organises his account around the outcome of the war.

EXTRACT 3.10. PARTICIPANT NUMBER 9, MALE, 41 YEARS OLD, UNIVERSITY STAFF; BASRA, IRAQ.

I: what do you think of the American invasion and why?
P: the American invasion was necessary
although the fighting has increased within our country
I still believe the invasion was necessary
who would forget our joy when Saddam's regime collapsed
we felt that America was supporting this nation
and was rescuing us from the injustice, oppression and death
the United States wanted to help us through all means
and we wanted the American forces to enter Iraq
and to stay in it

In the above extract, this time from an Iraqi, the participant warrants the American invasion of Iraq by describing it as "necessary". He then attends to the expected criticism organised around the negative consequences of that invasion. He admits that "the fighting has increased"; nonetheless, he "still believes that the invasion was necessary". By describing the dominant feeling when Saddam's regime collapsed as joy, he invokes positive implications of the invasion, and justifies that feeling by pointing out that "America was supporting this nation". In line 7, he continues justifying his endorsement of the American invasion through describing life under the ex-regime. He portrays it as being contaminated with "injustice, oppression, and death", using a three-part list to highlight the suffering the Iraqi people experienced under Saddam's rule. Describing the situation under Saddam in such a negative way enables the participant to present the invasion as a desired rescue. Importantly, the speaker uses the words "we" and "us" to imply that his view represents other people, in this case, the nation. In line 8, he describes the motive of the "United States" as helping them. He maintains that they "wanted the American forces to enter Iraq". The use of the term "enter" presents the advance of the American troops into Iraq as a mundane action. In line 10, the speaker asserts that they wanted the American forces to stay in Iraq, reinforcing how welcome they were. Through this account, the participant warrants the American invasion without being seen as unpatriotic, by describing it as necessary and in Iraqis' interests. By portraying the negative aspects of Saddam's regime, the positive aspects of the invasion are built up, despite the current difficult situation that he acknowledges.

Similar accounts are presented by the next two participants.

EXTRACT 3.11. PARTICIPANT NUMBER 10, 51 YEARS OLD, MALE, UNIVERSITY STAFF; BASRA, IRAQ.

I: what do you think of the American invasion and why?
P: I believe that the American invasion was right
for me as an oppressed Iraqi
I consider the American invasion liberation

EXTRACT 3.12. PARTICIPANT NUMBER 11, 32 YEARS OLD, MALE, UNIVERSITY STAFF; BASRA, IRAQ.

I: what do you think of the American invasion and why?
P: it was not an invasion it was liberation
under the previous regime I never felt that I was a real citizen
I always felt that I was a prisoner in a big prison

In Extracts 3.11 and 3.12, the two participants justify the American invasion of Iraq through invoking the nature of the ex-regime as oppressive and describing the situation under that regime as dominated by oppression. In the first extract, the participant characterises "the American invasion" as "right". In line 3, he defends this appraisal through introducing himself as "an oppressed Iraqi". Assuming the identity of "an oppressed Iraqi" allows the participant to describe the American invasion as "liberation" (line 4). The fact that the speaker mobilises the identity of being "oppressed" to defend his appraisal of the American invasion indicates that this appraisal might be problematic. In the second extract, the participant begins by objecting to the use of the term "invasion" to describe what happened in Iraq. He indicates that the right description is "liberation" and employs an *extreme case formulation* to describe his previous situation in Iraq, stating that "I never felt that I was a real citizen". The use of this extreme case formulation maximises the power of the claim that what happened in Iraq was liberation as opposed to invasion (Pomerantz, 1986). In line 4 of the second extract, the participant describes himself as having been a "prisoner" "in a big prison" during Saddam's rule. Again, by describing his subjective feelings and understanding of the situation under the ex-regime, the participant enhances the factuality of his evaluation of the American intervention as "liberation" (Wooffitt 1992; Potter 1996).

Summary and conclusion

This chapter shows that the participants in the above extracts convey their experience of war in ways that emphasise both its destructive and constructive aspects. Highlighting the destructive aspect of war performs specific rhetorical actions, such as blaming a specific side for the war, justifying a specific action, or portraying the speaker as a victim. In contrast, invoking constructive aspects of the war portrays the speakers as principled or resilient and presents an overall morally desired outcome of the war. It is important to stress that the participants who emphasize the constructive aspects of the war do not state that war is a pleasant experience; rather, they present and even amplify the deleterious consequences of the war but avoid being cast as defeated or resigned though invoking noble principles, notions of resilience, and so on. Throughout these accounts, there is a recurring theme of endurance; indeed, none of the speakers I interviewed indicated that they would be incapable of surviving the war.

These accounts, which portray the events of war not as wholly negative but rather as endurable overall, may have two possible effects. On the one hand, these accounts serve as a way for people portray their war experience – and themselves – in an appealing light. On the other hand, by presenting a constructive characterisation of armed conflicts, these accounts could have the effect of warranting the conflicts. This broader theme will be revisited in another chapter.

References

Achcar, G., & Warschawski, M. (2007). *The 33-day war: Israel's war on Hezbollah in Lebanon and its consequences.* New York, NY: Routledge.

Ajami, F. (2006) *The foreigner's gift: the Americans, the Arabs, and the Iraqis in Iraq.* New York: Free Press.

Billig, M. (1995). *Banal Nationalism.* London: Sage Publications.

Edwards, D. (1997). *Discourse and cognition.* London: Sage.

Edwards, D. (2005). Discursive psychology. In K. L. Fitch. & R. E. Sanders (Eds.), *Handbook of language and social interaction.* NY: Erlbaum.

Edwards, D., & Potter, J. (1992). *Discursive Psychology.* London: Sage.

Edwards, D., & Potter, J. (2003). Discursive psychology and mental states. In H. Molder & J. Potter (Eds.), *Conversation and cognition.* Cambridge University Press.

Genette, G. (1980). *Narrative Discourse.* Oxford: Basil Blackwell.

Graham, P., Keenan, T., & Dowd, A. (2004). A call to arms at the end of history: a discourse-historical analysis of George W. Bush's declaration of war on terror. *Discourse and Society 15*(2-3), 199-221.

Hammack, P. L. (2006). Identity, conflict, and coexistence: Life stories of Israeli and Palestinian adolescents. *Journal of Adolescent Research, 21*(4), 323-369.

Herrera, M. (2003). Constructing social categories and seeking collective influence: self-categorization and the discursive construction of a conflict. *International Journal of Psychology and Psychological Therapy, 3*(1), 27-57.

Hopkins, N., & Reicher, S. (1997). Constructing the nation and collective mobilization: A case study of politicians' arguments about the meaning of Scottishness. In C. C. Barfoot (Ed.), *Beyond Pug's tour: National and ethnic stereotyping in theory and literary practice* (pp. 313–337). Amsterdam: Rodopi.

Hutchby, I., & Wooffitt, R. (1998). *Conversation analysis.* Cambridge: Polity Press.

Kellezi, B., Reicher. D. & Cassidy, C. (2009). Surviving the Kosovo conflict: A study of social identity, appraisal of extreme events, and mental well-being. Applied Psychology; An international Review. *Special issue: Social Identity, Health and Well-being, 58*(1), 59-83.

Leudar, I. & Nekvapil, J. (2007). The war on terror and Muslim Briton's safety: A week in the life of a dialogical network. *Ethnographic Studies 9*, 44-62.

Lewis, B. (1998). *The multiple identities of the Middle East.* London: Weidenfeld & Nicolson.

Lifton, R. J. (1973). *Home from the war: Vietnam veterans: neither victims nor executioners.* NewYork: Touchstone.

Lomsky-Feder, E. (1995). The meaning of war through veterans' eyes: A phenomenological analysis of life stories." *International Sociology, 10*(4), 463-482.

Milgram, N. (1986). General introduction to the field of war-related stress. In N. A. Milgram (Ed.), *Stress and coping in time of war: Generalizations from the Israeli experience* (pp. 23-36). New York: Brunner/Mazel.

Muldoon, O. T. & Downes, C. (2007). Social identification and post-traumatic stress symptoms in post-conflict Northern Ireland. *British Journal of Psychiatry, 191*(8), 146–149.

Pomerantz, A. (1986). Agreeing and disagreeing with assessments: Some features of preferred/dispreferred turn-shapes. In J. M. Atkinson & J. Heritage (Eds.), *Structures of social action: Studies in conversation analysis.* Cambridge University Press.

Potter, J. (1996). Representing reality: *Discourse, rhetoric and social construction.* London: Sage.

Potter, J. (2005). Making psychology relevant. *Discourse & Society, 16*(5), 739-747.

Reicher, S. & Hopkins, N. (2001). *Self and nation.* London: Sage.

Sacks, H. (1984). On doing 'being ordinary'. In M. Atkinson & J. Heritage (Eds.), *Structures of social action.* Cambridge University Press.

Sacks, H. (1992). *Lectures on conversation.* Oxford: Basil Blackwell.

Schegloff, E.A. (1999). Discourse, pragmatics, conversation analysis. *Discourse Studies, 1*(4), 405 – 435.

Sifry, M. L., & Cerf, C. (Eds.). (2007). *The Iraq war reader: History, documents, opinions.* New York: Simon & Schuster.

Sokolovic, D. (2005). How to conceptualize the tragedy of Bosnia: Civil, ethnic, religious war or…? *War Crimes, Genocide & Crimes against Humanity 1*(1), 115-130.

Woodward, B. (2004). *Plan of attack.* New York, NY: Simon & Schuster.

Wooffitt, R. (1992). *Telling tales of the unexpected: the organization of factual discourse.* Hempstead: Harvester Wheatsheaf.

Chapter 4

Iraq: Invasion or liberation

Collective identity is arguably one of the most investigated topics in social psychology. It is reported that understanding collective identity allows us to comprehend the activities and characteristics associated with a group or individual (Antaki & Widdicombe, 1998). The importance of collective identity extends beyond providing a title that associates a certain group of people together and differentiates them from other groups. Collective identity is strongly related to the way people talk and interact with each other, especially in situations involving inter-group interaction. Several researchers argue that collective identity plays a central role in people's understanding and behaviour within armed conflicts (see Eglin & Hester, 1999; Gartzke & Gleditsch, 2006). Thus, examining the way in which people in armed conflicts deal with the issue of their own collective identity and that of the fighting sides is essential for any understanding of armed conflicts, social identity, and collective interaction.

Leudar, Marsland, and Nekvapil (2004) argue that framing the fighting sides along the lines of "us" and "them" is an important strategy in decision-makers' accounts of armed conflicts. Such accounts are fundamental in every war, since they are the means through which leaders convey the situation and mobilise people (Billig, 1995). Researchers have shown that influential individuals construct and use collective identities for themselves and their adversaries in ways that serve their interests. For example, studies indicate that politicians, when discussing conflicts, tend to portray their adversaries as evil and dangerous, whilst at the same time conveying their own group as benevolent (see Dower, 1986; Herrera, 2003; Leudar, Marsland & Nekvapil, 2004). Other studies have shown that different speakers construct varying collective identities for the same sides in a war (see Stevenson, Condor & Abell, 2007; Herrera, 2003). These collective identities are constituted and used to perform specific rhetorical functions, such as supporting and warranting specific positions, countering other positions, or preparing the ground for specific behaviours in relation to the conflict (see Castano, Leidner & Slawuta, 2008; Herrera, 2003).

In this chapter, I examine lay accounts of the American invasion of Iraq with a focus on collective identities. I analyse how lay Iraqi people build and utilise collective identities for themselves and for the other side in relation to the conflict. Through analysing several extracts, I show how Iraqi participants constitute and deploy rival collective identities in ways designed to advance specific stances in relation to the war or the involved sides. In doing so, I question the Social Identity Theory (SIT) and Self-Categorization Theory (SCT) understanding of collective identity. I therefore also address these theories' understanding of the categorisation process within conflicts and their conceptualisation of the relationship between collective identity and people's predispositions regarding the experience of armed conflicts.

Using national identity to portray events as an invasion

In this section, I present and discuss extracts in which the participants agree with the characterisation of events as an American invasion. They produce rhetorical accounts that are designed to denounce the invasion and reject arguments that warrant it. One of the main strategies the participants use to accomplish this is to invoke Iraqi national identity in a way that distinguishes the Iraqi people from the invading forces.

In the first extract, the participant discusses whether the war, which the researcher describes as an invasion, is right and explains why he holds this view.

EXTRACT 4.1. PARTICIPANT NUMBER 12, 37 YEARS OLD, MALE, UNIVERSITY STAFF; BASRA, IRAQ.

P: the occupying forces have committed grave blunders
they have dismantled the national institutions
and the ministries especially the ministry of defence
and ministry of interior and they delayed the formation
of an Iraqi government for more than a year
they have offended the people
they did not respect our culture and our customs
they have caused killing, destruction and looting
I want to say that the occupation came with a plan
to steal the oil and to serve their imperialist interests

In this extract, the participant forms an account that leads to a denunciation of the American invasion of Iraq. He starts by describing the deleterious consequences of the invasion, using that as a way to build up a distinction between "us" and "them" (Leudar, Marsland & Nekvapil, 2004). He distinguishes his group (us) from the opponent group (them) by formulating them as the "occupying forces" (line 1), the term he uses for the Western powers governing Iraq during the time of the interaction. This label entails category-bound activities and features, implying that these forces oppress the Iraqi people, control their land, and govern them against their free will. At the same time, it implies that the Iraqi people have the right to resist these forces based on common sense and international law. It is important to stress that the descriptor "forces" obscures several entities that are part of the occupation authority, such as the Iraqi government, the American civil administration, and various Western organisations that were in Iraq at the time of the interaction. Overlooking the existence of these entities enables the participant to construct the situation as a military occupation of Iraq carried out by foreigners against the will of the Iraqis. Through this formulation, the participant differentiates the occupation authority from the Iraqis, even though a significant number of Iraqis were working with the Americans, such as the Iraqi government, police, and army.

In line 2, the participant points out that one of the "grave blunders" of the "occupying forces" is the dismantling of "the national institutions". Here, the participant is invoking the value of these institutions, downplaying their role during the ex-regime era. One of the main category-bound characteristics of being nationalistic is being connected to the people, not just the regime. This formulation is designed to simplify the discussed event and portray it as an invasion of Iraq by foreign powers, without reference to internal factors that led to the invasion, such as the clash between the Iraqis and Saddam's regime.

In lines 3 to 4, he points to the Ministry of Defence and Ministry of Interior as examples of the national institutions that were dismantled by the occupying forces. Through describing these two institutions as national institutions, the participant is downplaying their role in causing suffering to the Iraqis during the ex-regime's reign. He constructs them as national Iraqi establishments, the dismantling of which is an aggression against Iraq.

In line 7, the participant invokes the cultural differences between the Iraqis and the occupying forces. He portrays the occupying forces as disrespectful to the "culture" and "customs" of the Iraqis, hence the accusation in line 6 that the occupying forces have offended the people. In line 8, he presents a three-part list to describe the effects of the invasion, stating that it "caused killing, destruction and looting". Atkinson (1984) demonstrates that the function of this list is to present the speaker's portrayal of the issue as comprehensive and indisputable. Here, the list is designed to amplify the deleterious implications of the invasion and portray it as destructive, helping to justify arguments that promote resisting the American presence. In lines 9 to 10, the participant presents negative and unacceptable causes of the invasion. He describes the motives behind the invasion as the desire to "steal the oil and serve their imperialist interests". This further constructs the notion that the war was an illegitimate invasion, and distinguishes between us and them on the basis of national interests.

In the next extract, the participant uses several different rhetorical techniques within his account of the American and allied military intervention.

EXTRACT 4.2. PARTICIPANT NUMBER 13, 21 YEARS OLD, MALE, STUDENT; BASRA, IRAQ.

I: do you think the American invasion was right and why?
P: of course it was not right who would accept
the occupation of his country by foreign powers
the ex-regime was a national Iraqi regime
even if we disagree with some of its acts
and it should be up to the Iraqi people to remove it
if they want
the Americans or anyone else do not have the right
to interfere
in our domestic matters
Iraq is a sovereign country and we do not accept
foreigners to dictate to us what to do

In the above extract, the participant provides an account that denounces the American invasion of Iraq. He distinguishes between two groups, "us" and "them", within this account. In line 2, he asserts that the American invasion was not right and asks "who would accept the occupation of his country by foreign powers". This rhetorical question strengthens the evaluation of the invasion as an unacceptable act (Wooffitt 1992; Potter 1996).

The speaker is also constructing two sides as relevant to the issue of the invasion – on one side is a group united by national identity ("his country"), and on the other side are the "foreign powers" – and he is associating himself with the country and against "foreign powers". This portrayal of the collective identities is designed to denounce not only the American side, but also the Iraqis who support it.

In line 4, the participant describes the "ex-regime" as "a national Iraqi regime", thus downplaying differences between the Iraqi people and the ex-regime, and invoking national identity as the most salient category in the attitude toward the invasion. This formulation emphasises the main theme that the invasion is an illegal action (Potter 1996). In lines 5 to 7, the participant attends to the expected arguments that distinguish the ex-regime from lay Iraqi people, but downplays that distinction by portraying it as a disagreement "with some of its acts", an implication that these are based on minor issues, rather than irreconcilable ones. In lines 6-7, he continues to downplay the tyrannical nature of the ex-regime, indicating that "it should be up to the Iraqi people to remove it if they want". This reformulates the situation prior to the invasion from one in which Iraqi people could not do anything to remove Saddam's regime into one in which the Iraqis are the only ones who have the right to eliminate the regime. The fact that they did not implies that they chose not to.

In lines 8 to 10, the participant emphasises the importance of collective identities, stating that the "Americans or anyone else do not have the right to interfere in our domestic matters" and in lines 11 to 12, the participant states that Iraq is "a sovereign country". This formulation establishes collective identity as the standard that indicates who has the right to do what, and uses the notion that the Americans are foreign to Iraq, thus it is not acceptable for them to interfere. Moreover, the ex-regime is framed in national terms, as part of the general portrayal of the invasion as occupation by a foreign power (Leudar & Nekvapil, 2007; Potter, 1996).

In the next extract, the participant also organises his account of the war around the notion of conflicting groups.

EXTRACT 4.3. PARTICIPANT NUMBER 14, 46 YEARS OLD, MALE, UNIVERSITY STAFF; BASRA, IRAQ.

I: do you think the American invasion was right and why?
P: no it was not since it destroyed the infrastructures
and dismantled the army and the police which made
the country live in chaos
and it brought people from outside Iraq
and gave them the power with no consideration for
the Iraqis who were inside Iraq and suffered from
oppression and hardships

In the above extract, the participant discusses the evaluation of the invasion through the lens of us and them. However, in this extract, the two rival groups consist of Iraqis. He starts in line 2 by focusing on the negative consequences of the invasion, namely the destruction of "infrastructures". This formulation makes the claim factual (Hutchby & Wooffitt, 1998). In line 3, he considers dismantling "the army and the police" as the cause of the "chaos" which "the country lives in". This formulation frames the Iraqi "police" and "army" prior to the invasion as efficient institutions, thus downplaying the criticisms of these two entities. Additionally, this formulation also portrays Iraq before the invasion as being in a better situation in these respects compared to afterwards, further stressing the negative consequences of the invasion.

In lines 5 to 6, the participant explicitly distinguishes between the Iraqi "people" who were "brought" from outside Iraq and the Iraqis who were inside Iraq. Though he does not use the word Iraqi here, the composition of the government (which is wholly composed of Iraqi exiles) makes the term "people" in this context unmistakably denote "Iraqi people". Indeed, it is significant that he refers to these exiled Iraqis who came to Iraq as a result of the invasion as "people", while he refers to the ones who were inside Iraq as Iraqis (line 7). This formulation functions as a way of presenting the people who were in Iraq before the invasion as more Iraqi in comparison to the ones who were living abroad. In line 6, the participant constructs the people who came to Iraq as a result of the invasion as being given the power by the Americans. In contrast, he presents the Iraqis who were in Iraq, and suffered from oppression and hardships, as currently marginalised. This formulation is designed to portray the current Iraqi government as part of the invasion. Furthermore, it implies that the way the power was divided among Iraqis was not fair, and it marginalised the true Iraqis.

Thus, in this account, the dispute is between two groups of Iraqis, and the participant associates himself with the ones who were in the country prior to the invasion. Here, the national identity is not the identity that differentiates between the two rival groups; rather it is the location prior to the invasion. The speaker associates location with suffering, describing the ones who were in Iraq as the ones who suffered while the ones who came from outside after the invasion benefited from the invasion and were favoured by foreign powers. This characterisation of these two sides is designed to function as a way of criticising the Iraqis who are in power, and it prepares the ground to resist the Iraqi government on the basis of them being part of a foreign invasion.

Using collective identities to warrant the invasion as liberation of Iraqis

In the following five extracts, several Iraqi participants provide accounts that warrant the American invasion of Iraq. They do so mainly through creating "oppressed" as a collective identity for themselves and their group, one that entails particular category-bound characteristics and features.

In the first extract, the participant creates an account that warrants the war, providing explanations for his position.

EXTRACT 4.4. PARTICIPANT NUMBER 15, 56 YEARS OLD, MALE, UNIVERSITY STAFF; BASRA, IRAQ.

1 I: do you think the American invasion was right and why?
2 P: yes it was right because it liberated us

from tyrannical, dictatorial and murderous regime
therefore removing it is a good thing
however it was inevitable that some mistakes would occur
when the allied forces entered
some people have benefited while others were harmed or
killed
this is a known thing and for sure it is bad
but if we were to look at the long term
we will see that potentially this country will nourish
and if we want happiness we need to taste bitterness
and if we wanted to have an advanced and stable country
we need to go through anarchy which we are in right now

In the above extract, the participant builds an account that warrants the American invasion of his country. He does so through invoking the situation under the ex-regime and making it relevant to the discussion of the invasion, focusing on the negative aspects of the situation prior to the war, when there was a "tyrannical, dictatorial, murderous regime". Here, the participant uses the three-part list formulation to amplify the harmful nature of the ex-regime and allow a positive comparison with the invasion which, the participant states in line 2, "liberated us". Again, through the use of the term "us" he implies the account reflects an opinion of a group of Iraqis rather than an individualistic point of view and also creates a distinction between Iraqis and the ex-regime, preparing the ground for detachment from both fighting sides. Note that although the participant provides a satisfactory answer to the question, he does not stop. In line 4, he implicitly equates the invasion with the removal of the ex-regime, further constituting the sides of the war as the ex-regime and the Americans, and allowing the participant, as a lay Iraqi, to detach himself from the war without risking being viewed as unpatriotic.

In line 5, he describes "mistakes" which took place because of the invasion as "inevitable". Here, the participant formulates what could be described as extremely negative implications, such as the destruction of infrastructure, the killing of thousands of people, and war crimes, into inevitable mistakes. This formulation entails acquitting the allied forces of intentionally harming Iraqis. In lines 7-8, the participant presents two categories: the first category consists of Iraqis who "benefited" from the removal of the ex-regime; the second is a group of people who were "harmed or killed" in the process. Considering that the participant portrays the ex-regime as a "tyrannical, dictatorial and murderous regime", people who benefited from its removal are expected to be identified as Iraqis who were oppressed under it. In contrast, those who were harmed or killed could be heard as being part of the "tyrannical" regime, with their injury and death seen as necessary for the greater good. However, in line 8, the participant protects himself from being seen as condoning the killing of other Iraqis by stating that it is "for sure a bad thing".

In lines 10 to 14, the participant provides an account that is designed to invoke positive prospects for the invasion. He suggests that in the "long term" Iraq will "nourish" and that the current suffering is a temporary stage that will end. Note that the participant constructs a positive ending on the basis of a forecast for the future rather than on things that are happening in the present. In line 12, he presents "happiness" as a reward if the Iraqis withstand the current "bitterness". In line 13, the participant portrays the suffering that is taking place at the time of the interview as something similar to a necessary path toward the desired goal of having an "advanced and stable country". Thus, the participant warrants the invasion by portraying the Iraqis as previously oppressed, and by portraying present suffering as a way to a better future.

In the next section of this chapter, I present three similar extracts that address the same question.

EXTRACT 4.5. PARTICIPANT NUMBER 16, 27 YEARS OLD, MALE, UNIVERSITY STAFF; BASRA, IRAQ.

1 I: do you think the American invasion was right and why?
2 P: I believe that the American invasion was right

for me as an oppressed Iraqi
I consider the American invasion liberation
from the ex-regime and all its aggressive behaviours
and tyrannical rules
the American invasion was a breakthrough from that
situation
regardless of all the negativities and
all the suffering that came with the invasion
and for the lack of security during the American era
for me I did not have security during the ex-regime's time
the difference is that it was not because of explosions
and bombs
it was because of the Ba'athist organisations'
security apparatus and policemen

EXTRACT 4.6. PARTICIPANT NUMBER 17, 29 YEARS OLD, FEMALE, UNIVERSITY STAFF; BASRA, IRAQ.

I: do you think the American invasion was right and why?
P: it was not an invasion it was liberation and everyone
knows that
under the previous regime I have never felt that I am
a real citizen
I always felt that I am a prisoner in a big jail
people were afraid to talk, to complain
we could not express our opinions
and we could not even leave the country
we were dragged into pointless wars
in which millions of people lost their lives
and millions were displaced and lost their incomes
so for me it was not an invasion since we got rid of
a criminal regime
the old regime did not represent me
I know the situation now is bad but it will get better
it just needs some time
in the end we will have a fair and strong government
and Iraqis' lives will improve

EXTRACT 4.7. PARTICIPANT NUMBER 18, 29 YEARS OLD, MALE, UNIVERSITY STAFF; BASRA, IRAQ.

I: do you think the American invasion was right and why?
P: for me as an oppressed Iraqi I consider
the American invasion is a release from the ex-regime
with all its aggressive acts and oppressing rules
the American invasion was a breakthrough from that
situation regardless of all the negatives
and the suffering which they have brought with them
and even if we want to talk about the loss of security
which we are living in for me
well I didn't have security during the ex-regime
but it was not because of explosions and bombs
but because of the Ba'athist

These three different participants also present the American invasion positively, using similar rhetorical techniques. They reformulate the invasion as "right", "liberation", and "release" (Extract 4.5, line 2; Extract 4.6, line 2; Extract 4.7, line 3). Within each of the above accounts, the participants build an argument that justifies and explains their support of the war – an indication that a positive portrayal of the invasion could be heard as problematic.

In the first extract, the participant describes the American invasion as "liberation from the ex-regime and all its aggressive behaviours" (Extract 4.5, lines 4-5). Similarly, the second participant warrants his assessment of the invasion through pointing to a positive outcome, stating that it was "liberation" (Extract 4.6, line 2). The third participant presents a similar notion by stating that what took place was "release from the ex-regime with all its aggressive acts and tyrranical rules" (Extract 4.7, lines 4-6). The reframing of the invasion as liberation is warranted by the introduction of the category of the "oppressed Iraqi". In line 3, the first participant uses the descriptive "oppressed Iraqi" as a label for himself. The third participant uses the same term, "oppressed", in line 2. By using this label, they provide a new category, one designed to create an identity alongside the conventional national identity. The second participant uses the similar term "prisoner" (line 6) to create a similar discursive account. This way of turning a description into a substantive collective identity is similar to Sacks' famous category of "hotrodder" (Sacks, 1992). Sacks showed that the "deployment of the term hotrodder as a description of people was an effective way of drawing boundaries around who did and did not count (for a current speaker, in the current talk) as a legitimate member of that category" (Edwards, 1998, p. 115). These speakers build up the oppressed identity through highlighting their life situation under the ex-regime, such as being in a "big jail", living under "aggressive behaviours and tyrannical rules", with no "security" (Extract 4.6, line 6; Extract 4.5, lines 4-6; Extract 4.7, line 8). By creating a collective identity based on the negative experience of the situation prior to the war, itself the result of the ex-regime, and the target of the invasion as that oppressive regime, the participants portray the invasion of Iraq as the liberation of Iraqis.

The three participants also attend to the negative aspects of the general situation in Iraq at the time of the interview. In lines 9 to 11, the first participant describes some of the "suffering that came with the invasion", such as the "lack of security during the American era", but he undermines the importance of these notions by indicating that he "did not have security during the ex-regime's time" (Extract 4.5, line 12). The second participant uses a similar discursive technique, indicating that the "situation now is bad", but counters this negativity by stating that "it will get better" (Extract 4.6, line 16). The third participant constructs a very similar account, indicating that the situation in which he now lives is not unprecedented, since he did not have security prior to the war (Extract 4.7, line 10). Thus, by appealing either to a darker past or to a brighter future, the problems of the present are put into context, and the negative aspects of the invasion are mitigated.

These four extracts present a similar argument that accomplishes several discursive actions simultaneously. The first action is to denounce the previous regime. This allows the participants to create and deploy the identity of the "oppressed", and by characterising the ex-regime as an aggressive and oppressive regime, they also subtly acquit the Iraqis of being portrayed as defeated by the Americans or as unpatriotic. This formulation performs an important discursive function of maintaining a positive self-presentation for Iraqi people (see Potter, 1996; van Dijk, 1992). The second function of the accounts is to portray the American invasion as targeted against the former regime rather than against Iraq as a country – as a war between the Americans and the ex-regime. Considering that they portray the ex-regime as the enemy to them not as individuals but as members of the Iraqi population, it is understandable that they would support the invasion. The third function is to portray the present as better than it was and en route to something better still. Like the participants who presented the invasion in negative terms, these accounts are bound up with notions of Iraqi identity that are based on different criteria, in this case, the relationship of Iraqis to the former regime rather than, say, whether one was living in Iraq prior to the invasion.

In the next extract, the participant warrants the invasion by portraying Iraqis as having benefited from it.

EXTRACT 4.8. PARTICIPANT NUMBER 19, 62 YEARS OLD, MALE, RETIRED; BASRA, IRAQ.

1 I: do you think the American invasion was right and why?
2 P: yes it was right
3 although it caused the deaths of many people
4 and the destruction of property
5 but who would have expected that the dictatorial regime
6 would be axed
7 and we would get rid of the injustice, fear and terror
8 which lived with us for 35 years
9 and caused mass graves
10 and the violation of honour
[entehak ala'arad – a term used to refer to rape]
11 is there an Iraqi house that does not have a evidence
12 that indicates the damage of Saddam
13 now there are several people who say that

the American invasion was not right
and we ask why?
the current situation which Iraqis are living through
is not new
we have seen it repeatedly so
why do we not let things take their natural course
without any objections and let's say that we will be patient
and god helps the ones who are patient and hopefully
we will get what we desire
whether by the Americans or others
and we will become like other nations
and live in peace, development and prosperity

In the above extract, the participant warrants the American invasion by building up positive outcomes of that invasion. He begins by describing the invasion as "right". Within the same sentence, in lines 2 to 4, he acknowledges the negative consequences of the war, stating that "it caused the deaths of many people and the destruction of property". In this formulation, the participant portrays a double-sided account of the invasion. He asserts that although it caused "the deaths of many people", he considers it a "right" action. In lines 5 to 12, the participant builds an account designed to justify the understanding that the invasion is "right", despite the deaths and destruction that were caused as a result. He describes the situation prior to the invasion using a three-part list, stating that they were living under "injustice, fear, and terror" (Atkinson, 1984), and implies that the "dictatorial regime" (line 5) is the one responsible for the rift between Iraqis and, consequently, the support for the invasion among them.

In lines 9 to 10, the participant presents evidence to support his account, indicating that the regime "caused mass graves" and used rape as a systematic policy to further its objectives. This portrayal functions as a way of distinguishing the ex-regime from the Iraqi people, which in turn justifies the participant's position on the ex-regime and the invasion. In lines 11 to 12, the participant extends this to all Iraqis, presenting Saddam as the criminal and the Iraqis as the victims, amplifying the suffering experienced by Iraqis and isolating Saddam as responsible for the suffering.

Although the participant has provided a complete answer addressing the issue of the invasion, he does not stop there. Rather, he moves on to discuss the present situation and provide a forecast for the future. In lines 13-14, he presents what can be described as his opponents' argument. He attributes this argument to "several people" who are saying that "the American invasion was not right". Attributing the counter-argument to several people indicates that it is not the opinion of the majority of Iraqis. He does not provide a direct answer but indicates that "the current situation which Iraqis are living through is not new" and that they "have seen it repeatedly". Moreover, by describing the criminal as just Saddam rather than the regime, the government, or other Iraqis, the participant warrants his account that all Iraqis were oppressed and thus happy when the ex-regime was axed. Thus, as in the previous extracts, the speaker isolates himself and his comrades from the ex-regime as part of the warranting of the invasion as liberation.

Summary and conclusion

Through analysing several accounts of the war, I have demonstrated that collective identities are a central factor in these accounts of armed conflicts that took place in Iraq and in Lebanon. Participants build various collective identities for themselves and others as part of their accounts (see Extract 4.2). Each one of these participants establishes a collective identity that is utilised as a discursive resource to provide a specific understanding of the war.

In the first part, several participants invoked specific national identities that allowed them to subtly defend the ex-regime in Iraq, denounce the invasion, and reject the current Iraqi government. By portraying Iraqi exiles as less Iraqi than those who lived in Iraq prior to the invasion, national identity is used to undermine the legitimacy of the current Iraqi government and the invasion that brought it into place, whilst avoiding explicit support for Saddam.

In the second part, I have shown that several lay Iraqi individuals opted to characterise themselves as "previously oppressed Iraqis". By drawing on the situation under the ex-regime, these individuals distinguished Iraqis from the former regime, and thus warranted the invasion of their country in a way that portrayed events as "pro-Iraqi" and in the national interest.

References

Antaki, C., & Widdicombe, S. (Eds.). (1998). *Identities in talk.* London: Sage.

Billig, M. (1995). *Banal Nationalism.* London: Sage.

Castano, E., Slawuta, P. & Leidner, B. (2008). Social Identification Processes, Group Dynamics and the Behavior of Combatants. *International Review of the Red Cross, 90*(870), 259-271.

Dower, J. W. (1986). *War without mercy: race and power in the Pacific War.* New York: Pantheon.

Edwards, D. (1998). The relevant thing about her: Social identity categories in use. In C. Antaki & S. Widdicombe (Eds.), *Identities in Talk* (pp. 15-33). London: Sage.

Eglin, P., & Hester, S., (1999). Moral order and the Montreal massacre: A story of membership categorisation analysis. In P.L. Jalbert (Ed.), *Media Studies: Ethnomethodological approaches* (pp. 195-230). Lanham: International Institute for Ethnomethodology and Conversation Analysis.

Gartzke, E. & Gleditsch, K. S. (2006). Identity and Conflict: Ties That Bind and Differences That Divide. *European Journal of International Relations, 12*(1): 53–87.

Herrera, M. (2003). Constructing social categories and seeking collective influence: self-categorization and the discursive construction of a conflict. *International Journal of Psychology and Psychological Therapy, 3*(1), 27-57.

Hutchby, I., & Wooffitt, R. (1998). *Conversation analysis.* Polity Press.

Leudar, I., Marsland, V. & Nekvapil, J. (2004). On membership categorization: 'Us,' 'them' and 'doing violence' in political discourse. *Discourse & Society, 15*(2-3), 243-266.

Potter, J. (1996). *Representing reality: Discourse, rhetoric and social construction.*

Sacks, H. (1992). *Lectures on conversation.* Oxford: Basil Blackwell.

Stevenson, C., Condor, S., & Abell, J. (2007). The Minority-Majority Conundrum in Northern Ireland: An Orange Order Perspective. *Political Psychology, 28*(1), 105–125.

van Dijk, T. A. (1992). Discourse and the denial of racism. *Discourse & Society, 3*(1), 87-118.

Wooffitt, R. (1992). *Telling tales of the unexpected: the organization of factual discourse.* Hempstead: Harvester Wheatsheaf.

Chapter 5

The 2006 war between Hezbollah and Israel

In this chapter, I present and analyse different interpretations of the 2006 war between Israel and Hezbollah by Lebanese decision makers. It is striking that the same rhetoric has been employed in relation to the 2024 war between Hezbollah and Lebanon.

By examining how various influential parties presented the conflict as it unfolded, we can connect these perspectives to developments over the past 18 years, thereby uncovering the psychological roots of the current situation. I will examine the primary narratives as they were expressed during the conflict, focusing on the influential figures who played significant roles in Lebanese politics at the time.

I will begin with a brief introduction of Hassan Nasrallah, the central figure in this context, before I discuss Hezbollah and then introduce the extracts.

Hassan Nasrallah is one of the most influential figures in the Middle East, recognized for his roles as a political leader, religious authority, and the head of Hezbollah – a powerful Shia Islamist organization based in Lebanon. Born in 1960 to a poor Shia family in the Beqaa Valley, Nasrallah claims lineage tracing back to the Prophet Muhammad, which has greatly enhanced his religious standing within the Shia community. Despite his family's modest means, he pursued religious studies in Iraq and Lebanon, which laid the groundwork for his rise within Hezbollah (Norton, 2007).

Nasrallah became involved with a group of Shia youths inspired by the Iranian Revolution and determined to create an Islamic state in Lebanon. This group sought support from Iran, which provided training, weapons, and financial assistance, leading to the formation of Hezbollah in the early 1980s. Hezbollah has since grown into one of the most formidable non-state actors in the world, wielding significant influence in Lebanon and across the Middle East (Levitt, 2013).

Hezbollah's political and religious agenda is deeply rooted in the principles of Shia Islam, heavily influenced by the Iranian Revolution and the teachings of Ayatollah Khomeini. The group's primary goals include establishing an Islamic state in Lebanon, resisting Israel, and opposing Western influence in the Middle East. These objectives are outlined in its 1985 "Open Letter," which remains a cornerstone of its ideological framework. The manifesto declared Hezbollah's loyalty to Ayatollah Khomeini and expressed its intention to create a society governed by Islamic law in Lebanon (Blanford, 2011).

Central to Hezbollah's agenda is its role as a "resistance" movement against Israel. The group views Israel as an illegitimate and oppressive state, and its military actions are framed as a righteous struggle not only for Lebanon but for the entire Arab and Muslim world. Hezbollah considers itself part of a broader "Axis of Resistance" that includes Iran, Syria, and various Palestinian factions, opposing Western influence in the Middle East and supporting armed resistance against Israel (Levitt, 2013). This anti-Western stance is further reinforced by Hezbollah's close and strategic ties with Iran, which provides substantial financial support, military training, and weaponry (Norton, 2007).

While Hezbollah's agenda is driven by religious and ideological commitments, the group has also sought to integrate itself into Lebanon's political system. Since the end of the Lebanese Civil War in 1990, Hezbollah has participated in elections and held seats in parliament and the cabinet, allowing it to influence national policy while maintaining its military independence (Harik, 2004). Its extensive social services network, which includes healthcare, education, and welfare programs, primarily targets Lebanon's Shia population, helping to secure a loyal base of support (Norton, 2007).

Hezbollah's rise has been marked by several high-profile terrorist attacks, including the 1983 bombing of the US Marine barracks in Beirut that killed 241 American servicemen. On the same day, a separate attack on French paratroopers killed 58 soldiers. These attacks targeted the Multinational Force in Lebanon, a peacekeeping mission invited by the Lebanese government to stabilize the country during its civil war (Blanford, 2011). Hezbollah has also been linked to terrorist attacks worldwide, such as the 1992 bombing of the Israeli Embassy in Buenos Aires and the 1994 bombing of the Argentine Israelite Mutual Association (Levitt, 2013).

The group has also been linked to the assassination of Rafic Hariri, the former Prime Minister of Lebanon, in 2005. Hariri's assassination led to widespread protests and the eventual withdrawal of Syrian troops from Lebanon in the Cedar Revolution. In 2020, the Special Tribunal for Lebanon convicted in absentia a Hezbollah member, Salim Ayyash, for his role in the assassination, though Hezbollah has consistently denied any involvement (Blanford, 2011).

Hezbollah's ability to sustain its operations and influence is largely due to its diverse funding sources. These include state sponsorship from Iran, charitable donations, illicit activities such as drug trafficking and money laundering, and legitimate business ventures in Lebanon and abroad. This funding network supports its military and political activities, allowing it to maintain influence in Lebanon and across the region (Levitt, 2013).

Hezbollah's involvement in the Syrian Civil War, beginning in 2011, further extended its regional influence. Nasrallah declared Hezbollah's support for the Assad regime, framing the conflict as part of a broader struggle against extremism and a defense of Shia communities. Hezbollah fighters played crucial roles in several key battles, deepening the group's ties to Iran and further polarizing the sectarian divide in the Middle East (Blanford, 2011).

Hassan Nasrallah's rhetoric has been a critical element of Hezbollah's strategy, combining religious authority, political messaging, and populist appeal to mobilize support and legitimize the group's actions. His speeches often invoke Shia religious imagery, portraying Hezbollah's struggle as a continuation of historic battles for justice and resistance against oppression. Nasrallah's rhetoric is also characterized by its strong anti-Israel and anti-Western themes, with his speeches broadcast widely through Hezbollah's media outlets, allowing him to reach a broad audience across the Middle East (Norton, 2007).

Nasrallah's leadership and rhetoric have been central to Hezbollah's rise as a significant political and military force in the Middle East. Through a combination of Iranian support, diversified funding sources, and a potent ideological narrative, Hezbollah has maintained its influence both in Lebanon and across the region. Nasrallah's speeches continue to shape the discourse of resistance and defiance against Israel and the West, ensuring Hezbollah's place as a key player in the region's ongoing conflicts.

Justification for triggering the war

The following extract is an essential part of Hassan Nasrallah's explanation of the 2006 war:

EXTRACT 5.1. HASSAN NASRALLAH, SECRETARY GENERAL OF HEZBOLLAH; 21 JULY 2006, AL-JAZEERA TV (N = NASRALLAH).

N: the Israeli reaction to the capture operation
could have been cruel but limited
if there had not been an international and Arab cover (.)
Israel did not receive a green light from America
Israel received an instruction from America
to go in, continue and finish
this is the issue in Lebanon now, what has been
the basis of that American decision?
this we leave till the time comes
when they will be held accountable
the international community did not give a green light to
Israel, the international community gave Israel instructions
to eradicate the resistance in Lebanon
more than that some Arabs came to give,
to provide a cover and to encourage Israel
to continue the battle and to tell Israel, Israel has been told
that this is the golden chance to eradicate the resistance in
Lebanon. I say it to you that they don't want Hezbollah's
resistance in Lebanon, they want to eradicate any will for
resistance in Lebanon whether it is Hezbollah or anyone else
they want to take the country to the point
where the word resistance is condemned
martyr, jihad, wounded, withstanding,
challenging, liberation, dignity, honour
all that should be removed from Lebanese discourse
from the political literature, the political mind
from the people's conscience
this is what Israel is doing and
this is what America needs
it wants to reconstitute the region

In this extract, Nasrallah uses evasive and obscure discourses to discuss the war. Bull (2003) showed that evasiveness and obscurity are usually used by politicians to guard against potential criticisms. Here, the speaker implicitly invokes the incident (line 1) which some media portrayed as the trigger for the war, yet the real focus of the account is on the Israeli reaction to that attack. He constructs the sides involved and the goal of each side in a specific way that warrants his organisation's activities. In the literature on war (e.g., DeRouen & Heo, 2007), the trigger incident represents a central factor used to identify the side responsible for the war. Usually, the side that initiates the first attack is considered to be the one culpable for starting the war and, therefore, considered responsible for its consequences. As I have shown in the introduction, Nasrallah and his organisation, Hezbollah, were widely described as the side that initiated the war and were consequently blamed for it by various countries. In this extract, the interviewee does not deny that his organisation carried out the first attack. Instead, the reaction to the incident is constructed in such a way as to make the Israeli reaction itself blameworthy and unreasonable, not the initial attack. Specifically, he says "the reaction to the capture operation could have been cruel but limited if there had not been an international and Arab cover" (lines 1-3). By describing his organisation's attack as a "capture operation", Nasrallah implies that this attack was carried out as a precise operation to accomplish a specific goal, which was to capture a number of Israeli soldiers. Therefore, it was not intended to start a war. Nasrallah focuses on the Israeli reaction to the attack. He indicates that the expected Israeli reaction to the "capture operation" carried out by his organisation was a "limited" one. He attributes the unexpected Israeli reaction, which was waging an open war, to the international and Arab complicity. This can be seen as a reference to the official Arabic position which condemned Hezbollah for attacking Israel.

In lines 4 to 6, Nasrallah builds up the responsibility of the United States specifically for the war, stating that "Israel did not receive a green light from America, Israel received an instruction from America to go in, continue and finish". The implication of "go in, continue and finish" is to portray the role of these countries as an active, aggressive stance, rather than a response to a provoking incident. In this formulation, Nasrallah apportions the blame for the war on the United States and the Arabs. He constructs these sides as the ones that caused the war between Israel and Hezbollah. This formulation is repeated in lines 11 to 12, but here the intentions are escalated by referring to "the international community" and using the term "eradicate" rather than finish. He portrays this campaign as orchestrated by several sides in addition to Israel to "eradicate the resistance in Lebanon". This formulation portrays Hezbollah as not accountable for the war, since it is planned by America, covered by Arabs, and executed by Israel to accomplish specific goals. This acquits Hezbollah of the responsibility for causing the war and consequently any blame for its consequences. At the same time, it accuses Arab countries of being accomplices with Israel and America in the war against Lebanon. This consequently apportions the blame to these countries along with Israel and the US. In line 7, Nasrallah indicates that the support which Israel has received "is the issue in Lebanon now".

In lines 8 to 10, the interviewee initiates a subtle threat against certain sides, stating that he does not want to discuss the "basis of that American decision" to push Israel into war. He indicates that when "the time comes", some people "will be held accountable". This warning, which can be seen as directed against Lebanese sides that collaborate with Arab states, the US, and possibly with Israel against Hezbollah, has several discursive functions. Firstly, it implies that the interviewee has specific information sufficient to hold these people accountable. This is designed to make his account seem factual (cf. Edwards & Potter, 1992; Potter, 1996). Secondly, it portrays the interviewee as confident that his organisation will come out of the war strong enough to hold its enemies accountable.

In lines 12 to 16, Nasrallah presents a detailed account of the collaboration between "Israel", "Arabs", and the "international community" in the war against his organisation. He accuses the "international community" of being the side that "gave Israel instructions to eradicate the resistance in Lebanon" (lines 11-12).

This formulation characterises the war in a way that minimises Hezbollah's role significantly. It frames the Western governments as the culpable side in relation to the war. In lines 13 to 16, Nasrallah presents another side as responsible for the war, by portraying some Arab states as actively supporting Israel in its effort to "eradicate the resistance". He states that "some Arabs came to give, to provide a cover, and to encourage Israel to continue the battle" (lines 14-15). In line 16, Nasrallah presents a detailed account of the Arab message to Israel, indicating that they have told Israel that this war is "the golden chance to eradicate the resistance". This frames the Arab countries as actively pursuing the eradication of the resistance movement in Lebanon. This portrays these countries as being against Lebanon's interests.

In lines 17 to 29, Nasrallah builds an account that highlights Israel's and America's strategic goals for the war. He implies that Israel's goal in the war is larger than defeating Hezbollah, stating that it "want[s] to eradicate any will for resistance in Lebanon whether it is Hezbollah or anyone else" (lines 19-20). Here, he is implying that it is not Hezbollah *per se* that is significant but their stance. In other words, it is not their identity, policies, beliefs, actions, or any other attribute of Hezbollah. It is simply because they are standing up to Israel, and Israel would attack any Lebanese group that resists its dominance. Further, the use of words such as "eradicate" is designed to maximise the intensity of Israeli activity. He continues building up Israel as an enemy to Lebanon, not just Hezbollah, indicating that it wants to remove notions such as "challenging, liberation, dignity, honour". Here, Nasrallah constructs the ultimate Israeli goal of the war as removing ideas and beliefs that are associated with liberties and the right of self-determination. In this way, the speaker portrays the goal of eradication of resistance in the broadest way: not just crushing fighters but even the will or notion of freedom. He indicates that the concepts "martyr, jihad, wounded, withstanding, challenging, liberation, dignity, honour" are what Israel wants to erase "from Lebanese discourse, from the political literature, the political mind" (lines 23-26). Here, through deploying this report which contains vivid descriptions and strong, specific accusations, the interviewee is building up the factuality of his argument (cf. Edwards & Potter, 1992; Potter, 1996).

In lines 28 to 29, Nasrallah indicates that Israel's actions serve the United States' desire "to reconstitute the region". This account builds a stake for all Lebanese in resisting Israel. It also implies that Hezbollah is protecting all Lebanese people from Israel's hegemony. It discursively prepares the ground for warranting Hezbollah's activities, associates them with all Lebanese, and makes them more appealing. Note that he extends the argument to include other Middle Easterners who are not Lebanese by mentioning the region, which can be seen as a reference to the Middle East, particularly since these events are taking place while American forces are in Iraq. Thus, through this formulation Nasrallah is creating a stake for the Lebanese and other Middle Easterners in supporting the resistance. Supporting the resistance in Lebanon can be seen as a means to prevent America and Israel from establishing control over all the countries in the region. To summarise, this account downplays the potential role of Hezbollah's capture operation as being responsible for the violence that followed. Instead, it portrays Israel's actions as driven by a mutual American and Israeli goal to end the resistance in order to reconstitute the region. The implication is that Hezbollah's responsibility for the war is denied and their actions in resisting Israel and America are presented as being in the interests of all Lebanese people.

Distancing yourself from the war: "Not our war"

In the next extract, an influential Christian Lebanese politician accounts for the war by discussing the appropriate stance in relation to the ongoing war. He also discusses the social structure of Lebanese society and the different points of view on the war. He constructs the situation in a way that, like the first extract, warrants Hezbollah's activities and holds Israel solely responsible for the war.

EXTRACT 5.2. GHASSAN TUENI, FORMER MP AND PUBLISHER OF AL-NAHAR NEWSPAPER; 27 JULY 2006, AL-ARABIYA.

I: some people are saying that this is a surrogate war,
it is on behalf of others
do you believe that? And who are those others?
T: there are many (.) let me be clear here I do not wish to acquit
the Lebanese from going into wars (.) they have fought
against each other however unfortunately this is because
the multi-sectarian nature of the Lebanese society
allows regional and international powers to infiltrate it
and break it down and the side that recruited the Lebanese
the most to work for its causes is Israel. If we read
the classified documents which were [published recently]
I: [about the war?]
T: no not about the war about the negotiations which led
to Israel's declaration we would see that they were trying
to draw a specific sector to create a sectarian state
I: yes but now the situation is different
there is a consensus among the Lebanese
that Israel is the biggest [enemy]
T: [not the] biggest enemy
there is no such thing as big and [small enemies]
I: [there are no small]
enemies?
T: there are small enemies but they are (.)
I do not know how to say this
the enemy is Israel.
and this is why I warn the Lebanese who
distrust Shiites for sectarian reasons or distrust Hezbollah
because of its weapons. They should not forget
that Hezbollah is fighting Israel
whether that was legitimate or not
it is fighting the enemy
and that enemy is the enemy of all of us
and it is the greatest enemy to the Christians
whom it tried to pull in

and [recruit them]
I: [so Ghassan] Tueni thinks that the issue today
is not capturing two Israeli soldiers
and whether that operation was right or not,
what you see is that Hezbollah is resisting Israel?
T: yes the issue is that Hezbollah is fighting Israel
and it is fighting better than all the [Arab armies]
I: [for what]
T: for what (.) for the cause and we are all in this together

In this extract, the speakers address the issue of accountability and discuss whose war it is. In lines 1 to 3, the interviewer presents an assessment of the war as "a surrogate war", a war "on behalf of others". She attributes this assessment to "some people". This device allows the interviewer to avoid being seen as responsible for this notion, which is a controversial accusation. She subsequently asks Tueni if he agrees with this assessment and if he can identify the sides that the Lebanese parties are proxies for. The term "surrogate" and the accompanying explanation are inference-rich formulations designed to assign blame to the Lebanese side, Hezbollah, for the war. This framing suggests that Hezbollah's actions were driven by serving the interests others rather than by their own intentions or objectives or those of their country. This can be seen as portraying the involvement of Lebanese factions in the war as more reasonable, as they are depicted as taking their country to war to serve the interests of others. It is worth noting, however, that the nature of these others remains unspecified.

In lines 4 to 7, Tueni's response addresses the issue of war but overlooks the question whether Lebanese factions are acting as proxies for others. This is done through a two-part answer. In the first part, Tueni acknowledges that Lebanese parties have acted as proxies, indicating that these sides are numerous. In the second part of his answer, he indicates that he "do[es] not wish to acquit" the Lebanese from responsibility for wars by blaming foreign actors. He points out that the Lebanese "have fought against each other" (lines 5 to 6), which is designed to portray the Lebanese as responsible for the wars. Tueni attributes the Lebanese tendency to become involved in wars to the nature of Lebanese society rather than to the weakness of the state or the nature of the region. Specifically, he says that the "multi-sectarian nature of the Lebanese society allows regional and international powers to infiltrate it". By characterising conflict in this manner, he implies that there is nothing that can be done about conflict: it is an inherent feature of Lebanese society which invites external interference. The implication is that war is caused by outsiders, with the help of the Lebanese themselves.

In lines 9 to 10, Tueni accuses Israel of being "the side that recruited the Lebanese the most to work for its causes". Here, Tueni can be seen as shifting the focus from Hezbollah, which is reported to be a surrogate for Iran and Syria, to Israel, which has historically been associated with the Lebanese Phalangists. This shift is designed to blame Israel for the civil wars that previously occurred in Lebanon. It also constructs Israel as an enemy that exploited the divisions among the Lebanese people. In lines 9 to 10, this claim is warranted with reference to the evidence provided by "the classified documents which were published recently". The speaker states these documents indicate "that they [Israel] were trying to draw a specific sector and create a sectarian state". This refers to the relationship between Israel and the Phalangists in the 1940s, prior to the establishment of Israel. The implication is that Israeli intentions are transparent, thus constructing the claim as factual (cf. Potter, 1996).

The interviewer in lines 16 to 18 initiates a counter-argument, stating that "now the situation is different; there is a consensus among the Lebanese that Israel is the biggest enemy". Here, she implies that the interviewee's assessment is obsolete and not applicable to the current situation. Nonetheless, within her account, she describes Israel as the "biggest enemy", suggesting that Israel is not the only enemy at present. By distinguishing between "big" and "small" enemies, she implies that other factions within Lebanon are aligned with "small enemies" who are also culpable for instigating wars. This can be seen as an implicit reference to Hezbollah's alliances with Iran and Syria. Tueni rejects this, stating that "there is no such thing as big and small enemies". In lines 18 to 24, the two engage in a debate around the existence of different types of enemies. In line 25, the interviewee states that "the enemy is Israel". By constructing Israel as the enemy, the speaker negates the notion of multiple enemies and, consequently, the idea of several blameworthy parties. This statement thus warrants Hezbollah's activities against Israel and justifies backing Hezbollah.

In lines 26 to 28, Tueni initiates a warning to the Lebanese people about losing sight of the core of the matter. He states that "the Lebanese who distrust Shiites for sectarian reasons or distrust Hezbollah because of its weapons. They should not forget that Hezbollah is fighting Israel". This suggests that sectarian differences or concerns about Hezbollah's military capabilities should not distract from the fact that Hezbollah is fighting their common enemy. This serves to encourage Lebanese people to put their differences aside and unite in support of Hezbollah. In lines 30 to 31, Tueni indicates that the Lebanese should support Hezbollah in this war "whether that [war] was legitimate or not". The consequence of this formulation is that it counters potential criticism of Hezbollah's actions based on their legitimacy. This formulation is designed to downplay divisions among the Lebanese in relation to the stance of Hezbollah and, consequently, of the war. In lines 31 to 32, Tueni reiterates the notion that Hezbollah "is fighting the enemy and that enemy is the enemy of all of us [Lebanese]". This formulation functions as a way to reinforce the representation of the war as a conflict between Hezbollah and a common enemy, thereby rallying Lebanese support for Hezbollah. In lines 33 to 35, Tueni addresses the relationship between Christian Lebanese and Israel. He indicates that Israel is "the greatest enemy to the Christians, whom it tried to pull in and recruit". In this formulation, the speaker negates the stereotypical image of Lebanese Christians as less antagonistic toward Israel. It is important to note that this image stems from the civil war in Lebanon during which several Christian parties, such as the Phalangists, collaborated publicly with Israel. Tueni counters this by indicating that Israel attempted to "recruit" Christians for its own purpose.

In lines 36 to 39, the interviewer produces a summary of the argument: "So Ghassan Tueni thinks that the issue today is not capturing of the two Israeli soldiers and whether that operation was right or not, what you see is that Hezbollah is resisting Israel?" This formulation suggests that there are two main stances in relation to the war in Lebanon. On one hand, there is the understanding that Hezbollah is the one that caused the war by capturing two Israeli soldiers. This implies that Hezbollah is responsible for all the subsequent ramifications and should therefore be held accountable. By contrast, the second perspective views Hezbollah as "resisting Israel", which is in the interest of all Lebanese. Thus, the Lebanese need to support Hezbollah's activities. Note the contrast between the two reasons and how one is dismissed. The first explanation makes the cause situation-specific (capturing soldiers), whereas the second provides a more general rationale for the war. Thus, Hezbollah cannot be blamed for its actions since it is a reaction to Israeli aggressions: they were self-defence.

In lines 40 to 41, Tueni rejects the first position and affiliates himself with the second one. He shows unequivocal support for Hezbollah, indicating that "the issue is that Hezbollah is fighting Israel". He continues praising Hezbollah for its military performance, indicating that "it is fighting better than all the [Arab armies]". This is designed to cement the notion that Hezbollah is deserving of support from all Lebanese people.

In line 42, the interviewer challenges Tueni's positive appraisal of Hezbollah by questioning the motive behind Hezbollah's activities, asking "for what" Hezbollah is fighting. In line 43, Tueni replies by stating that Hezbollah is fighting "for the cause". This simple formulation serves as an effective rhetorical device; it implies that Hezbollah is motivated by principles other than self-interest and at the same time leaves the nature of the cause unstated. Tueni then reemphasises the notion that "all [Lebanese] are in this together". Here, Tueni affirms, again, the notion that Hezbollah is fighting on behalf of all the Lebanese, therefore its activities are justifiable and the Lebanese have a stake in supporting it (cf. Potter, 1996).

The Lebanese government searching for a role

In the extract that follows, the interviewee, the Lebanese Minister of Defence, builds an account of the war that is designed to acquit Lebanon and the Lebanese resistance from responsibility in relation to the war. He constructs the events and the roots of the ongoing conflict in a way that legitimises the attack carried out by Hezbollah against Israel and apportions the blame for both the attack and the war solely to Israel.

EXTRACT 5.3. ELLEAS ALMOR, MINISTER OF DEFENCE; 23 JULY 2006, AL-ARABIYA TV.

I: Good evening, more than 300 people have been killed
and more than a 1000 wounded since the beginning
of the war against Lebanon (.)
how would you describe the situation on the ground?
A: the current situation can be summarised in two words
there are more than 300 to 350 martyrs
and more than 1000 wounded
and I believe the war has not started yet
since there is no balance of power in this war (.)
Israel is committing a massacre against the Lebanese people
Israel is attacking our bridges,
Israel is destroying our villages
it is killing and displacing our people
Israel attacked the infrastructure
which the Lebanese have been building
for the last 10 to 15 years (.)
Israel has attacked all
components of Lebanese society
under a pretext that there was a capture operation

carried out by Hezbollah
in which two Israeli soldiers were kidnapped
the question I want to ask is ok
there was a military operation against soldiers (.)
two soldiers were kidnapped (.) were captured
the reason for that is we have prisoners in the Israeli jails
they have been there for 20 to 30 years
the government, the resistance and United Nations
have been demanding their release
and everyone was demanding that
to solve the problem but that did not happen
so the resistance kidnapped and captured these two
there was a capture and kidnap operation
we have been taken by surprise that Israel waged a war
against the civil Lebanese people
it destroyed the country (.) it killed the people
it brought Lebanon 20 to 30 years backward

The interviewer starts in lines 1 to 3 by reporting the casualties on the Lebanese side, stating that "300 people have been killed and more than 1000 wounded". This report is designed to highlight the deleterious effects of the war on Lebanon exclusively. Note that the interviewer does not discuss the effects of the war on Israel. In line 4, she asks Almor to "describe the situation on the ground". In lines 6 to 7, Almor upgrades the number of deaths, stating that there "are more than 300 to 350 martyrs and more than 1000 wounded". Almor recharacterises the interviewer's reference to "people killed", using instead the term "martyrs". In contrast to "people killed", martyrs refers to people who have been killed for a worthy, even sacred, cause. He then escalates the severity of the situation by stating that "I believe the war has not started yet" (line 7). This formulation suggests that despite the numbers killed and wounded, the war and its destructive effects are still to come. The interviewee in line 9 explains why he thinks that the war has not started, by indicating that "there is no balance of power in this war". He characterises the fighting sides as not equals in terms of the military power each one is exercising and, consequently, the harm each side is inflicting or would inflict on the other side. Thus, it is implied that Lebanon is sustaining greater casualties due to its military inferiority in comparison to Israel. In lines 10 to 15, he discusses the Israeli action as "against the Lebanese people". He describes the Israeli activities as "killing and displacing our people", "attacking our bridges", and "destroying our villages". This account emphasises the ferocity of the Israeli attacks. It also portrays these attacks as targeting people in addition to a range of widespread, vital civil infrastructure. Almor further reinforces this notion in lines 14 to 16, in which he states that Israel "attacked the infrastructure which the Lebanese have been building for the last 10 to 15 years". Constructing "people", "bridges", and "villages" as targets of the attacks implies that Israel is attacking civilians, not soldiers or resistance fighters. Civilians and civil infrastructure are not conventionally or legally regarded as legitimate targets of war attacks; he thus implies that the attacks are illegitimate. It is important to stress that in this account Almor uses the term "our" to associate himself with the affected people and attacked infrastructure. This functions as a way of increasing his credibility as a source of information (cf. Edwards & Potter, 1992; Potter, 1996).

In lines 17 to 18, Almor produces a summary claim of the Israeli attacks, stating that "Israel has attacked all components of Lebanese society". This reinforces the disproportionate nature of the attacks. It implies that the Israeli attacks did not target a specific group of Lebanese; rather, they affected all areas and all Lebanese, regardless of their sectarian identity, as well as bridges, villages, and infrastructure.

Having built up the extent of Israeli action, Almor then produces an account for those actions: "under the pretext that there was a capture operation carried out by Hezbollah" (lines 19-20). This inference-rich formulation entails that Hezbollah's initial attack was used by Israel as an excuse to justify attacking Lebanon. The attack is described as a military operation against soldiers. This description of the nature of the attack as "military" and the characterisations of the target as "soldiers" portrays the attack as a legitimate activity, and, compared with attacking "people", these actions are constructed as reasonable activities that were not intended to be a cause for war. Here, Almor reconstructs Hezbollah's actions from being the cause of the war to being an excuse which Israel exploited to massacre Lebanon's people, villages, and infrastructure. This is designed to construct Israel as the side that is responsible for the war and its ramifications, such as the unjustified killing and destruction. It acquits Hezbollah from starting the armed conflict, apportioning the blame to Israel. In lines 25 to 26, the interviewee constructs an account that explains the motives behind Hezbollah's conduct. He indicates that "the reason for" the attack is the Lebanese "prisoners in the Israeli jails, they have been there for 20 to 30 years". He continues, asserting that several civil means were used to release "them and solve the problem, but that did not happen". He indicates that the "United Nations", the Lebanese "government", the "resistance," and other sides have been calling for the release of these Lebanese prisoners. As in the previous part, here Almor acknowledges the potential provocation, but in the way he describes the incident, it does not merit the degree of retaliation that followed. In lines 31 to 32, he portrays Hezbollah's attack as a reasonable act to release the prisoners by using violence since non-violent means did not deliver the desired end. In other words, he portrays extensive efforts to release the prisoners and claims that these were unable to resolve the problem. In this context, the use of specific and limited force is warranted as a last resort.

In line 33, the interviewee depicts Israel's activity as an unforeseeable and unwarranted reaction. This formulation is based on the narrative the participant has constructed throughout the extract. In lines 34 to 36, he presents a formulation of the war that portrays the Lebanese civilians as the target of the Israeli attacks. He concludes that these attacks have "destroyed the country" and "killed the people". Here, by presenting the consequences of the attacks in an extreme form – "destroyed the country" – the participant is deploying a rhetorical cover against potential counter-arguments. To sum up, in this extract, the interviewee constructs an account that is designed to apportion the blame for the war to Israel. He does this by downplaying Hezbollah's role in the war, the "trigger incident," and emphasising the Israeli actions as being against the Lebanese civilian state. He thus re-characterises the war from being a battle between two armed sides to being a massacre committed by Israel against Lebanese civilians. The Lebanese Minister of Defence counters the argument that blames Hezbollah for the war by constructing Hezbollah's activity as both limited and justified.

In this reply, Almor does not present the account of the Lebanese government, nor does he position himself as an active agent in the conflict. Instead, he assumes the role of a spectator or an impartial arbiter rather than that of the head of the Lebanese armed forces.

Constructing boundaries of identity and allegiance

The participant in the next extract, a former president of Lebanon during the civil war, is known for his criticism of Hezbollah and has been accused of allying with Israel.

EXTRACT 5.4. AMIN GEMAYEL, FORMER PRESIDENT, CURRENT MP, CHRISTIAN LEADER; 10 AUGUST 2006, AL-ARABIYA TV.

G: the one that is paying for all that
are the poor Lebanese people who are suffering
who we live with in their suffering.
I don't think there is a country that has lived (.)
has suffered in such a short period
we have given a thousand martyrs, a million refugees
which means one fourth of the Lebanese nation
this tragedy must end. [lines 9-12 omitted]

G: the problem is that we in Lebanon are paying the price
Lebanese people are displaced, the Lebanese people
are getting killed and their houses are being destroyed
I: Mr President are you demanding that Hassan Nasrallah
give up his weapons
G: where is the problem, we have been demanding
this since 2000
I: that means defeat if he gives up the weapons now
G: listen there is the original situation and the new situation
which means there is the internal political
situation and the war
there is no doubt and we have said
that and we repeat it again that
we are 100 times against the Israelis' aggression
and when it is between Israel and any Lebanese party
especially Hezbollah
we are with Hezbollah against the Israelis' aggression
this should be clear
however if it is between the project of Hezbollah and
the project of the state of Lebanon
then we are with the state
the state of Lebanon should regain its control
over all of Lebanon's territories
and it should be the only one who can
take the decision of peace or war

In this extract, the interviewee, the former Lebanese president, focuses on the "suffering" of the "poor Lebanese", whom he describes as the group that is most affected by the war ("paying for it"). He explicitly associates himself with them by indicating that he "live[s] with them in their suffering". This allows the interviewee to assume the right to speak on behalf of the people who are suffering. In lines 4 to 7, he amplifies the suffering of the Lebanese people, stating that it is unprecedented and that "a thousand martyrs, a million refugees" is the result of the war so far. In line 8, he describes their situation as "a tragedy [that] must end". Similarly, in lines 13 to 15, the interviewee reemphasises the suffering of the Lebanese, saying that "we in Lebanon are paying the price," and this price is then specified through a three-part list: "Lebanese people are displaced, the Lebanese people are getting killed, and their houses are being destroyed". The three-part list is used here to underline the suffering of the Lebanese due to the war. As Jefferson (1984) indicated, this device's function is to present the general class of the objectives listed. Here, the list is designed to frame the situation in Lebanon as unbearable. In lines 14 to 15, the interviewee presents what is happening in Lebanon in a grim way, indicating that "Lebanese people" "are displaced", "getting killed," "and their houses are being destroyed". This implies that the Lebanese people cannot long withstand such circumstances, suggesting that the war must end at any cost, even through capitulation.

The interviewer's response to this state of affairs is very important from a discursive point of view. Rather than, for instance, producing an assessment or comment on the people's suffering, she responds with the question, "Are you demanding that Hassan Nasrallah give up his weapons?" This implicates a relationship between "giving up weapons" and alleviating the suffering of the Lebanese. That is, it may be inferred that Hassan Nasrallah's use of weapons is contributing to the attacks on Lebanon. In other words, without stating this directly, it is implied that Hezbollah (Nasrallah's party) is contributing to the situation. However, asking this question is ambiguous. It could function as seeking clarification or as an expression of incredulity. Gemayel's response treats it as the latter, and this is not challenged by the interviewer.

In lines 18 to 19, Gemayel portrays his demand as legitimate by saying, "Where is the problem? we have been demanding this since 2000". Here, the speaker implies that his demand is independent of the war and it should not be viewed as his taking any sides. By framing his argument as predating the war, the speaker suggests that Hezbollah's weapons are problematic regardless of current hostilities. This formulation also implies that the interviewee is criticising Hezbollah's position in the war and suggests that they could contribute to ending the war by disarming. Thus, in line 20, the interviewer re-characterises the interviewee's demand, indicating that such an action "means defeat, if he gives up the weapons now". In this formulation, she is subtly accusing the interviewee of being against the resistance and seeking to undermine it by arguing for its defeat. In lines 21 to 30, he counters that accusation, saying, "We are 100 times against the Israelis' aggression, and when it is between Israel and any Lebanese party, especially Hezbollah, we are with Hezbollah against the Israelis' aggression". Here, he invokes national identity as the salient and relevant categorisation within the war with Israel. This also functions as a way of countering potential accusations that might portray him as working for Israel against his country.

Thus, Gemayel rejects these potentially difficult inferences that arise from the proposed solution to suffering and claims solidarity with the diverse groups of Lebanese, in contrast to Israel. However, in lines 31 to 37, he draws a different contrast, this time between Hezbollah and Lebanon, saying, "if it is between the project of Hezbollah and the project of the state of Lebanon". This construction implies that Hezbollah is not identical with the state of Lebanon. This can be seen as framing Hezbollah as a separate entity from Lebanon. In line 33, he associates himself with the state and against Hezbollah, saying "we are with the state". In lines 34 to 37, he creates an account of how the state should behave in relation to Hezbollah, arguing that the "state of Lebanon should regain its control over all of Lebanon's territories and it should be the only one who can take the decision of peace or war". This formulation suggests that the state does not have control over all of Lebanon's territories and that this is problematic. Moreover, by indicating that the country should be the only one that can make the decision of peace and war, he is suggesting that Hezbollah is currently making that decision, and this is not acceptable. This account is designed to portray Hezbollah as an independent group that has a different agenda than the government. It implies that Hezbollah's campaign is not reflective of Lebanon. This negotiates the blameworthiness of Hezbollah's activities and dissociates Lebanon from their project while portraying Gemayel as against Israel and its "aggression". In this extract, we can see that the complete task of accountability is fraught with potential inferential difficulties related to identifying with Lebanon and supporting Hezbollah's cause, while also acknowledging its contribution to the Lebanese people's suffering. The speaker has made, implicitly and explicitly, several discursive formulations that deal with multiple issues related to the discussed topics and to the speaker.

Lebanon as a hostage

In the following extract, the speaker is Walid Jumblatt, a central figure in Lebanese politics and the leader of the Druze community since 1977, following the assassination of his father, Kamal Jumblatt. Kamal Jumblatt was a prominent politician and the founder of the Progressive Socialist Party (PSP), a secular and leftist political party that has been a significant force in Lebanese politics since its establishment in 1949. After his father's assassination, Walid Jumblatt inherited leadership of both the Druze community and the PSP.

Walid Jumblatt has been a pivotal figure in Lebanon's complex and often volatile political landscape. His influence extends beyond the Druze community, as he has consistently played key roles in the broader political alliances that have shaped the country's history. Known for his pragmatic and sometimes unpredictable political manoeuvres, Jumblatt has shifted alliances multiple times, always with an eye toward maintaining the stability and influence of his community and political party.

Jumblatt's leadership is particularly significant given the strategic importance of the Druze community in Lebanon. Although a minority, the Druze have wielded considerable political power, especially in the mountainous Chouf region where they are concentrated. Jumblatt's ability to navigate the intricate web of Lebanese sectarian politics has made him an essential player in the country's power dynamics.

EXTRACT 5.5. WALID JUMBLATT, MP AND DRUZE LEADER; 20 JULY 2006, AL-ARABIYA TV (I = INTERVIEWER, J = JUMBLATT).

1 I: good evening Walid Bek [Bek is an old Turkish title]
2 who is the enemy of Lebanon?
3 J: the enemy of Lebanon first is Israel, the second enemy
4 in the current state of affairs is the Syrian regime and
5 those two regimes Syrian and Iranian cooperate together
6 one way or another with Israel in destroying Lebanon
7 I: can you please explain what you said
8 how come Israel is striking them
9 it is primarily striking the Iranian missiles
10 and striking Hezbollah the main ally of the Syrian regime
11 I: in Lebanon, how are they cooperating to destroy Lebanon?
[lines 12 -19 omitted]
20 J: today Syria and Iran are conducting a new military
21 experiment in Lebanon, it is called a balance of fear
22 the Syrians/Iranians are using Lebanon's territories
23 to say to Israel and America we are here
24 with a disregard of Lebanon's interests
25 I: yes but also the Americans seem to have
26 given a green light to the
27 Israelis to continue, they don't want a cease-fire
28 J: this is true (.) why we gave Israel an excuse to destroy
29 it is an Iranian agenda and Syrian agenda
30 to dominate and re-control Lebanon

The first point of interest in this extract is in line 2, where the interviewer raises the question, "Who is the enemy of Lebanon?" This is designed to present the main topic of the interview as identifying the sides that are against Lebanon in the ongoing war. Considering that this interview took place during the war between Hezbollah and Israel, raising such a question implies that the situation might not be as straightforward as it seems. In lines 3 to 4, Jumblatt responds by saying, "The enemy of Lebanon first is Israel; the second enemy in the current state of affairs is the Syrian regime". Here, he indicates that Israel is not the only side harming Lebanon. In lines 5 to 6, he says, "the two regimes Syrian and Iranian cooperate together one way or another with Israel in destroying Lebanon". This account constructs the war as an assault against Lebanon carried out by Israel, Syria, and Iran, portraying the Lebanese people as victim of these competing powers. Consequently, this suggests that all these powers are responsible for the war rather than the Lebanese.

In lines 7 to 10, the interviewer presents an exclamatory question that frames Jumblatt's assessment as problematic. She asks, "Can you please explain what you said? how come?" By deploying this question, the interviewer is showing disagreement with the assessment, not asking for clarification. Thus, she does not wait for Jumblatt to provide clarification. Instead, she reformulates her argument, stating that Israel "is primarily striking the Iranian missiles". The implication is that if Israel is attacking Syria and Iran, then they cannot be cooperating against Lebanon at the exact same time. This addresses and rejects the possible counter-argument that Israel is not attacking Iran. She then produces a second argument which, like the first, takes the form of a logical assessment: "[Israel] is striking Hezbollah, the main ally of the Syrian regime in Lebanon; how are they cooperating to destroy Lebanon?" Again, the implication is that one does not attack collaborators. Thus, her statement demonstrates that she has examined possible bases for the claim of cooperation and found no evidence to support it. She asks rhetorically, "How are they cooperating to destroy Lebanon?" (line 11).

In lines 20 to 30, Jumblatt justifies his notion that Israel, Syria, and Iran are cooperating to destroy Lebanon. He does this by portraying them as jointly responsible. He claims that the consequences of Syrian and Iranian activities have provided

Israel with an excuse to attack Lebanon. Specifically, he says that "Syria and Iran" are conducting a "new military experiment in Lebanon", in which "the Syrians and Iranians are using Lebanon's territories to send a message to Israel and America" (line 23). The message relates to fear, implying that Iran and Syria are responsible for the war. Additionally, he claims that this goal is advanced with "a disregard of Lebanon's interest". He thereby constitutes Lebanon as uninvolved in the conflict. In other words, the interviewee frames this war in a way that insulates Lebanon from it. This attribution of responsibility to the alliance of Syria and Iran for causing the war is questioned by the interviewer. She says, "Yes, but also the Americans seem to have given a green light to the Israelis to continue; they don't want a cease-fire" (lines 25-27). This implies that there are other countries that are equally involved in the state of affairs and should also be held accountable, in particular America and Israel. The implication is that responsibility is distributed among America and Israel along with Syria and Iran. This can be seen as an indirect accusation that the speaker is providing a biased view of the conflict. Jumblatt's response in lines 28 to 30 acknowledges American involvement ("this is true") while maintaining the accountability of Syria and Iran, who "gave Israel an excuse," and by re-specifying their aims "to dominate and re-control," further warranting his claims. To sum up, in this extract, the interviewer constructs the war and the involved sides in a way that portrays Hezbollah, Syria, and Iran as contributing to the war and the consequent suffering of the Lebanese people.

They support us despite their suffering

The following two extracts were taken from the first media interview conducted with Hassan Nasrallah during the war. In these extracts, Nasrallah and the interviewer address the issue of public support for Hezbollah's conduct. The consequence of discussing public support is an assessment of the legitimacy of

Hezbollah's activities. In the extract that follows, the interviewer builds an account that is organised around the relationship between Hezbollah and specific Lebanese groups prior to the war. He then presents a key question designed to imply that Hezbollah is ostracised in Lebanon. Nasrallah responds to this question by creating an account that is designed to portray his organisation as being supported by the Lebanese laypeople.

EXTRACT 5.6. HASSAN NASRALLAH, 23 JULY 2006, AL-ARABIYA TV (I = INTERVIEWER, N = NASRALLAH).

I: we will discuss the political issues
but what you have just mentioned about
people enduring is important,
it is known that in the areas
where the resistance fighters and Hezbollah are
there is a real popular incubator
now this incubator is displaced,
expatriated, exhausted,
there is a state of complete devastation
I: frankly, do you still trust that popular incubator?
don't you think that you may win militarily
but you have lost the popular support
even among your own sector
even among your own incubator,
not just among the other sides?

In this extract, the interviewer addresses the issue of support for the resistance. Public support is crucial for any group involved in armed conflict. It is more so in the case of Hezbollah because it is an organisation that decisively depends on the support and cooperation of the lay population (see Achcar & Warschawski, 2007). In line 3, the interviewer shows agreement with what he describes as the interviewee's prior claim "about people's enduring" during the war, describing it as "important". He does not explain why it is important; rather, he frames it as a known fact. In lines 4 to 6, the interviewer establishes two categories: the first includes "the resistance fighters, Hezbollah," and the second category is "the popular incubator (hadena)". The word *hadena* in Arabic usually is not used to describe people, and its literal translation is incubator. It is derived from the act of incubating (haden). The interviewer uses this unconventional descriptive term "popular incubator" to build specific social identities for the people who support the resistance (cf. Edwards & Potter, 1992; Potter, 1996; Sacks, 1992). The use of the word "popular" as part of the descriptive term implies that this group is composed of laypeople, in contrast to the fighters, who are known to be devoted members of the Hezbollah organisation. The term implicates safe-keeping, security, and insulation from outside dangers. Thus, "popular incubator" suggests that Hezbollah fighters enjoy significant support from the local laypeople. It is important to stress that the interviewer does not provide any reference or evidence to support this claim. Instead, he frames it as general knowledge or a known fact. It can be suggested that the term "incubator" is used as an alternative to the potentially relevant term "Shiite," as it is from this group that Hezbollah derives much of its popular support. This category term was used by different media networks such as Al-Arabiya TV, CNN, and BBC (2006-2008). The category "Shiite", however, suggests that Hezbollah's supporters are just one sector of the Lebanese people. It implies that this group could be united by an identity or causes that are not necessarily shared by other Lebanese people. This can be seen as problematic for Hezbollah, considering it categorises itself as an Islamic, Arabic, and Lebanese resistance movement, which broadens its appeal. Thus, portraying its supporters as only Shiites would deprive it of an important mandate.

In lines 7 to 8, the interviewer discusses the current situation of "the incubator" group. He uses a three-part list, saying that "this incubator is displaced, expatriated, exhausted". The discursive function of the three-part list device is to intensify the assessment and inoculate against potential counterarguments. In this case, the interviewer uses this formulation to highlight the severity and the seriousness of the suffering that people are experiencing. In line 9, the interviewer presents the final assessment of the "incubator" group's current situation. He uses an *extreme case formulation*, stating that there is "complete destruction". Pomerantz (1986) points out that extreme case formulations strengthen the speaker's claim and inoculate against potential disagreement. Here, this formulation is used to highlight and amplify the severity of the situation that traditional Hezbollah supporters are experiencing. This suggests that one consequence of the war is the loss of popular support for Hezbollah.

The interviewer finishes this part of his utterance with a question based on the picture he portrayed earlier. In line 10, he raises the question of trust between Nasrallah and the "incubator". Raising this question underlines the importance of popular support for the resistance. In lines 11 to 12, the interviewer presents a discursive contrast, asking, "Don't you think that you may win militarily but you have lost the popular support?" Here, the interviewer frames the goals and desired outcomes of Hezbollah as extending beyond military victory. By constructing the group that traditionally supports Hezbollah as being severely affected by the ramifications of the war, the interviewer portrays Hezbollah as compromised. This account prepares the ground for demanding actions such as apologising to the people, giving up weapons, accepting defeat, and most importantly, accepting responsibility for the damage inflicted on Lebanon.

In lines 13 to15, the interviewer continues building on the notion that Hezbollah is losing the people's support, stating that it is losing "even among your own sector, even among your own incubator, not just among the other sides". He constitutes the decline in Hezbollah's support among people as extreme to the degree that even those expected to be most connected to it – its "own sector" and "own incubator" – are turning away. This formulation highlights both the importance of popular support and amplifies Hezbollah's lack of it. Moreover, it implicitly invokes the sectarian identity of both groups. By highlighting the sectarian identity, he invokes a category-bound attribute of the "own sector" and "own incubator," which is that of loyalty and solidarity. This employment of sectarian collective identity downplays the importance of the ideological basis for supporting the resistance in comparison to the identity basis. It emphasises the gravity of the resistance's situation.

In the next extract, Hassan Nasrallah responds to this account.

EXTRACT 5.7. HASSAN NASRALLAH, 23 JULY 2006, AL-ARABIYA TV (I = INTERVIEWER, N = NASRALLAH)

N: before I met with you the brothers told me
and they are of course visiting all the areas
where the refugees and the displaced are
they meet with the people and ask the people
but most importantly they told me
that Western embassies are sending teams
to ask the people about their opinions
and when they ask
they ask the people about their sector
and their religious sector
they are mostly interested in Shiite opinions
based on the classification of the country
because they think if Shiite started to dismantle
and back down from supporting
the resistance this is an indication
that other sectors will back down
because this is the composition of the country
these teams were shocked
from their visits and meetings
they found that there is very strong
support for the resistance
there is a will to withstand and to sacrifice
they have listened to many women
who said "we are willing
to give up our children

and willing to give, to fight
and we will withstand and sacrifice
and suffer but
we don't accept the defeat of the resistance
or that it would be humiliated or be hit"
anyway instead of me going or anyone else
people can go but in an objective and decent way
to meet with those people
and not to take one person who may
not be one of the displaced
who says that I speak in the name of the refugees
all our information on the ground
and we are in continuing contact
because they are our folk
the definite impression and I'm sure it now exists
among the Western embassies
which monitor and follow and give information
to the Israelis and the decision capitals in the world

It is worth noting that the interviewee does not disagree with interviewer's assessment, which presents a specific sect of the Lebanese people as supporters of the resistance. Instead, he focuses in his response on negating the interviewer's final assessment that he is losing the support of his "own sector", let alone other Lebanese. He does so by portraying himself as someone who knows what is happening and is able to gauge popular views. Specifically, he describes the basis of his information, stating that, "before I met with you, the brothers told me". This portrays the information as recent ("before I met with you"). In addition, he uses the term "brothers" instead of more conventional terms such as "members of Hezbollah". This term allows listeners to notice the close relationship between Nasrallah and his informants. Thus, by describing these individuals as brothers, the speaker implies that they are an important and credible source of information. In lines 17-18, he builds up the credentials of the "brothers", saying that "they are of course visiting all the areas where the refugees and the displaced are" and "they meet with the people and ask the people". This formulation portrays the "brothers" as in close contact with the people whose views are sought and therefore as knowledgeable. It provides the informants, and consequently Hassan Nasrallah, with what Potter (1996) calls an *entitlement* to speak on behalf of the "refugees and displaced". However, their opinion is not stated. Instead, in lines 16-26, he introduces another category, "Western embassies", stating that they are sending teams "to ask people about their opinions". By invoking this category, the interviewee pre-empts the potential accusation that the brothers' report is a self-interested one, as they have a stake in portraying support for Nasrallah. The Western embassies are reported as asking about the sectarian identity of Hezbollah's supporters. They are described as being "interested in Shiite opinions". By invoking Western embassies as information-gatherers (and the source of information), and by taking on the role of reporter of that information, Nasrallah is able to portray that information as neutral and objective rather than influenced by his own and Hezbollah's interests. In these ways, Nasrallah is able to present and discuss sensitive accounts without assuming responsibility for them. Although he portrays the Western embassies' interest in Shiite opinion as understandable, he does not state his position. Instead, he moves to tackle the main question, which is whether the Shiites are backing down from supporting the resistance or not. He answers this question by reporting that the Western teams "were shocked" because "they found that there is very strong support for the resistance". He adds that they found that "there is a will to withstand and to sacrifice".

Here again, the interviewee does not take the role of the composer of the claim; instead, he attributes this claim to the Western embassies' teams. They "support the resistance" and they are willing "to withstand and sacrifice". This depiction of the laypeople's position challenges the more conventional portrayal of laypeople in wars. Laypeople are usually constituted as passive recipients of war events, or as victims who do not have any say in what is happening. In line 38, he invokes another category: "women". He reports that "many women" said they are "willing to give up their children", to "fight", "withstand and sacrifice and suffer" in order to prevent "the defeat of the resistance". The use of the category "women", who are not typically expected to support a war, let alone give up their children, implies that Hezbollah enjoys significant support even among groups that are less likely to back its cause. The implication is that support would be even greater among traditional supporters. In this way, he accomplishes support for Hezbollah, countering the interviewer's claim of declining popular support. More significantly, he frames extreme suffering, even the loss of one's children, as the lesser of two evils. These women would rather lose their children than witness the defeat of the Islamic resistance.

In lines 46-50, the speaker invites "people" to go in a "decent way to meet with" the displaced people. This invitation functions as a way of reinforcing the factuality of the claim that the displaced still support the resistance. It is important to note that the speaker does not use the word Shiite to describe this group. Instead, he refers to them simply as "people". In lines 49-51, he warns against making generalisations based on isolated cases, such as one person who may not be one of the displaced but claims, "I speak in the name of the refugees". This warning is designed to pre-empt any potential counter-argument that some of the people suffering due to the war may not share the interviewee's assessment that they are willing to sacrifice and withstand. In lines 52-54, Nasrallah produces a summary which warrants his assessment by affiliating himself with these people, stating that he is "in continuing contact" with them and that these people are "our folk". This affiliation entitles the interviewee to speak on their behalf. He further supports his assessment by saying, "the definite impression – and I'm sure it now exists – among the western embassies, which monitor and follow and give information to the Israelis and the decision capitals in the world". Here, he describes them as a hostile side that cooperates with Israel and provides information to it. That description strengthens the claim the interviewee made earlier and formulates it as a fact that could be confirmed by adversaries. Moreover, by inviting people to go and see for themselves, the speaker constructs the 'out-thereness' of popular support, which in turn deflects the idea that Hezbollah is itself responsible for the events in Lebanon.

Summary and conclusion

In this chapter, I have shown how various Lebanese politicians dealt with issues of accountability in relation to the war. I demonstrated how they warranted some actions while not warranting others. In Extract 5.1, we saw how the Secretary General of Hezbollah built up the attack carried out by his organisation in a way that made this attack appear discursively righteous. In Extract 5.2, the speaker constructed the sides of the war and the audience's stake in a way that positioned support for Hezbollah as a desired end. This also applies to Extract 5.3, where the Lebanese Minister of Defence created an account of the war designed to denounce Israel and revere Hezbollah. In contrast, in Extracts 5.4 and 5.5, two prominent Lebanese politicians constructed the war in a way that is designed to primarily apportion the blame to Hezbollah. In both of these extracts, Hezbollah was constructed as the side that needed be stopped. The speakers in both extracts created opposing Hezbollah as the acceptable and reasonable stance.

In all the extracts discussed, it is evident that speakers used the 2006 Lebanon-Israel war as a vehicle for advancing social and political agendas. The narratives surrounding the events, the parties involved, and the causes of the conflict were constructed as discursive resources (Potter & Wetherell, 1987). These resources were strategically employed to justify specific stances in the conflict, thereby legitimizing particular actions related to the war and the involved parties. This analysis underscores that to truly understand any account of war, it is crucial to consider it within its broader context, with particular attention to the discursive actions it seeks to accomplish (Edwards & Potter, 1992).

As demonstrated, the accounts of the 2006 war are not neutral reflections of the events but rather complex, multi-layered narratives crafted to serve specific psychological and social purposes. These narratives shape the meaning of the conflict in ways that align with the interests and agendas of the speakers (Billig, 1996). The analysis of the extracts reveals how different influential figures emphasized various aspects of the war, using them as discursive tools to either justify the conflict and Hezbollah's role or to reject Hezbollah by condemning the war (Wetherell & Potter, 1992). Thus, these war accounts are interest-driven formulations rather than objective descriptions.

Moreover, it is evident that some influential speakers manipulated the narrative, concealing their true motives and presenting identities that did not accurately reflect themselves or their groups. These manipulations and fabrications help explain why the conflict between Hezbollah and Israel did not conclude. Hassan Nasrallah's justification of Hezbollah's initial attack on Israel laid the groundwork for justifying further aggression. The absence of a principled rejection of these attacks by other parties contributed to the continuation and escalation of the conflict.

This pattern of justification was a key factor in the dynamics of the 2006 war. The analysis highlights the importance of critically examining war narratives, recognizing that they are constructed with specific goals in mind—often to justify or condemn particular actions or ideologies. They also play a crucial role in normalising aggression and suffering. Understanding these narratives within their discursive context is essential for gaining deeper insights into the underlying motivations and potential long-term implications of such conflicts.

References

Achcar, G., & Warschawski, M. (2007). *The 33-day war: Israel's war on Hezbollah in Lebanon and its consequences.* New York: Routledge.

Billig, M. (1996). *Arguing and thinking: a rhetorical approach to social psychology* (2nd ed.). Cambridge University Press.

Blanford, N. (2011). *Warriors of God: Inside Hezbollah's thirty-year struggle against Israel.* New York, NY: Random House.

Bull, P. (2003). *The microanalysis of political communication: Claptrap and ambiguity.* London, UK: Routledge.

DeRouen, K., & Heo, U. (2007). *Civil wars of the world: Major conflicts since World War II.* Santa Barbara, CA: ABC-CLIO.

Edwards, D., & Potter, J. (1992). *Discursive Psychology.* London: Sage.

Harik, J. P. (2004). *Hezbollah: The Changing Face of Terrorism.* I.B.Tauris.

Jefferson, G. (1984). On the organization of laughter in talk about troubles. In J. M. Atkinson & J. Heritage (Eds.), *Structures of social action: Studies in conversation analysis* (pp. 346-369). Cambridge University Press.

Levitt, M. (2013). *Hezbollah: The Global Footprint of Lebanon's Party of God.* Georgetown University Press.

Norton, A. R. (2007). *Hezbollah: A Short History.* Princeton University Press.

Pomerantz, A. (1986). Agreeing and disagreeing with assessments: Some features of preferred/dispreferred turn-shapes. In J. M. Atkinson & J. Heritage (Eds.), *Structures of social action: Studies in conversation analysis.* Cambridge University Press.

Potter, J., & Wetherell, M. (1987). *Discourse and social psychology: Beyond attitudes and behaviour.* London: Sage.

Potter, J. (1996). *Representing reality: Discourse, rhetoric and social construction.* London: Sage.

Sacks, H. (1992). *Lectures on conversation.* Oxford: Basil Blackwell.

Chapter 6

War between hope and violence: In favour of suffering

As I have argued in Chapter 2, the ongoing war in Iraq is a clear example of the volatile nature of modern wars. It is also a prime example of how difficult it is to understand the dynamics of modern conflicts. This war began on 20th March 2003 as an armed campaign intended to remove Saddam Hussein and his regime from power using a coalition of several Western countries led by the US and the UK. A significant segment of the Iraqi people welcomed the American intervention; the Iraqi Army abandoned Saddam's regime. However, soon after the fall of the regime and the establishment of the Coalition Provisional Authority to administer Iraq, a fierce and well-organised insurgency movement emerged. This movement started as a resistance-like campaign led by ex-Ba'athist, radical Sunni Muslims, and former Iraqi soldiers who were mainly Sunni Arabs. As this movement gained momentum, it shifted its goals from fighting American and British forces to carrying out genocide against Iraqi Shiites, Christians, and Kurds. By 2006, Iraq was in a situation that resembled civil war. Fighting between different Iraqi groups and looting became the norm. According to the Iraq Body Count Project, more than 188,000 civilians have lost their lives in violent events related to fighting in Iraq since 2003 (Iraq Body Count website, 2024). Countless accounts intended to explain what has been taking place, who the fighting sides are, and what the potential outcomes might be were broadcast worldwide. These accounts are contrasting and often contradictory. The starting point for this chapter is a discursive understanding of rhetorical accounts. I examine these accounts not as reflections of the situation but as constructions of the situation intended to perform specific rhetorical actions (see Antaki & Widdicombe, 1998; Billig, 1995; Edwards & Potter, 1992, 2003; Edwards, 2005; Potter, 1996; Sacks, 1992).

In this chapter, I use discursive psychology (Potter, 1996, 2003) to analyse how a number of Iraqi politicians and decision makers account for the violence through dealing with various aspects of the ongoing war within their rhetorical accounts. I show that these various Iraqi individuals construct and deploy different accounts to justify or reject violence and violent attacks. Each one of these accounts is designed to establish and argue for a specific position in relation to war through building up violent events in a specific way. Here, I focus on how the different speakers warrant or reject specific types of violence within their account of the war. I also discuss how they construct and deploy specific collective identity, and why they do so.

The extracts I use in this chapter are taken from different interviews conducted by TV and radio stations, such as Al-Arabiya, Al Jazeera, and Radio Free Europe, with various Iraqi politicians, from March 2003 to August 2009. Some of these interviews were conducted in English, and their transcripts are available on the media outlets' websites; however, I reviewed and edited these transcripts. I have transcribed and translated all the other ones. It is important to stress that there were several limitations in the transcripts provided by the various media outlets, as most of them contain literal translations that do not accurately reflect the meaning of the talk. Moreover, I have excluded data that cannot be translated into English accurately without including discursive formulations that the speakers did not utter. All the extracts are taken from interviews that were conducted in Iraq with prominent Iraqi politicians. In this chapter, I analyse extracts that contain accounts of violent activities related to the war. I focus on how the various Iraqi politicians and decision makers warrant, deny, explain, or reject violence and specific violent activities and groups.

Rejecting the conventional implications of being a victim

The following extract is taken from an interview conducted a few hours after the interviewee survived an attempt on his life. The interviewee is Mithal al-Alousi, a prominent Iraqi politician and the long-time head of the De-Ba'athification Committee in the Iraqi Parliament. On the morning of 8th February 2005, a group of armed men fired on his car. Two of al-Alousi's sons, Ayman and Jamal, along with a bodyguard, who were all inside his vehicle, were instantly killed in the incident. Several media reporters came to the scene of the attack and asked Mr al-Alousi to speak about the incident. The extract is all that was broadcast by Radio Free Europe. The interviewee starts by talking freely before being asked a few questions by the reporter.

EXTRACT 6.1. MITHAL AL-ALOUSI, IRAQI POLITICIAN; 8 FEBRUARY 2005, RADIO FREE EUROPE; BAGHDAD, IRAQ.

A: again, the ghosts of death are going out
they are ready to kill a human being,
ready to kill the peace,
ready to kill the victory of Iraqis and their right to life

5 again (.) henchmen of the Ba'ath and the dirty terrorist
6 gangs Al-Qaeda and others, are going out convinced
7 that they can determine life and death as they desire (.)
8 Iraq will not die
9 my children (.) three people one (.) of my bodyguards and
10 two of my children (.) died as heroes, not differently from
11 other people who met their heroic deaths but we will not,
12 I swear by God, hand Iraq over to murderers and terrorists
13 we will pave the road for peace if they thought that
14 by attempting to kill Mithal al-Alousi, the advocates of peace
15 in Iraq will be stopped, then they have made a grave mistake
16 we will be calling for peace. We will be calling for peace
17 with all neighbouring countries, we will be calling for peace
18 with all countries of the region and we will be calling for
19 fighting terrorism by any means (.)
20 against all forms of terror
21 they claim that Islam is a message of killing, while Islam
22 is a message of peace. They claim that its principles
23 encourage killing, while the only principles that encourage
24 killing are the principles of the Ba'ath and of the
25 heathens from Al-Qaeda groups.
26 the Sunni areas groan under the hands of murderers and
27 criminals who are neither Sunnis nor Iraqis.
28 they are intruders in Iraq from Al-Qaeda groups
29 and Ba'ath henchmen. They are the ghosts of death.
30 we will be building Iraq.
31 we will be building Iraq despite all that has happened.
32 may God help us.
33 I: How long do you expect some political circles to continue
34 speaking the language of violence and terror?
35 do they have any political programme?
36 do they have any clear goals?
37 do they have any slogan which they might bring forward
38 to discuss, and lead a dialogue?
41 A: that would not excuse them.
42 if they have a slogan, a goal, a language,

and an activity, it is killing.
they were killing us for more than three decades
they want to kill us and enslave us, over and over again
that is why I have always urged politicians to avoid trying
to lead a dialogue with terrorists
any kind of inviting murderers to dialogue
means giving them a little bit of legitimacy,
which they do not have
they do not have the right to play with us.
consequently, I ask my friends and colleagues in the
political leadership inside or outside the government...
to take a clear, frank, and firm position to enforce the law
over all, whoever it is (.) be it a religious
or non-religious party.
there should be no debate or dialogue with a murderer
who calls for killing. This cannot be the [right] way
the way is the way of law, the way of dialogue,
the way of building, and the way of leading the Sunni areas
out of confusion. I would like to focus on that very clearly
the Sunni areas groan under the hands of murderers and
the criminals who are neither Sunnis nor Iraqis.
they are intruders in Iraq from among Al-Qaeda groups
and Ba'ath [Party] henchmen. They are the ghosts of death.
I: you have been the target of repeated assassination attempts
do you believe the reason is your opinions and political
attitudes, or is there another factor that has made you
such a target?
A: they do not spare anyone
they target laypeople on the way to do shopping
in the market. they target hospitals and schools
they target everyone
on the fact that I have been targeted personally, I have kept
saying, there is no way for Iraq but the way of peace

This extract contains an interesting and important account of the violence associated with war. Here, the speaker, a prominent

Sunni politician, discusses the killing of his two children. Speaking shortly after this traumatic event took place, he constructs an account designed to perform several social actions. Firstly, it reports and explains how he perceives what happened. Secondly, it denounces the killers and the killing of his sons. Thirdly, it identifies the killers in a way that encourages listeners to view the killing as a matter that concerns many Iraqis, not just the speaker himself. Finally, it portrays the speaker as resilient and implies that he will continue fighting those involved in the insurgency movement. For practical reasons, I will divide this excerpt into smaller extracts.

A: again, the ghosts of death are going out
they are ready to kill a human being,
ready to kill the peace,
ready to kill the victory of Iraqis and their right to life
again (.) henchmen of the Ba'ath and the dirty terrorist
gangs Al-Qaeda and others, are going out convinced
that they can determine life and death as they desire (.)
Iraq will not die
my children (.) three people one (.) of my bodyguards and
two of my children (.) died as heroes, not differently from
other people who met their heroic deaths but we will not,
I swear by God, hand Iraq over to murderers and terrorists

In lines 1 to 4, the interviewee frames what happened to his sons as a matter that concerns the general Iraqi public. He begins by presenting what seems like a vague label for the killers of his sons, describing them as "ghosts of death" (line 1). He indicates that these killers are "ready to kill a human being", and more than that, they are ready to kill principles and tenets. In particular, they are "ready to kill the peace, ready to kill the victory of Iraqis and their right to life". In these lines, the interviewee constructs the killing of his sons as part of a campaign against the Iraqi people in general, by people who want to eradicate essential principles, such as "victory", "peace", and free choice in "life". These notions are inherently valuable to most, if not all, people. They have been invoked throughout history by various politicians as objectives worth sacrificing one's life for (cf. Billig, 1995; Dower, 1986; Herrera, 2003; Leudar, Marsland & Nekvapil, 2004). Constructing these notions as the ultimate target of the attack that claimed the lives of the interviewee's sons extends its impact beyond the speaker and his family. It implicates many other Iraqis in the attack, suggesting that Iraqis who support peace, victory, and the right to life are all potential targets for the killers. It also implies that the victims are innocent and that the killing is unjust and unwarrantable. This reformulates the killing from being an accomplishment from the point of view of the attackers into a means for them to achieve a further goal, making that goal harder to accomplish. In lines 5 to 7, the interviewee puts a face to the killers, identifying them as members of the Ba'ath party and Al-Qaeda. He constructs the members of the Ba'ath party as "henchmen" and uses the inference-rich label "gangs" to denote Al-Qaeda members. The title "henchmen" is an inference-rich descriptor that implies the Ba'ath party members are anti-religion and criminals. This discards the Ba'ath members' campaign against the new Iraqi government. Similarly, describing Al-Qaeda members as "gangs" is designed to undermine the credibility of these people, thereby discrediting their activities. This formulation is designed to reject the whole insurgency movement in Iraq by depicting the main two factions involved as murderers and terrorists.

In lines 6-7, al-Alousi begins identifying the motive of the killers, stating that they "are going out convinced that they can determine life and death". Here, the interviewee is building up the rationale of the killers as a general desire to establish absolute control over the "life and death" of the Iraqis. This depiction presents the killers as zealous people who seek hegemony, rather than being driven by specific causes. This formulation also provides solid justifications for many of the Iraqi listeners to affiliate with the victims and view the assassination as an incident that concerns them. In other words, the speaker is establishing a stake for the audience in opposing the insurgency through the way he constructs the killing of his two children. He has transformed the issue from a specific event in which he lost his two sons into a struggle that concerns other Iraqis. He also constructs the insurgency movement as the enemy, not just the individuals or the faction that carried out the attack.

In line 8, al-Alousi states that "Iraq will not die". This reformulates the issue of the interview from the killing of the speaker's sons into the goal of the attackers. The interviewee frames the unknown attackers as part of the insurgents whose goal is to rule Iraq. He asserts that they will not succeed in achieving this goal even if they manage to kill some Iraqis. This reemphasises the argument that the killers want to harm Iraq, not just the interviewee or his family. It also implies that the speaker is resilient and still willing to challenge these killers despite losing his sons. In fact, he does not construct the murder of his children as a personal loss at any point in this extract. This can be seen as a way of resisting and refusing to be seen as defeated or resigned. This is similar to the account in Extract 3.3, where the speaker constructed his brother, who was killed as a result of the war, as not dead. The interviewee here invokes the notion that "Iraq will not die" as a way of signifying his loss and the death of his sons as part of the greater issue of the battle against the insurgents. This, in turn, constructs the killings as a failure to achieve the killers' desired goals. Analysing this and similar formulations may help researchers understand the vicious circles that occur in armed conflicts, where killing often leads to more killing, and the violence continues over a long course of time. In most armed conflicts, it seems as though people have developed a bewildering tendency to overlook the immediate deleterious effects of their actions. This extract provides some explanation of how people in war can appear indifferent to what seems unintelligible to outside researchers. On the one hand, this rhetorical account functions as a way of mitigating the loss caused by the conflict; on the other hand, it prolongs conflict by diminishing its consequences.

In lines 9 to 11, al-Alousi returns to the death of his two sons and his bodyguard, describing their deaths as "heroic". He further indicates that the way his children and bodyguard died is not different from the deaths of other Iraqis who have been killed in insurgents' attacks. This formulation is designed to portray the deaths of the interviewee's sons, his bodyguard, and the rest of the Iraqis victims as sacrifices for the same just cause. It elevates the victims from being powerless individuals who could not protect themselves and lost their lives tragically, to heroes. It also binds the killing of his sons to the numerous other victims, often Iraqis, who have lost their lives in the conflict. This can be seen as a way of alleviating the potential emotional and psychological extremes that are conventionally attached to such occurrences. Moreover, by describing the deaths of his sons and other Iraqis as heroic, al-Alousi transforms sadness into pride. Here, the three victims, as well as all the other victims, deserve admiration, not just empathy. This is designed to show solidarity with other victims of the violence. It is important to stress that the killing is associated with pride and resilience rather than sadness and horror. In lines 11 to 12, the interviewee indicates that he is not defeated or deterred due to the killing of his children, promising that he will not "hand Iraq over to murderers and terrorists". By describing his opponents as "murderers and terrorists", the speaker prepares the ground for denouncing them and for actively continuing to fight them. This formulation is similar to the rationale used by fighting sides in Yugoslavia to warrant the war (see Glenny, 1992). This account constructs the murder of the speaker's sons as a reason for continuing to fight rather than as a deterrent to the continuation of the conflict.

In the next part of the extract, the interviewee builds up the sides that are involved in the violence.

13 A: we will pave the road for peace if they thought that
14 by attempting to kill Mithal al-Alousi, the advocates of peace
15 in Iraq will be stopped, then they have made a grave mistake

we will be calling for peace. We will be calling for peace
with all neighbouring countries, we will be calling for peace
with all countries of the region and we will be calling for
fighting terrorism by any means (.)
against all forms of terror
they claim that Islam is a message of killing, while Islam
is a message of peace. They claim that its principles
encourage killing, while the only principles that encourage
killing are the principles of the Ba'ath and of the
heathens from Al-Qaeda groups.
the Sunni areas groan under the hands of murderers and
criminals who are neither Sunnis nor Iraqis.
they are intruders in Iraq from Al-Qaeda groups
and Ba'ath henchmen. They are the ghosts of death.
we will be building Iraq.
we will be building Iraq despite all that has happened.
may God help us.

In this segment of the extract, the interviewee constructs the rival sides of the conflict. He constructs his group as "the advocates of peace" (lines 13-17), placing them in contrast with the rival category, "ghosts of death" (line 1). Here, he builds a moral contrast between the two groups. Note that both rival groups are composed of Iraqis; the Americans or any other sides involved in the conflict are rendered irrelevant in this extract. Al-Alousi does not blame the occupation forces, even for the lack of security or their inability to protect the civilian population. This shows that people involved in war can depict the situation in a way that may not be obvious to outside observers. In lines 14 to 15, he asserts that killing him will not make other "advocates of peace" stop. Here, he affiliates himself with a group that he frames as advancing peace. Consequently, the activity he is carrying out is not exclusive to him; rather, it is shared by many others. This is designed to further alienate the insurgents' violence and activities. He implies that the matter is bigger than him and his life or death. In lines 18 to 20, the interviewee indicates that he intends to continue "fighting terrorism by any means". This formulation portrays the speaker as resolute and determined, despite losing his two sons. Despite these personal losses, he does not show sadness, rancour, or desperation, even at the point of the incident. On the contrary, in this extract, al-Alousi presents as unswervingly dedicated to his cause.

In lines 21 to 29, the interviewee constitutes an account that dismisses the insurgents. He begins by indicating that they misinterpret and misrepresent the ideas of Islam, stating that that "Islam is a message of peace," while they present Islam as "a message of killing" (lines 21-22). In lines 23 to 25, he states that the two groups with an ideology that encourages killing are the "Ba'ath" party and the "heathens from Al-Qaeda". In lines 26 to 27, he presents an account which rejects the notion that the insurgents are fighting on behalf of the Sunni community in Iraq. He argues that "the Sunni areas groan under the hands of murderers and criminals". He then indicates that these "killers" and "criminals" "are neither Sunnis nor Iraqis", but "intruders in Iraq from Al-Qaeda and Ba'ath henchmen". In this formulation, the speaker detaches the members of the Ba'ath and Al-Qaeda from Islam and from Iraq and constructs them as intruders. This warrants fighting these groups and adopting strong measures against them. Indeed, this and the previous segments of the extract warrant fighting against the insurgents. Hence, the interviewer picks up on this notion and presents a question and response, in lines 33 to 51, designed to explore the possibility of a peaceful way of dealing with the insurgents.

33 I: How long do you expect some political circles to continue
34 speaking the language of violence and terror?
35 do they have any political programme?
36 do they have any clear goals?
37 do they have any slogan which they might bring forward
38 to discuss, and lead a dialogue?
41 A: that would not excuse them.
42 if they have a slogan, a goal, a language,

and an activity, it is killing.
they were killing us for more than three decades
they want to kill us and enslave us, over and over again
that is why I have always urged politicians to avoid trying
to lead a dialogue with terrorists
any kind of inviting murderers to dialogue
means giving them a little bit of legitimacy,
which they do not have
they do not have the right to play with us.

In lines 33 to 38, the interviewer presents a question that discusses the possibility of the insurgents and terrorists employing civil means instead of violence. He uses the term "political circles" as a label to denote the insurgents. This term is an effective device that encompasses all the different sides involved in violence in Iraq while at the same time avoiding the controversy attached to naming these groups. In line 34, the interviewer clarifies what he meant by "political circles", indicating that they are "speaking the language of violence and terror". Here, the speaker gradually introduces the groups carrying out attacks like the one that claimed the lives of the interviewee's sons, without using conventional labels. The interviewer asks if the terrorists and insurgents "have any political programme" or "clear goals" and if they can "lead a dialogue" (lines 35-38). This formulation implies that the violence these groups employ represents a means to achieve specific goals. In line 41, the interviewee begins answering the question by indicating that even if they have goals or a programme, that would not justify their acts. In lines 42 to 43, he indicates that "if they have a slogan, a goal, a language, and an activity, it is killing". Here, the interviewee frames the goals of these groups as killing. This transforms killing from a means, as suggested in the interviewer's question, into the goal of the insurgents. This formulation implies that the insurgents cannot be part of a peaceful process, since violence is their goal, not just a means to accomplish further goals. The interviewee supports his argument by invoking a historical account of the insurgents' acts (lines 44-45). He states that "they were killing us for more than three decades; they want to kill us and enslave us, over and over again". This formulation portrays the current attacks of the insurgents as a continuation of the conduct of the ex-regime, identifying the insurgents as being members of the "Ba'ath". In lines 46 to 51, the interviewee presents an appropriate way for Iraqi "politicians" to deal with the insurgents. He argues that there should not be a "dialogue with terrorists". He justifies this position by warning that dialogue would give the "murderers" "a little bit of legitimacy" (lines 48-49). In line 51, he indicates that the terrorists "do not have the right" to be part of the political process in Iraq. Here, by constructing what seems like a factual account that portrays the insurgents as "murderers and terrorists", al-Alousi frames talking to these groups as an erroneous act with negative consequences. To sum up, in this segment, the interviewee frames the insurgents as lacking legitimacy and the will to abandon violence. This constitutes these people as an existential threat to the Iraqi people. Al-Alousi discards arguments that call for reconciliation between the Iraqi government and the insurgents.

In the last segment of this extract, I will discuss how the speakers deal with the attack that specifically targeted al-Alousi.

66 I: you have been the target of repeated assassination attempts
67 do you believe the reason is your opinions and political
68 attitudes, or is there another factor that has made you
69 such a target?
70 A: they do not spare anyone
71 they target laypeople on the way to do shopping
72 in the market. they target hospitals and schools
73 they target everyone
74 on the fact that I have been targeted personally, I have kept
75 saying, there is no way for Iraq but the way of peace

In line 66, the interviewer indicates that al-Alousi has been a target of "repeated assassination attempts". This sentence functions as the basis for the question posed in lines 67 to 69 – whether "the reason" for these assassination attempts is al-Alousi's "opinions and political attitudes". This question implies that the interviewee is responsible for being targeted by the assassins. It further suggests that the attack is part of a limited conflict between al-Alousi and the insurgents. In line 70, the participant replies, stating that "they do not spare anyone". This response is designed to absolve the speaker of any responsibility for the attacks by indicating that the insurgents are killing people indiscriminately. It also implies that the killing was not an isolated incident that is motivated by a specific reason or individual conduct; rather, it reflects a systematic behaviour. In lines 71 to 72, the interviewee cements the notion that these killers are targeting Iraqis without specific reason. He says, "they target laypeople on the way to do shopping in the market, they target hospitals and schools". Here, by reporting that the killers are targeting people going about their mundane activities such as "shopping", al-Alousi advances and reinforces the notion that the victims are innocent and that the killers have no valid justification for their acts. This is designed to portray the killers as enemies to all Iraqis by nature. It is also designed to solicit empathy from the audience for the Iraqi people in general, not just for the interviewee. In line 73, the speaker presents an ultimate conclusion, stating that "they target everyone". This conclusion functions as a way of suggesting that the killing of al-Alousi's sons is related to the nature of the killers and their goals, rather than being connected to the speaker's activities. Further on, al-Alousi attends to the fact that he has been specifically targeted by the insurgents (lines 74-75), indicating that he was promoting "peace". This implies that his endeavours do not justify targeting him or killing his sons.

To conclude, the analysis of this extract shows that despite the severe context of the interview, the interviewee conveyed his personal experience in the form of a coherent narrative that served several specific important social functions. Firstly, this account transforms the meaning of the attack on the interviewee. Secondly, it frames the attack as an event that concerns the general Iraqi population through presenting it as part of a broader campaign that targets all Iraqis. Thirdly, it portrays the interviewee and his supporters as peaceful while it depicts the insurgents as criminals. More than that, it implicitly warrants the use of force against the insurgents. Finally, it suggests that the Iraqi people will prevail over the insurgents despite the losses.

Warranting disregard of law and human rights

In the next extract the interviewee, who is heading an armed militia that has been fighting the insurgents in Iraq, speaks about the conflict between his militia and Al-Qaeda.

EXTRACT 6.2. ALI SULAIMAN, LEADER OF THE AWAKENING GROUPS; 12 MARCH 2003, AL-ARABIYA TV; IRAQ (I = INTERVIEWER; S = SULAIMAN).

S: we are going to wipe them out, with God's help
and with complete disregard of human rights.
when the Al-Qaeda organisation kills 20 or 30 human beings
and cuts off their heads and throws them
in the street no one talks about human rights
and when the Americans arrest a leader of Al-Qaeda
they look after him (.) they feed him meat and give him Pepsi
and lock him up in an air-conditioned room
when we kill Al-Qaeda, a senior member of Al-Qaeda
they accuse us of violating the law
which law is this and what nonsense is this
I: you do not want this law
S: let me tell you something, we are not afraid
we are vengeful people we are not school pupils
I swear to God wherever we spot Al-Qaeda or any member
of Al-Qaeda we are going to kill them
we are not willing to put our project at risk because of

human rights
we were not even given animal rights
our dead bodies were tossed up in the streets in hundreds

In this extract, Sulaiman creates an account designed to warrant the killing of members of Al-Qaeda without trial or any legal procedures. He does this through two rhetorical techniques: firstly, by portraying the killing of Al-Qaeda members as a natural and valid response to Al-Qaeda's own conduct; and secondly, by downplaying the effectiveness of the American army's actions and the validity of human rights laws. He begins in line 1 with an extreme formulation of his intended act, indicating that "we are going to wipe them [Al-Qaeda] out". In this formulation, he assumes the role of a group representative (the Awakening Movement). This is designed to give his account more weight on the basis that it reflects the decision of a group directly involved in the issue (cf. Edwards & Potter, 1992; Potter, 1996). He indicates that he is going to carry out his fight against Al-Qaeda with complete disregard for human rights (line 2). This implies that he does not intend to grant his enemies the legal rights to which they are entitled by law. This formulation suggests that he is capable of fighting Al-Qaeda independently, which portrays the speaker and his group as powerful and independent. It also suggests that the speaker and his group are confident they can defeat Al-Qaeda.

Throughout lines 3 to 10, the interviewee presents the justification for his extreme intended act by describing Al-Qaeda's conduct. Providing justification for the intended act implies that the act is problematic (cf. Potter, 1996). Here, Sulaiman presents three parties as related to the struggle. The first is Al-Qaeda, which he portrays as a ferocious organisation that "kills 20 or 30 human beings and cuts off their heads" (lines 3-4). The second party is the Americans, whom he builds up as ineffectual in dealing with Al-Qaeda. He criticizes the way the Americans handle the terrorists, stating that when they "arrest a leader in Al-Qaeda, they look after him" and they provide him with "meat", "Pepsi", and "an air-conditioned room" (lines 6-8). The interviewee constructs a factual account by listing specific details of how the Americans treat Al-Qaeda members (cf. Potter, 1996). This account portrays the Americans' treatment of Al-Qaeda leaders as unacceptable and unjust from the perspective of the victims of Al-Qaeda. It implies that justice is not served by the Americans in relation to Al-Qaeda terrorists. Most importantly, it implies that the way the Americans treat Al-Qaeda members will not deter them from continuing to slaughter Iraqi people. This functions as a warning to the Iraqi audience that Al-Qaeda members arrested by the Americans may still pose a danger, thus justifying the extreme measures Sulaiman proposes.

In line 8, the interviewee presents his group as the one that kills Al-Qaeda members, indicating a dispute with the Americans over this act. He states that the Americans accuse his group "of violating the law" when they kill "a senior member of Al-Qaeda" (lines 9-10). The use of the word "senior" is designed to warrant the killing on the grounds that the person is expected to have been involved in the deaths of many people. The interviewee describes the law that prohibits him from killing Al-Qaeda members as "nonsense", further warranting his stated intention to kill them without trial.

The interviewee constructs an inference-rich category for his group, referring to them as "vengeful people" (line 14). This category entails that they are determined to retaliate against Al-Qaeda and its members. In the subsequent sentences, he explains how he intends to fight against Al-Qaeda, indicating that the members of his group "are going to kill them". In line 17 to 20, he justifies killing Al-Qaeda members by portraying them as a threat to his "project" and by indicating that Al-Qaeda members have not granted his group "even animals' rights". In the last sentence of this extract, the interviewee presents an image of how Al-Qaeda members treated the Iraqi people, saying that "our dead bodies were tossed up in the streets in hundreds". This extreme discursive formulation is designed to portray Al-Qaeda members as lawless and dangerous, deserving to be killed. This, in turn, justifies the argument the interviewee has constructed throughout his account: killing Al-Qaeda members without granting them their basic legal rights. The account is designed to portray the speaker and his group as independent from the Americans, capable of fighting Al-Qaeda, and fighting for legitimate reasons.

Manufacturing suicide bombers

In this extract, the speaker, who served as the final Minister of Foreign Affairs under Saddam, discusses the training of suicide bombers. He builds up an account that is designed to characterise suicide attacks as warrantable activities and ultimately glorifies suicide bombers.

EXTRACT 6.3. NAJI SABRI AL-HADITHI, IRAQI FOREIGN MINISTER DURING SADDAM'S REGIME; 12 MARCH 2003, AL-JAZEERA TV; BAGHDAD, IRAQ.

I: yesterday you granted access to international media outlets
to film Arab volunteers who came from all over the Arab
world to carry out martyr operations
[amlyat isteshhadya – suicide bombings]
against the American forces if they invaded Iraq
also the CIA published a report last Sunday
which indicated that active terrorists
who belong to Al-Qaeda will launch attacks from Iraq
yesterday you disclosed these camps and this
created a great buzz and became the centre of attention
aren't you afraid that Iraq will be accused of being
headquarters of terrorism and of exporting terrorism?
A: before these Arab volunteers arrived we had
tens of thousands of Iraqis
who have volunteered to become martyrs
and the State is currently training them to do that

in addition to that our heroic army is preparing and
also other armed forces
and members of the civil armed party organizations
and they are all over Iraq and there are Saddam's Fedayen
and Al-Quds Army and as I have said there are
tens of thousands of Iraqis
who have volunteered to defend their land, women,
and honour by being martyrs
and for months tens of thousands of Arabs have been
contacting us
so they could come and fight with their brothers in Iraq
I: this is the first time you disclose such an issue
A: yes in fact we were hesitant, very hesitant, but
under the pressure of of thousands of Arabs and I will say
something that might surprise you
someone has contacted us saying that
he has a list of 20,000 volunteers
who are ready to come to Iraq, I won't disclose the name
but they are waiting for us to allow them to come
I: this is from just one country?
A: yes just one country yes
I: this is an army
A: yes this is from just one country and there are many
thousands of Arabs and Muslims who [want, want to, to]
I: [but what does]
that mean?
A: they want to show the whole world that they are with Iraq
for them this is a national, religious, and Islamic position
they want to defend the land of faiths, land of prophets
the land of Abraham the father of all prophets
they want to defend the land that contains the graves
of Mohammad's family
they want to defend the centre of the Arabs and Muslims
thousands of Arabs and Muslims have been persisting in
asking to allow them to join
now we are training them and we are honoured to have them

The first point of interest in the above extract is the account in lines 1 to 11. In these lines, the interviewer gradually constructs a factual report of the establishment of suicide training camps in Iraq by the Iraqi government. He discusses the Iraqi decision to publicise these camps. He starts by establishing the topic of the discussion as allowing "access to international media outlets to film Arab volunteers who came from all over the Arab world to carry out martyr operations". In line 5, he continues building up this account as factual by stating that there was a CIA report accusing Iraq of establishing connections with terrorists belonging to Al-Qaeda. In lines 10 to 11, he asks whether the Iraqi government is not afraid of being accused of supporting terrorism. Here, the interviewer does not question the factuality or legitimacy of such activity; rather, he focuses on the expected implications of allowing media outlets to film these camps. This account implies that publicising such activities can produce undesirable consequences for Iraq.

Al-Hadithi replies in lines 12 to 26 by constructing an account aimed at normalising suicide operations. He begins by indicating that before training non-Iraqis to carry out such operations, the Iraqi regime had already prepared thousands of Iraqis "to become martyrs". Note that both speakers describe suicide bombers as martyrs. This inference-rich descriptive term implies that the suicide bombers are fighting for a legitimate cause according to Islamic doctrine, and this consequently qualifies them to enter heaven upon completing their missions. In lines 16 to 20, the interviewee lists several organisations, describing them as armed and ready to fight in the anticipated war. By naming these organisations, he creates a factual account designed to portray Iraq as ready for the war (cf. Edwards & Potter, 1992; Potter, 1996). It also implies that the Iraqi people support Saddam and are willing to fight under his leadership. More than that, by naming institutions such as the Iraqi Army, the interviewee frames suicide operations as analogous to lawful military activities. All of this functions as a warning to the Americans and the British against attacking Iraq.

In lines 21 to 23, he identifies the motivation behind these people's willingness to fight and carry out suicide missions. Rather than associating it with loyalty to the regime, he indicates that "being martyrs" is the way to protect "land, women, and honour". This formulation frames suicide bombing as martyrdom. It legitimates these attacks by portraying them as a means to protect crucial objectives: land, women, and honour. It is designed to create a stake for Iraqi laypeople to join the training camps (cf. Potter, 1996). These objectives have been repeatedly used by politicians to justify wars (see Billig, 1995). Notably, when constructing the legitimacy of suicide attacks, the interviewee avoids discussing the specific targets of such attacks. This allows him to sidestep the problematic notions associated with such attacks, which, if addressed, could undermine his argument.

In line 27, the interviewer returns to the issue of disclosing the suicide training camps. This implies that the problem lies not in the activity as much as in its disclosure. This subtly implies that supporting suicide attacks and mobilising people to execute them is a virtuous action, as long as it should remain clandestine. In lines 29 to 34, the interviewee discusses why the Iraqi regime is engaging in this activity. He assigns the responsibility for establishing such training camps to "the pressure of thousands of Arabs". Here, he portrays the creation of the suicide training camps as a response to public demand. This is designed to absolve the Iraqi regime of responsibility. It also furthers the notion that both Iraqi and Arab people are willing to give up their lives. In lines 31 to 33, he strengthens his argument by presenting a narrative about the number of volunteers from just one country who want to join the fight against the Americans. In lines 38-39, he delivers the central argument of his account, stating that there are "many thousands of Arabs and Muslims who want" to participate.

In lines 40-41, the interviewer asks why they want to do so. In lines 42 to 50, the interviewee builds up the causes that drive these Arab and Iraqi people to willingly sacrifice their lives, indicating that it is a "national, religious, and Islamic position".

Here, he portrays suicide attacks as legitimate because it is the way "to defend the land of faiths". The speaker characterises the war as legitimate by associating it with notion of defending the land, which is designed to justify the war from the Iraqi position. Furthermore, it implies that the war carries both national and religious dimensions.

In lines 44 to 48, the speaker builds up the importance of Iraq and, in turn, the need to defend it. He describes Iraq as "the centre of the Arabs and Muslims", a description intended to build up a stake for Arabs and Muslims in defending Iraq by constituting its defence as the protection of their spiritual and cultural capital. Furthermore, the interviewee employs emotional rhetoric designed to affiliate Muslims with Iraq and, in turn, encourage them to support the Iraqi position. In line 51, he describes Iraq's role in regard to the suicide bombers as providing them with training and being "honoured to have them". This formulation is designed to portray these fighters as having the leading role in the matter, thereby encouraging the audience to join the camps. It also attributes the establishment of these camps to the volunteers themselves, rather than to the Iraqi government.

To sum up, in this extract, Al-Hadithi warrants and promotes suicide attacks as legitimate means of fighting against foreign invasion. He constructs them in such a way that makes them seem a legitimate and natural way of defending and protecting valuable objectives. This account represents a good example of how rhetorical accounts can justify and endorse actions that are normally rejected and abhorred.

In the next and last extract, I examine how the Iraqi president addresses the conflict taking place in his country.

Invaded by foreigners, not by Americans

In the extract below, the speaker, who is the Iraqi President, constructs and deploys a discursive account that is laden with rhetorical formulations to describe the situation in his country. He warrants the American invasion while at the same time constructing the insurgency movement as an invasion originating from other countries, aimed at destroying Iraq. He invokes a stake for Arab countries in preventing Iraq from becoming a stable country, using several effective rhetorical formulations. He attributes the killing of Iraqi people to non-Iraqis.

EXTRACT 6.4. JALAL TALABANI, PRESIDENT OF IRAQ; 12 MARCH 2003, AL-ARABIYA TV; BAGHDAD, IRAQ.

T: this terrorism is coming from abroad
we are under a foreign invasion
I: who is the foreign
T: Please let me (.) the terrorists admitted that 4,000 of them
who were killed were foreigners 4,000 have been killed
in Iraq and we believe that the number is higher
more than 10,000 foreigners have been killed
we are facing a foreign invasion and it is causing the problems
we do not have enough forces to counter this foreign invasion
so the Americans are countering it although in a very
limited way
I do not think that the Americans want chaos
I do not agree with that I think that
there are mistakes (.) they have committed mistakes
we do not have enough Iraqi forces
there is not an adequate plan to counter terrorism
but the Americans do not want to create chaos
I: Mr President what does it mean, a foreign invasion?
who are the foreigners? When we hear foreign invasion
we think (.) many people would think
where are they coming from?
T: the foreigners who are in Iraq now
are from all Arab countries
there is not one single Arab state that does not have
hundreds of fighters in our country
Islamic countries also have

some Islamic countries have (.) there are people coming
from Afghanistan we are facing a campaign
at one point 200 terrorists were entering Iraq daily
there is an international coalition and international crusade
against Iraq because a united democratic Iraq
would influence the people of the East towards
democracy and prosperity
this is why there is a conspiracy against the new Iraq
and these terrorists who are coming from abroad
have declared all the Shiites as infidels
they considered them rejectionists
they have considered all Kurds as traitors
they have considered all the Sunni Arabs who do not agree
with them as unbelievers
I: you are talking about Al-Qaeda?
T: this is [genocide against the Iraqi] people
I: [you are talking about Al-Qaeda?]
T: yes Al-Qaeda
I: yes but what about the foreign invasion
T: [and the other terrorists not just Al-Qaeda]
there are troops from other radical Islamic organisations
that came to Iraq to fight us
I: like whom (.) do you mean Iran?
T: Iran does not attack us
I: when we are talking about foreign invasion we think of
the Americans and the British they are the foreigners
when we are talking about invasion shouldn't we talk
about the alliance forces?
T: Yes they are foreigners who came and liberated Iraq
from the most savage dictatorship which left hundreds of
thousands of Iraqis in jails and in the mass graves
those foreigners do not kill Iraqi people
did not kill the Shiites or the Sunnis or the Kurds
the ones that are killing us are terrorists, invaders
who have come from abroad to fight the Iraqi people

In this extract, the Iraqi President acquits Iraqis of responsibility for the violence, allocating the blame to non-Iraqis. He warrants the American invasion and praises the American and the British forces, framing them as liberators. Talabani denounces Arab and Muslim fighters in Iraq, constructing them as terrorists and bloodthirsty foreigners who are killing innocent Iraqi people. He apportions the culpability exclusively to radical Muslims and Arab countries while acquitting the Americans and the British forces of being responsible for the ongoing violence in Iraq.

In the first sentence, he presents the situation: "terrorism is coming from abroad, we are under a foreign invasion" (lines 1-2). Invasions must have victims and perpetrators, thus, the interviewee asks in line 3, who the invaders or foreigners are. In lines 4 to 17, the Iraqi President builds up an account that explains his use of the term "invasion". He introduces the categories "foreigners" and "terrorists" (lines 4-5) as the enemy invading Iraq. By using the labels "foreigners" and "terrorists", Talabani constructs the notion that these people are not Iraqis but come "from abroad".

The way Talabani builds up and uses the category "terrorists" resonates with Sacks' (1992) concept of category construction and deployment, where a speaker creates a label and constructs specific features and activities as related to the label. Distinguishing "terrorists" from Iraqi people functions as a way of de-legitimising the existence of this group in Iraq. This in turn renders their activities unwarrantable, since they do not have the right to be in Iraq in the first place.

The participant uses several discursive techniques to make his account seem factual. He does so by presenting his account as based on the enemy's own admission of the number of foreign fighters killed in Iraq (cf. Potter, 1996). Mentioning the number 4,000 bolsters the factuality of his account (Potter, 1996). The interviewee also provides his own estimation of the number of these fighters, indicating that he believes "more than 10,000 foreigners have been killed" (line 7).

This implies that the speaker possesses independent data in relation to the terrorists and their activities. Here, the interviewee constructs himself as knowledgeable on the subject (see Potter, 1996).

In line 8, Talabani places the blame for Iraq's problems on the "foreign invasion". However, he portrays "the Americans" as liberators (line 55), indicating that they are "countering it [terrorism], although in a very limited way". Here, he identifies foreign terrorists as the cause of Iraq's problems while simultaneously constructing the Americans as allies helping the Iraqi people. In lines 11 to 17, the Iraqi President reinforces that notion. He does this by constructing the idea that the Americans are restoring order (line 10-12). The interviewee does, however, acknowledge that the Americans "have committed mistakes". This lends his argument greater realism and thus makes it more convincing (cf. Potter, 1996). In lines 15 to 16, he describes the lack of "Iraqi forces" and the absence of "an adequate plan to counter terrorism" as factors enabling terrorists to implement their agenda. This implies that if Iraqi people wish to eliminate terrorism, they must join and support the Iraqi police and army, and that the Americans will not counter terrorism on behalf of the Iraqi people. Most importantly, this legitimises the presence of foreign forces in Iraq on the grounds that Iraq cannot defend itself against terrorists.

The interviewer asks the President of Iraq to clarify whom he means by "foreigners" and where they are from (lines 18-21). This suggests that the term "foreigners" needs justification, since it seems the president is using it to refer to fellow Arabs and Muslims. The interviewer here implies that considering Arabs and Muslims to be foreigners in Iraq is problematic. In line 22, the Iraqi President reasserts his characterisation of these Arabs as foreigners. He states that they are from "all Arab countries" and that "there is not one single Arab state that does not have hundreds of fighters in our country". This formulation accuses Arab countries and Arab people of supporting the terrorists. It also implies that even though these people are Arabs and

Muslims, they are foreigners because they are not Iraqis and are harming Iraqi people.

In line 28, the interviewee constructs what is happening as a "campaign" against Iraq. He supports this claim by indicating that "200 terrorists were entering Iraq daily" (line 29). Talabani presents a final conclusion, describing the situation as "an international coalition and international crusade against Iraq" (31-32). He constructs the reasons behind this campaign as fear of the influence of a "united democratic Iraq". He argues that these countries are afraid that the existence of a united and democratic Iraq would inspire the people in the East to opt "for democracy and prosperity". This argument implies that the general public in the East is living without democracy or prosperity. The participant suggests that terrorists and their sponsors fear Iraq's potential to become a democratic country and therefore have an interest in preventing this from happening (see Potter, 1996, for how people attend to the issue of stake within their accounts). This formulation is designed to portray the terrorists and their supporters as the culpable side, motivated by self-interest rather than principles.

In lines 35 to 40, the interviewee constructs the terrorists as enemies of all Iraqi people by showing that they are attacking the three main sub-groups that constitute Iraqi society. He indicates that they are against all Shiites, as they "have declared all the Shiites as infidels" and "rejectionists" (line 37). Note that describing a group of people as infidels effectively warrants waging an annihilation war against that group, according to radical Sunni doctrines. Talabani thus constructs the terrorists as an existential threat to all Shiites in Iraq and beyond. He also highlights the terrorists' use of the term "rejectionists" to describe Shiites, a derogatory term used by fundamental Sunnis to imply that Shiites have rejected the true doctrine of Islam, making them a legitimate target. The speaker further indicates that the foreign terrorists "have considered all Kurds as traitors" (line 38). This implies that the terrorists aim to obliterate all Iraqi Kurds as well. In lines 39 to 40, he discusses how the terrorists perceive the third major Iraqi group, stating that "they have considered all the Sunni Arabs who do not agree with them as unbelievers". Note that, unlike their approach toward Shiites and Kurds, Talabani indicates that the terrorists are not against each and every Sunni; rather, they are against those ones who do not agree with them. By highlighting this distinction, the speaker seeks to counter the stereotypical notion that Sunni Iraqis are supporting the terrorists. He implies that the foreign terrorists are willing to kill even Sunnis who do not agree with them.

In lines 41 and 43, the interviewer attempts to limit the terrorists to one specific organisation by asking the Iraqi President if he is referring to Al-Qaeda. Talabani describes what is going on in Iraq as "genocide against the Iraqi" (line 42), framing the Arab terrorists as enemies to the entire Iraqi population. He indicates that other terrorist groups besides Al-Qaeda are involved (lines 44-46). Thus, it is "not just Al-Qaeda" that is killing Iraqis but also "there are troops from other radical Islamic organisations that came to Iraq to fight us" (lines 47-48). This constructs the terrorists as powerful and numerous, which implies that the Iraqi government cannot defeat them alone.

In line 49, the interviewer asks the Iraqi President if he accuses Iran of fighting the Iraqi people. He replies firmly stating that "Iran does not attack us". Here, the interviewer, an Arab working for a Saudi-owned TV station, is attempting to accuse Iran of supporting terrorism in Iraq. In response, the Iraqi President affirms the notion that terrorism in Iraq is a product of Arab countries. In the next sentence, the interviewer raises the issue of the Americans and British, stating that "they are the foreigners" (line 52). This implies that the Americans and British do not have the right to be in Iraq. This subtly suggests that the insurgency's argument, based on rejecting the presence of American and British troops in Iraq, is legitimate. The Iraqi President counters this argument, which is extensively used to validate the insurgency's activities (lines 55-61). He indicates that although the Americans and the British are foreigners, "they came and liberated Iraq" (line 55). Here, he warrants the

American and British presence in Iraq by describing what they have done as "liberating Iraq from the most savage dictatorship". This constructs the Americans and the British as legitimate actors in Iraq, as they are portrayed as having helped the Iraqi people by rescuing them from the former regime. The interviewee supports his characterisation of the ex-regime as the most savage dictatorship by highlighting "mass graves" and the imprisonment of hundreds of thousands of Iraqis. He rejects the notion that Americans and British are enemies of the Iraqis by stating that they "do not kill Iraqi people" (line 58). He further builds up this argument by stating that the American and British forces "did not kill the Shiites or the Sunnis or the Kurds". Here, he affirms that the American and British soldiers are not hostile to any Iraqi sub-group. This counters the argument that characterises the American forces as being against Iraq or certain groups of Iraqis. In the final two lines, Talabani identifies the true enemies of Iraq as the "terrorists, invaders who have come from abroad to fight the Iraqi people". This sentence encapsulates the main argument the Iraqi President has been building up gradually throughout his account.

To sum up, the Iraqi President builds up what is happening in Iraq as an international campaign, led by Arabs and Muslims, aimed at preventing Iraq from becoming a democratic and united state by murdering Iraqi people and destroying infrastructure. Killing and terrorism are constructed in this account as a means used by Arab states and radical organisations to accomplish specific goals in Iraq. The Iraqi President constructs the motive behind this campaign against Iraq as the vested interest that these Arab countries and radical Muslims have in blocking democracy in their own countries through extirpating Iraq's democratic experiment. He defends the American and British armies by describing them as liberators who did not seek to annihilate any Iraqi faction. This, in turn, also warrants the American invasion by characterising it as liberation. The account of the war is thus organised around the interests of the Iraqi people.

Summary and conclusion

The analytical focus of this chapter has primarily rested upon highlighting the ways in which various prominent Iraqi politicians attended to the events in Iraq following the 2003 war. If we considered wars to be essentially about killing and violence, then understanding how people present and justify violence is essential. Here, the different speakers, who have faced life-threatening situations, constructed coherent narratives that incorporated redeeming and inspirational aspects and notions into the otherwise grim picture of the situation in Iraq. More than that, each speaker constructed their accounts to attend to the future as much as the present and the past.

The interviewee in the first extract manages to create an account that presents him as resilient, the Iraqi people as virtuous, and Iraq as a country with potential. At the same time, he constructs Al-Qaeda and members of the Ba'ath party as bloodthirsty criminals who will be defeated. The speaker in Extract 6.2 presents a similar account of Al-Qaeda as ruthless criminals. However, he does so as a means to convince the audience of the legitimacy of his intentions to kill Al-Qaeda members. In this extract, killing is presented as a right and necessary action. In Extract 6.3, the interviewee constructs an account designed to warrant and promote suicide bombers by employing certain rhetorical techniques. In the final extract, the Iraqi President accounts for the conflict in Iraq as an invasion by fanatical Muslims against the country and its people. He re-characterised the fighting from an insurgency movement against the Iraqi government and Western forces into an Arab campaign against Iraq and its interests.

These multiple accounts demonstrate that different speakers employ discursive techniques to support their own versions of the conflict and to achieve certain desired ends. Killing and suicide attacks are constructed, presented, and defended in some of these extracts. The loss of one's sons is presented in a way that appeared patriotic. Moreover, in all the extracts discussed, the speakers consistently seek to present themselves and their groups as resilient, moral, and enduring, while at the exact same time they portray their opponents as aggressive, culpable, and morally defeated. Finally, in this chapter, I have demonstrated that categories, events, and conducts are flexible resources, constructed and employed by the speakers to accomplish specific ends.

References

Antaki, C., & Widdicombe, S. (Eds.). (1998). *Identities in talk.* London: Sage.

Billig, M. (1995). *Banal Nationalism.* London: Sage Publications.

Dower, J. W. (1986). *War without mercy: race and power in the Pacific War.* New York: Pantheon.

Edwards, D., & Potter, J. (1992). *Discursive Psychology.* London: Sage.

Edwards, D., & Potter, J. (2003). Discursive psychology and mental states. In H. Molder & J. Potter (Eds.), *Conversation and cognition.* Cambridge University Press.

Edwards, D. (2005). Discursive psychology. In K. L. Fitch. & R. E. Sanders (Eds.), *Handbook of language and social interaction.* New York: Erlbaum.

Herrera, M. (2003). Constructing social categories and seeking collective influence: self-categorization and the discursive construction of a conflict. *International Journal of Psychology and Psychological Therapy, 3*(1), 27-57.

Iraq Body Count. (2024). *Documented civilian deaths from violence.* Retrieved from https://www.iraqbodycount.org/

Leudar, I., Marsland, V. & Nekvapil, J. (2004). On membership categorization: 'Us,' 'them' and 'doing violence' in political discourse. *Discourse & Society, 15*(2-3), 243-266.

Potter, J. (1996). *Representing reality: Discourse, rhetoric and social construction.* London: Sage.

Potter, J. (2003). Discursive psychology: Between method and paradigm. *Discourse & Society, 14*(6), 783-94.

Sacks, H. (1992). *Lectures on conversation.* Oxford: Basil Blackwell.

Chapter 7

Gaza War: Normalising suffering and aggression

The Gaza War, which erupted on 7th October 2023, drew significant international attention, becoming one of the most publicized conflicts in recent history. Tens of thousands of protesters took to the streets of Europe, Canada, USA, New Zeeland, Australia supporting Hamas and the Palestinian resistance, and calling for a ceasefire. Actors, intellectuals, and journalists have discussed this war at length, lamenting the losses and the suffering it has caused.

While this war has resulted in considerable loss of life and widespread destruction, it is crucial to recognize that other ongoing conflicts around the world – particularly in regions like Sudan, Mali, Burkina Faso, Myanmar – have been equally or even more devastating in terms of casualties and humanitarian impact. These conflicts, however, receive far less media coverage and international focus, leaving millions without the desperately needed support.

The civil war in Sudan, which began in April 2023, has already claimed over 20,00 lives and injured 33,000 people. It has displaced more than 7.7 million people internally and forced over 2 million to flee to neighbouring countries, according to UN reports. The humanitarian crisis in Sudan is severe, with millions facing acute food insecurity, yet it remains underreported compared to the Gaza conflict. Not a single protest has taken place anywhere in the world to call for a ceasefire or to show sympathy with the victims.

Similarly, ongoing conflicts in the Central African Republic, Ethiopia's Tigray region, the Democratic Republic of Congo, and Myanmar continue to cause significant loss of life and mass displacement, yet none of these wars receive even a fraction of the attention or financial support that the Gaza War does.

The Gaza War began when Hamas launched a sudden and unprovoked attack against Israel from the Gaza Strip, resulting in over 1,400 casualties and the kidnapping of 250 civilians. Hamas fighters recorded and broadcast themselves shooting at civilians in their homes and in the streets and kidnapping women, children, and elderly Israelis and taking them to Gaza. Israel responded by declaring war with the stated goals of dismantling Hamas and rescuing the hostages. The conflict has since escalated, causing a worsening humanitarian crisis in the region.

Despite the Gaza War dominating global headlines, its psychological dimensions – especially the pivotal role of identity – remain surprisingly underexplored. From a social psychology perspective, **identity stands as one of the most critical factors** in understanding this conflict.

In this chapter, I will explore how the Gaza conflict has been framed by influential actors and the implications of these narratives. I will begin by providing a historical background of the conflict.

How far back should we go in history?

The ongoing conflict between Hamas and Israel is a manifestation and continuation of a much broader and historically entrenched struggle that has persisted for over a century. While the immediate roots of this conflict can be traced back to the early 20th century, particularly with the decline of the Ottoman Empire, the rise of nationalist movements in the Middle East, and the establishment of the State of Israel in 1948, the underlying tensions have much deeper historical antecedents.

One perspective views this conflict as a continuation of religious and territorial disputes that have marked the region for over 1,400 years. This view situates the Gaza conflict within the broader context of the Arab conquests of the 7th century, during which Islamic armies rapidly expanded their territories, including the capture of Jerusalem in 638 CE. These conquests brought the Islamic world into direct and often conflictual contact with other religious populations, particularly Christians and Jews who had lived in the region for centuries.

The region that is now Israel and the Palestinian territories has long been a focal point for religious and cultural identities, serving as a crossroads of civilizations and a land of significant religious importance for Judaism, Christianity, and Islam. The Arab-Israeli conflict is thus not merely a political or territorial dispute but part of a larger, ongoing struggle involving deep-seated religious identities. Historical events such as the Crusades and the various conflicts over control of Jerusalem are often cited as earlier chapters in this enduring struggle.

In the modern era, the late 19th and early 20th centuries witnessed the rise of nationalist movements among both Jews and Arabs. For Jews, this period marked the beginning of Zionism, a movement advocating for the return of Jews to their ancestral homeland in Palestine, which was then under Ottoman rule. For Arabs, the end of Ottoman rule and the subsequent British mandate in Palestine sparked aspirations for independence and self-determination. The Balfour Declaration of 1917, in which the British government expressed support for the establishment of a "national home for the Jewish people" in Palestine, further intensified tensions between Jewish and Arab communities.

The establishment of Israel in 1948 and the subsequent wars with neighbouring Arab states in 1948, 1956, 1967, 1973, and 1982 cemented the conflict as a central issue in Middle Eastern politics. The displacement of hundreds of thousands of Palestinian Arabs during the 1948 Arab-Israeli War, known to Palestinians as Nakba or "catastrophe," created a refugee crisis that remains unresolved to this day. This event continues to fuel resentment and conflict in the region. Conversely, the expulsion of around a million Jews from Arab countries and the confiscation of their properties by various Arab regimes forced these Jews to seek refuge in the newly established state of Israel, further complicating regional dynamics.

Islamic armed movements were established in Palestine in the 1930s, engaging in attacks against both Jews and the British administration. From the 1950s to the 1980s, the Palestine Liberation Organization (PLO) was the primary Palestinian organization involved in armed conflict against Israel. The PLO's activities also extended beyond Israel, as they attempted to overthrow regimes in Lebanon and Jordan, leading to significant regional conflicts, including the Lebanese Civil War and the Black September conflict in Jordan.

Hamas, an Islamist militant group that emerged in the late 1980s during the First Intifada – a Palestinian uprising against Israeli occupation – is one of the more recent actors in this long-running conflict. While Hamas frames its struggle as resistance to Israeli occupation and a defence of Palestinian rights, its ideological roots are also tied to a broader Islamic narrative that seeks to re-establish an Islamic empire governed by Sharia law.

Constructing identity and the nature of Gaza War

In analysing the Gaza War, I will examine how identity and the nature of the conflict are constructed through key speeches and communications by influential figures. Specifically, I will analyse the following:

1. **An intercepted phone call between one of the Hamas fighters and his family during the attack** - this personal communication offers a unique perspective on how the militants themselves perceive their actions and their role in the conflict.

2. **The first speech by the leader of Hamas following the 7th October attack** - crucial in understanding how Hamas justifies its actions and frames the conflict within its ideological and religious narrative.

3. **The reaction of the President of the United States to the attack** - this speech provides insight into how the conflict is framed from a Western perspective, particularly in terms of counter-terrorism and the defence of democratic values. It also highlights the special relationship between the US and Israel.

4. **A speech by the Israeli Prime Minister in response to the attack** - it reflects Israel's position, focusing on national security, the right to self-defence, and the broader implications for Israeli society and its international standing.

5. **An interview segment with an Israeli female hostage who was released after six months in captivity** - this account provides a humanized view of the conflict's impact on civilians and how they construct their identity and experience in relation to the broader war.

Through these analyses, I aim to explore how these narratives shape public perceptions, influence international responses, and contribute to the ongoing cycle of violence and retaliation. The construction of identity and the framing of the conflict are not mere rhetorical exercises – they have real and profound consequences in terms of policy decisions, military strategies, and the lived experiences of those caught in the crossfire.

Hamas fighter's conversation with family

The first extract is a phone call between one of the Hamas fighters who took part in the October 7th attack and his family. The phone call was intercepted by Israeli intelligence and broadcasted. In the call, the Hamas fighter (Mahmoud) speaks with his father, mother, brother, and sister.

EXTRACT 7.1. HAMAS FIGHTER, 7 OCTOBER 2023, PHONE CALL. (T=TERRORIST; F=FATHER; M=MOTHER; B=BROTHER; S=SISTER)

T: Hello dad. Dad I am inside Mefalsim.
Open your WhatsApp right now
and see all the killed.
Look at how many I killed with my own hands,
your son killed Jews.
F: Allahu Akbar, Allahu Akbar.
May God protect you. My God protect you, my son.
T: This is inside (.) Mefalsim, father.
I am talking to you from the phone of a Jewish woman.
I killed her and I killed her husband.
I killed ten with my own hands.
F: ↑Allahu↓ Akbar. Allahu Akbar, thank God.
T: Open your phone and see how many I killed (.)
Father, open your phone, I am calling you on WhatsApp.
F: ((unintelligible))
T: I am in Mefalsim, father. I killed ten.
Ten! Ten with my own bare hands.
Their blood is on my hands, let me talk to Mom.
M: Oh, my son, may God protect you.
T: I killed ten all by myself, mother. Ten I killed.
F: I am praying for you. May God bring you home safely.
T: Father, go back to WhatsApp!
I want to call you live from Mefalsim.
M: I wish I was there with you.
T: Mother, your son is a hero. I was the first
to enter under the guidance (.) and with the help of Allah.
Father, lift your head, lift your head.
((Talking to terrorists on the scene: Kill! Kill! Kill!
Kill them! Inside, inside, into the city.))
B: Mahmoud, Mahmoud. Where are you?
T: I am inside, in Mefalsim, Alaa. Inside. I killed ten. Ten

with my hand.
I am talking to you from the Jewish woman's phone.
B: You killed ten?
T: I killed ten, I swear to Allah.
B: Where are you, in Zikim, in Zikim?
T: I am in Mefalsim, not Zikim.
I was the first one to enter under the protection of Allah.
Hold your head up, father, hold your head up.
B: You are inside, you are inside.
T: Inside the city. Look at the WhatsApp,
see those whom I have killed, see the WhatsApp.
B: Come back [to Gaza], that's enough, return.
T: Return? There is no return, it is victory or martyrdom.
My mother gave birth to me for Islam, Alaa.
Are you serious, how will I return?
Look at WhatsApp, look at your phone, look at all the killed
B: Ok, Ok enough come back, come back
T: What do you mean come back? There is no going back.
It is either victory or martyrdom [shahadah]
My mother gave birth to me for the religion, Alaa.
What's with you Alaa, how will I return?
B: Mahmoud, Mahmoud
T: Yes
B: Pray for us Mahmoud
T: open, open the WhatsApp and see the killed.
Open my cell phone
S: Mahmoud should I open your cell phone?
T: open my cell phone and [see] the ones I killed with my hand
S: Well, promise to come Back.
T: came how (unintelligible)
S: (unintelligible)
T: I will come back

The intercepted phone call between a Hamas fighter, Mahmoud, and his family provides a deeply revealing case study of how language is used to construct identities, justify violence, and frame the ongoing conflict. The conversation exemplifies the use of various discursive techniques and devices to shape the speakers' understanding of themselves, their enemies, and the broader events surrounding them. This analysis will explore how these discursive practices are employed to construct identities, others, events, and violence, drawing on key concepts from discourse analysis and sociolinguistics.

Construction of identity

Mahmoud's identity as a militant and religious warrior is meticulously constructed throughout the conversation using a range of discursive strategies. One of the primary techniques employed is *action description as identity construction*. Mahmoud repeatedly describes his violent actions in specific and graphic terms, such as when he declares, "Your son killed Jews" (line 5). This act of killing is not presented merely as an incident in the conflict but as a core component of the speaker's identity. By defining himself through his actions, Mahmoud uses his brutal behaviour as a way to assert his position within the conflict.

This identity construction is further reinforced by the use of *religious framing*, a discursive technique that links his actions to a divine mission. Mahmoud and his family members invoke religious phrases such as "Allahu Akbar" (lines 6, 12) and express prayers for divine protection (lines 7, 19). According to Fairclough (1992), religious language in discourse often serves to legitimize actions by embedding them within a broader ideological or divine framework. In this context, Mahmoud's identity as a warrior is not just self-proclaimed but is sanctified by religious discourse, positioning him as a figure carrying out the will of a higher power. This religious framing transforms his violent actions from mere acts of aggression into acts of faith and divine duty, effectively elevating his identity within both his family and the broader militant community.

Mahmoud's assertion, "There is no return, it is victory or martyrdom" (line 44), exemplifies the use of *binary opposition* as a discursive technique. This framing device reduces the complex realities of conflict to a simple dichotomy, where the only possible outcomes are either victory or death. As van Dijk (1998) notes, such binary framing is a powerful discursive strategy in ideological rhetoric, as it simplifies decision-making processes and eliminates middle-ground options. By presenting his situation in these stark terms, Mahmoud constructs his identity as unwaveringly committed to the cause, with no room for doubt or retreat.

The *performative nature of the language* in this conversation is evident in the terrorist's use of imperatives and directives. It is highlighted in his interaction with other terrorists on the scene, where he tells them to "Kill! Kill! Kill! Kill them!" (lines 28-29). This use of language is not merely descriptive but directive, actively shaping the behaviour of others and reinforcing the collective identity of the group as active participants in the violence. Chilton (2004) explains that performative language in political and militant discourse serves to enact the very reality it describes. In this case, Mahmoud's commands are both a reflection of his commitment to violence. It is also a reinforcement of his identity as a Hamas fighter.

Moreover, Mahmoud's repeated reference to the *physicality of the violence*, such as "I killed ten with my own hands" (lines 11, 17, 31-32), emphasizes the personal involvement in the acts of violence. This discursive focus on the physical act of killing highlights the aggressive aspects of his identity, further embedding him within the archetype of the militant warrior. Goffman (1974) describes this as "frame alignment," where an individual's actions and identity are continuously aligned with a broader narrative or role – in this case, that of a religiously motivated militant.

Construction of others

The construction of the enemy in this conversation is achieved primarily through applying a title designed to dehumanise the members of that group. *Dehumanization* and *othering* are key discursive techniques that serve to justify violence by stripping victims of their individual identities, and these were used interactionally by the speakers. Mahmoud and his family refer to the people he has killed simply as "Jews" (line 5). They do not explain to each other or build up a reason for the killing beyond the title "Jews" or "Jewish". In lines 9-10, the speaker informs his father that he killed a Jewish woman and her husband and took her phone. Neither the terrorist nor his father provide or seek justification for the killings.

In lines 3, 13, 42, 47, the victims are further reduced to faceless members of a collective enemy group that can be exterminated without justification. This reductionist labelling is a common technique in conflict discourse, as it simplifies the moral landscape, making it easier to justify violence against those who are not seen as individuals but as part of an evil group (Wodak & Meyer, 2009).

The act of using a Jewish woman's phone to make the call (lines 9 and 33) serves as a symbolic erasure of the victims' rights and identities, transforming them into mere tools within Mahmoud's narrative. By informing his father that he is using the phone he appropriated, without justification or an objection from his father, Mahmoud further dehumanizes the woman he has killed. The discourse is designed to transform the murder of civilians inside their homes and theft of their property from something intrinsically evil and reprehensible into a banal, if not virtuous, act.

The family's reactions, particularly the father's emotional and religiously charged exclamations (lines 6, 12), further reinforce this dehumanization. By celebrating the deaths of the victims as a cause for religious exultation, the family collectively constructs the victims as deserving of their fate. This is a clear example of *discursive legitimization*, where violence is framed as not only justified but necessary within the context of a broader religious or ideological struggle (Fairclough, 1992).

Construction of events and conflict

The conversation also constructs the events of October 7th and the broader conflict in ways that align with the speakers' ideological positions. Mahmoud's focus on the number of people he has killed (lines 11, 16, 20) serves to amplify the significance of his actions, portraying them as substantial contributions to the war effort. This emphasis on quantity is a discursive strategy that seeks to maximize the perceived impact of his actions, thereby constructing the event as a significant victory.

The use of *technology as a discursive tool* is particularly noteworthy. Mahmoud's repeated instructions for his family to "open WhatsApp" to view images of the dead (lines 2, 13, 22, 42) illustrate how modern communication tools are used to validate and disseminate acts of violence. This reflects what Fairclough (1992) describes as the "intertextuality" of discourse, where different texts (in this case, the phone call and the WhatsApp images) intersect to create a more compelling narrative. By insisting on the visual confirmation of his actions, Mahmoud constructs the event as not just a physical reality but a documented and shared experience, further embedding it within the collective consciousness of his family and, by extension, the militant community.

Mahmoud's framing of the attack as being carried out "under the guidance and with the help of Allah" (lines 26) is another significant discursive strategy. This statement aligns the event with a divine mission, constructing it as part of a larger, sacred conflict rather than a mere battle. Chilton (2004) notes that such religious framing is a powerful tool in political and militant discourse, as it provides a moral and ethical justification for actions that might otherwise be seen as reprehensible. By linking the event to divine will, Mahmoud elevates the conflict from a territorial dispute to a cosmic struggle, where the stakes are existential and the outcomes predetermined by a higher power.

The binary opposition of "victory or martyrdom" (lines 44, 50) further simplifies the conflict into a narrative of absolutes, where there is no middle ground or possibility of negotiation.

This discursive technique is effective in creating a clear, unambiguous framework within which the conflict is understood, both by Mahmoud and his family. It reduces the complexity of the situation, making it easier to maintain commitment to the cause without the burden of moral ambiguity.

Legitimising the killing of innocent people

The role of the family in reinforcing the terrorist's actions and identity is a crucial aspect of this conversation. The father's repeated use of "Allahu Akbar" (lines 6, 12) and the mother's expressions of pride and support (lines 19, 24) serve to legitimize the terrorist's actions within the family context. This familial reinforcement is not only emotional but also ideological, as the parents' responses align with the broader religious and political narratives that justify the violence.

The brother's intervention (line 43), in which he urges the terrorist to return home, introduces a momentary challenge to the prevailing narrative. However, the terrorist quickly dismisses this suggestion, asserting, "There is no return, it is victory or martyrdom" (lines 44, 50). This response reasserts the dominant narrative of the conversation, framing the violence as a binary choice between success and sacrifice, with no room for retreat or doubt.

The interaction between the terrorist and his family illustrates how social and familial contexts can play a critical role in sustaining violent ideologies. The parents' responses provide emotional and moral support for the terrorist's actions, reinforcing his identity as a "hero" and validating the ideological framework that underpins the violence.

Construction of agency and responsibility

Agency is a key theme in this conversation, with the terrorist repeatedly asserting his personal involvement in the killings.

His statements, such as "I killed ten with my own hands" (lines 11, 16-17) and "Their blood is on my hands" (line 18), emphasise his active role in the violence. This *self-attribution of agency* is critical in constructing his identity as an empowered and effective actor within the context of the conflict.

However, this assertion of personal agency is juxtaposed with references to divine guidance (lines 26), which serve to distribute responsibility between the individual and the divine. By attributing his actions to the "guidance and help of Allah," the terrorist simultaneously claims personal agency and absolves himself of full responsibility, suggesting that his actions are part of a larger, divinely sanctioned plan.

This dual construction of agency is significant in understanding how individuals involved in extremist violence navigate the tension between personal responsibility and ideological justification. The terrorist's language allows him to maintain a sense of personal power and achievement while also framing his actions as part of a collective religious duty.

Conclusion

The phone call between Mahmoud and his family offers a rich case study in the use of discursive techniques and devices to construct identities, other people, events, and violence in the context of conflict. Through action description, religious framing, dehumanization, binary opposition, and the strategic use of technology, Mahmoud constructs his identity as a religious warrior committed to a divinely sanctioned mission. His family members reinforce this identity through their responses, collectively constructing the violence as a legitimate and noble act within their ideological framework.

This analysis underscores the complex interplay between language, identity, and violence in the construction of militant mentality. By examining the specific discursive strategies used in this conversation, we gain a deeper understanding of how individuals and groups justify and perpetuate violence in the context of conflict.

This understanding is crucial for developing strategies to counteract extremist narratives and promote more peaceful conflict resolutions.

Hamas leader's justification of the attacks

Khalid Mashal's speech, delivered on 10th October 2023, two days after the attack, provides a profound example of how language can be used to construct identities, justify actions, and mobilize support within a conflict setting. This speech is not just a reflection of pre-existing beliefs but an active construction of social reality designed to influence the audience's perception of themselves, their enemies, and the broader conflict. Most importantly, the speaker used his description of the events to demand future action from the targeted audience. The analysis will focus on how Mashal employs discursive techniques to build collective identity, legitimize violence, and invoke emotional and psychological engagement.

EXTRACT 7.2. KHALID MASHAL, SENIOR HAMAS LEADER; PUBLIC SPEECH BROADCAST ON 10 OCTOBER 2023.

1 My brothers and sisters, my folks, and people in this Ummah [Islamic nation],
2 These are your brothers and sisters who created this glory,
3 created this flood.
4 The flood of al-Aqsa.
5 They fought for al-Aqsa when they saw it being defiled
6 for long months
7 and they saw that al-Aqsa was in danger of being demolished
8 or divided and of building the fake temple,
9 they fought victoriously for liberating the homeland and the land
10 from this criminal occupation.
11 These are your brothers who did all that.
12 This flood in which they sank the dignity of the occupation.
13 This flood rekindled in us life, it brought back to us
14 pride and dignity...

Let's talk about what is most important and more urgent.
My Brothers, al-Aqsa is the trust of Mohammad,
the place from which he ascended and traveled to.
Al-Aqsa is the trust of our master Omar who got its keys
and walked half the way to it.
It is the trust of Saladin who liberated it.
It is the trust of Sultan Abdulhamid who protected it.
So it is our duty today. Our duty is much bigger than
what I have said previously.
Allah will ask everyone. He will ask the rulers of the Ummah,
will ask the kings and princesses and the presidents
and the leaders,
He will ask the leaders of Islamic, national movements,
He will ask everyone, He will ask the scholars.
This is the time for the Ummah to get involved
in the battle we fight with them.
Abdullah Azam, that martyr, the leader, he is a Palestinian,
but he moved to Afghanistan
and made it the Ummah's struggle.
Where is the Jurist who would issue a decree obligating
for every Muslim, male and female, to fight in Palestine
What are you waiting for? To lose al-Aqsa,
to see it demolished,
for the synagogue to be built, for the temple to be built?

Constructing collective identity

Mashal begins his speech by designating the audience he is addressing: "My brothers and sisters, my folks, and people in this Ummah" (line 1). This opening immediately serves to establish a shared identity among his listeners, positioning them as part of the global Islamic community (Ummah). The use of *inclusive pronouns* like "my" and collective terms like "brothers and sisters" is a powerful discursive technique that fosters a sense of belonging and unity. This linguistic strategy is crucial in discursive psychology, as it helps to align individual identities with a collective cause, thereby framing personal actions as contributions to a broader communal effort (Fairclough, 1992). Most importantly, by addressing only those who share his collective identity, the speaker excludes the people who are not part of this group. This exclusion is a powerful technique to supress anticipated opposition to both the attacks and the subsequent construction of these attacks.

The repetition of the phrase "your brothers and sisters" (lines 2 and 11) further reinforces this collective identity. Here, Mashal connects the audience directly to the actions of Hamas fighters on 7th October, suggesting that the militants' deeds represent the will of the entire Ummah. This collectivization minimizes individual agency and differences, instead emphasizing collective action and accountability. By framing the fighters as representative of the audience's own identity, Mashal effectively dissolves the boundary between the militant group and the broader population, constructing a shared identity rooted in religious and ideological solidarity. It underscores the idea that the actions of a few are reflective of a broader communal obligation, making it more difficult for the audience to dissociate from the violence or the cause it is meant to serve.

The title "flood of al-Aqsa" (lines 4 and 12) serves as another key discursive device in constructing collective identity. This name, given by Hamas to their attack, refers to the large-scale mobilization to defend the al-Aqsa Mosque in Jerusalem – a significant religious site for Muslims – from the Jews, who want to destroy it or build a synagogue on that ground. By invoking the metaphor of a "flood," Mashal not only evokes a sense of an overwhelming, unstoppable force but also frames the actions of Hamas as a natural, spontaneous, justified, and almost inevitable response to the perceived desecration of a sacred site. Describing the militants' actions as a "flood" further reinforces the idea that these actions are not isolated or individual but part of a broader, divinely sanctioned mission. Moreover, this title is designed to mobilise support, as it taps into deep-seated religious narratives that resonate with the audience's sense of self and community.

Legitimizing aggression through religious and historical references

Mashal's speech is rich in *religious and historical references*, which serve to legitimize Hamas's actions by placing them within a broader sacred narrative. By invoking revered Islamic figures like Mohammad, Omar, Saladin, and Sultan Abdulhamid (lines 16-21), Mashal positions Hamas's actions as a continuation of a legacy of defending Islam and its holy sites. This discursive strategy aligns current events with revered Islamic traditions, making it difficult for the audience to question or oppose the actions being advocated.

The reference to al-Aqsa Mosque as "the trust of Mohammad" and other Islamic leaders establishes a direct link between the past and present, suggesting that the current conflict is a fulfilment of religious duty and historical destiny. This elevates the stakes of the conflict and frames it as a sacred obligation, thus creating a moral imperative that discourages dissent or inaction. In discursive psychology, such references are a way to construct a narrative of inevitability, making it appear as though the actions being taken are the only legitimate course of action available (van Dijk, 1998).

Moreover, by positioning al-Aqsa as a trust given to the Ummah, Mashal transfers the responsibility of its protection from Hamas to the entire Muslim community. This rhetorical move broadens the scope of the conflict, implicating all Muslims in the struggle and thereby amplifying the sense of urgency and duty among the audience. The speech constructs Hamas's actions not just as political or military but as a divine obligation that the audience is morally and religiously bound to support (Wodak & Meyer, 2009).

Moral imperatives and rhetorical questions

Mashal's use of *rhetorical questions* (lines 36-38) is a key discursive strategy designed to provoke reflection and action from the audience. Questions like "What are you waiting for? To lose al-Aqsa?"

serve to challenge the audience's commitment and loyalty. These rhetorical questions are not seeking answers; instead, they function as discursive tools that reinforce the urgency of the situation and the necessity of immediate action. By asking these questions, Mashal shifts the responsibility for the outcome of the conflict onto the audience, making them complicit in the future of al-Aqsa.

In discursive psychology, rhetorical devices such as these are understood as ways to construct and manage accountability. By posing these questions, Mashal creates a discursive environment where inaction is equated with betrayal, effectively closing off any alternative courses of action. The implication is clear: the only acceptable responses are those that align with Hamas's objectives, thereby framing the conflict as a zero-sum game where the only outcomes are victory or religious and moral failure (Fairclough, 1992).

The repetition of "Allah will ask everyone" (lines 24-28) further intensifies the moral pressure on the audience. This statement is not merely a religious assertion; it is a discursive construction that frames the conflict as a test of faith, where each individual will be held accountable by divine judgment. This strategy serves to mobilize the audience by tapping into their religious beliefs and fears, making the call to action not just a political or social imperative but a religious duty that cannot be ignored.

Emotional and psychological engagement

Khalid Mashal's speech is carefully constructed to evoke strong emotional responses, particularly feelings of pride, fear, and religious duty. The phrase "rekindled in us life, it brought back to us pride and dignity" (line 13) is designed to evoke a sense of empowerment and resurgence among the audience. This emotional appeal is a key component of the speech's effectiveness, as it aligns the audience's emotional responses with the goals of Hamas.

In discursive psychology, emotions are understood as products of social interactions and language use, rather than purely internal experiences. Mashal constructs emotions such as pride and fear to serve specific social and political functions. By framing the conflict as a battle for dignity and survival, Mashal taps into deep-seated emotional currents that resonate with the audience's sense of identity and moral values. This emotional engagement is crucial for sustaining support and ensuring continued commitment to the cause.

The construction of emotions like pride and fear reinforces the collective identity established earlier in the speech, creating a unified and emotionally charged community ready to act in defence of al-Aqsa and the broader Islamic nation. This use of emotional appeals is a common discursive strategy in political and militant rhetoric, as it helps to solidify group cohesion and motivate collective action (Chilton, 2004).

The role of historical continuity and appeals to authority

Throughout the speech, Mashal employs *historical continuity* and *appeals to religious authority* as central and powerful discursive strategies. By referencing figures like Saladin and Sultan Abdulhamid, he positions Hamas as the rightful heirs to a long tradition of defending Islamic holy sites. This appeal to authority not only legitimises Hamas's actions but also frames them as part of an inevitable and divinely sanctioned historical process.

Discursive psychology highlights the importance of such appeals in constructing narratives of inevitability and moral certainty. By framing the current conflict as a continuation of historical struggles, Mashal diminishes the perceived agency of the audience and suggests that there is only one correct course of action – supporting Hamas. This discursive move effectively reduces the space for dissent and increases the likelihood of collective action, as the audience is positioned not as passive observers but as active participants in a divine and historical mission (Wodak & Meyer, 2009).

Conclusion

Khalid Mashal's speech on 10th October 2023 demonstrates the power of language in constructing collective identities, legitimizing violent actions, and mobilizing support within the context of the Israeli-Palestinian conflict. Using inclusive/exclusive language, religious and historical references, rhetorical questions, and emotional appeals, Mashal effectively constructs a narrative that aligns his audience with the goals of Hamas and presents the attacks as glorious acts.

The speech creates a shared identity, evokes strong emotional responses, and frames the conflict as a moral and religious duty. This discursive approach highlights the power of language in shaping social reality and influencing behaviour. It offers valuable insights into the mechanisms through which militant groups like Hamas mobilize support and sustain their cause in a deeply divided and conflict-ridden region.

Benjamin Netanyahu's account

Prime Minister Benjamin Netanyahu's speech following the Hamas attack on 7th October 2023 is a sophisticated example of political rhetoric designed to unify the Israeli public, construct a clear enemy, and justify military action. Through various discursive techniques, Netanyahu carefully crafts a narrative that frames the situation as a dire, existential threat while also positioning the Israeli state and its people as morally justified in their response.

EXTRACT 7.3. SPEECH BY PRIME MINISTER BENJAMIN NETANYAHU FOLLOWING THE HAMAS ATTACK (7 OCTOBER 2023).

Dear citizens of Israel,
This morning, on Shabbat and a holiday,
Hamas invaded Israeli territory and murdered
innocent citizens including children and the elderly.

Hamas has started a brutal and evil war.
We will be victorious in this war despite an unbearable price.
This is a very difficult day for all of us.
Hamas wants to murder us all.
This is an enemy that murders children and mothers
in their homes, in their beds,
an enemy that abducts the elderly, children, and young women,
that slaughters and massacres our citizens, including
children, who simply went out to enjoy the holiday.
What happened today is unprecedented in Israel –
and I will see to it that it does not happen again.
The entire government is behind this decision.
The IDF will immediately use all its strength
to destroy Hamas's capabilities.
We will destroy them, and we will forcefully avenge this dark day
that they have forced on the State of Israel and its citizens.
As Bialik wrote: "Revenge for the blood of a little child
has yet been devised by Satan."
All of the places in which Hamas is deployed, hiding, and
operating, that wicked city, we will turn them into rubble.
I say to the residents of Gaza: Leave now
because we will operate forcefully everywhere.
At this hour, the IDF is clearing the terrorists out of
the last communities.
They are going community by community, house by house,
and are restoring our control.
I embrace and send heartfelt condolences
to the bereaved families whose loved ones were murdered
today in cold blood and endless brutality.
We are all praying for the well-being of the wounded
and all those who are being held hostage.
I say to Hamas: You are responsible for their well-being.
Israel will settle accounts with anyone who harms
one hair on their heads.
I appeal to the residents of the south: We all stand alongside
you. We are all proud of your heroism and your fighting.

To our beloved IDF soldiers, police officers,
and security forces personnel, remember that you are
the continuation of the heroes of the Jewish people,
of Joshua, Judah Maccabee, and the heroes of 1948
and of all of Israel's wars.
You are now fighting for the home and future of
us all. We are all with you. We all love you. We all salute you.
To the medical and rescue teams, and the many volunteers
who came out in force in a long list of locations today,
the people of Israel salute you. With your spirit,
we will overcome our enemies.
Today, I spoke with US President Biden and
with other world leaders in order to ensure freedom of action
for Israel in the continuation of the campaign.
I thank President Biden for his strong and clear words.
I thank the President of France, the Prime Minister of
Great Britain, and many other leaders for their
unreserved support for Israel.
I now appeal to all citizens of Israel.
We stand together in this campaign.
This war will take time. It will be difficult.
Challenging days are ahead of us.
However, I can promise one thing: With the help of G-d,
the forces that we all have in common, and
our faith in the Eternal One of Israel, we will win.

Constructing national identity and unity

Netanyahu opens his speech with the phrase "Dear citizens of Israel" (line 1), immediately establishing a collective identity that includes himself and his audience within a unified national group. The use of the collective "we" throughout the speech, such as in "We will be victorious in this war despite an unbearable price" (line 6), serves as a discursive tool to foster a sense of solidarity and shared purpose. By repeatedly using the pronouns "we" and "our," Netanyahu blurs the line between the speaker and the audience, creating a collective "us" that stands in opposition to the external threat posed by Hamas (Billig, 1995).

These collective pronouns function as what Sacks (1992) describes as *membership categorization devices*. They categorise individuals into groups – in this case, Israeli citizens and their government – who are portrayed as united against a common enemy. This categorization is essential for rallying public support, as it delineates clear boundaries between the in-group (Israelis) and the out-group (Hamas). This technique not only strengthens internal solidarity but also serves to legitimize the government's actions by presenting them as a collective will of the people.

Constructing the enemy

Netanyahu constructs Hamas as a clear and morally unequivocal enemy through the use of *emotionally charged language*. Phrases like "Hamas invaded Israeli territory and murdered innocent citizens including children and the elderly" (lines 3-4) and "Hamas has started a brutal and evil war" (line 5) exemplify *othering*, where the out-group (Hamas) is depicted as fundamentally different and morally corrupt compared to the in-group (Israelis). By using words like "brutal," "evil," and "murder," Netanyahu not only demonises Hamas but also justifies the need for a strong military response.

The strategic repetition of graphic and emotive descriptions of Hamas's actions – such as "murders children and mothers in their homes, in their beds" (lines 9-10), "abducts the elderly, children, and young women" (line 11), and "slaughters and massacres our citizens" (line 12) – serves to evoke strong emotional responses from the audience, including fear, anger, and moral outrage. This aligns with Potter's concept of action orientation, where the speaker's language is deliberately crafted to justify and motivate specific actions – in this case, military retaliation against Hamas.

Moreover, Netanyahu's statement, "What happened today is unprecedented in Israel – and I will see to it that it does not happen again" (lines 14-15), employs *extreme case formulation*. This technique emphasizes the uniqueness and severity of the situation, underscoring the necessity of a decisive response. By framing the events as unprecedented, Netanyahu elevates the stakes, making the audience more likely to support extraordinary measures to prevent such occurrences in the future.

Justifying military attacks

Netanyahu constructs a narrative that justifies military action as both a moral imperative and a defensive necessity. His declaration that "The IDF will immediately use all its strength to destroy Hamas's capabilities" (lines 17-18) is framed as a necessary response to the "dark day" that Hamas has "forced on the State of Israel and its citizens" (lines 19-20). The invocation of Bialik's quote, "[No such revenge –] revenge for the blood of a little child – has yet been devised by Satan" (lines 21-22), serves as a powerful cultural reference that resonates with the collective memory of the Israeli people, framing the military response as not only justified but righteous.

This approach aligns with Wetherell and Potter's (1988) concept of *interpretative repertoires*, where the speaker draws on culturally resonant narratives to frame the current situation within a broader moral and historical context. By invoking the concept of revenge, Netanyahu taps into deep-seated cultural and historical narratives that frame the military response as not just a strategic necessity but a moral obligation.

The use of phrases like "We will destroy them and we will forcefully avenge this dark day" (line 19) and "We will turn them into rubble" (line 24) exemplifies the discursive device of militaristic rhetoric, where language is used to normalize and legitimize violence as a necessary and justified response. This rhetoric serves to align the audience's emotional response with the political and military objectives of the state, making the idea of violent retribution not only acceptable but expected.

Invoking historical and religious narratives

Netanyahu's speech is deeply embedded in historical and religious narratives, which serve to elevate the current conflict to a broader, almost existential struggle. By referencing figures like Joshua, Judah Maccabee, and the heroes of 1948 (line 44), Netanyahu taps into the collective memory of Israel's historical struggles and triumphs. This use of intertextuality, where the speaker draws on existing texts and narratives, gives greater meaning to the present situation, framing it as part of a continuous historical and religious struggle.

The appeal to divine support – "With the help of G-d, the forces that we all have in common, and our faith in the Eternal One of Israel, we will win" (lines 63-65) – further amplifies the stakes of the conflict, framing it not just as a political or military struggle, but as one with religious and moral dimensions. This aligns with Wetherell and Potter's (1988) concept of *interpretative repertoires*, where certain discourses are used to frame events within culturally resonant narratives. By invoking religious faith, Netanyahu strengthens the moral justification for military action and appeals to the deep-seated religious beliefs of his audience.

Netanyahu skilfully manages issues of accountability and responsibility throughout his speech. By directly holding Hamas responsible for the well-being of hostages – "You are responsible for their well-being" (line 36) – Netanyahu shifts the burden of responsibility onto Hamas, framing any future harm to hostages as a result of Hamas's actions rather than Israel's military response. This is an example of the discursive device of attribution of blame, where responsibility is assigned in a way that supports the speaker's narrative and justifies subsequent actions.

Moreover, Netanyahu's expression of gratitude to international leaders for their "unreserved support for Israel" (line 58) serves both to bolster the legitimacy of Israel's actions and to share the moral and political responsibility with Israel's allies. This strategy can be seen as a form of rhetorical alignment, where the speaker seeks to align his position with that of influential others to strengthen his own stance.

Netanyahu also employs *temporal framing* as a discursive technique to manage expectations and prepare the audience for the prolonged nature of the conflict. Phrases like "This war will take time. It will be difficult. Challenging days are ahead of us" (lines 61-62) serve to frame the conflict as an ongoing and inevitable process, thereby managing the audience's expectations about the duration and intensity of the military response. This technique of future projection (Fairclough, 2003) helps to prepare the public for the challenges ahead while reinforcing the notion that the current course of action is both necessary and unavoidable.

Conclusion

Netanyahu's speech following the Hamas attack is a carefully constructed piece of political rhetoric that employs a wide range of discursive techniques to construct a narrative of victimization, moral righteousness, and military justification. Through the use of collective pronouns, emotionally charged language, historical and religious references, and strategic attribution of blame, Netanyahu constructs a powerful narrative that aligns the audience's emotions and beliefs with the political and military objectives of the Israeli state.

This analysis demonstrates how discursive psychology can provide valuable insights into the ways in which language is used to shape perceptions, justify actions, influence emotions, and mobilize collective identities in times of crisis. By focusing on the performative aspects of language, discursive psychology reveals the complex interplay between discourse, power, and social action in political communication. It also allows us to understand human behaviour in a more comprehensive way.

The US President's account of October 7th attack

President Joe Biden's speech on 10th October 2023, following the terrorist attacks in Israel, exemplifies the effective use of language in political discourse to construct realities, evoke emotions, and shape public perceptions during crises. This analysis explores the discursive strategies Biden employed to frame the events, establish moral boundaries, mobilize international and domestic support, and reaffirm alliances. Through these techniques, Biden effectively communicates a clear stance, aligning the United States with Israel against terrorism while justifying the actions taken in response to the attacks.

EXTRACT 7.4. REMARKS BY PRESIDENT BIDEN ON THE TERRORIST ATTACKS IN ISRAEL; THE WHITE HOUSE, 10 OCTOBER 2023.

Good afternoon. You know, there are moments in this life – and I mean this literally – when the pure, unadulterated evil is unleashed on this world. The people of Israel lived through one such moment this weekend. The bloody hands of the terrorist organization Hamas – a group whose stated purpose for being is to kill Jews. This was an act of sheer evil. More than 1,000 civilians slaughtered – not just killed, slaughtered – in Israel. Among them, at least 14 American citizens killed. Parents butchered using their bodies to try to protect their children. Stomach-turning reports of being – babies being killed. Entire families slain. Young people massacred while attending a musical festival to celebrate peace – to celebrate peace. Women raped, assaulted, paraded as trophies. Families hid their fear for hours and hours, desperately trying to keep their children quiet to avoid drawing attention. And thousands of wounded, alive but carrying with them the bullet holes and the shrapnel wounds and the memory of what they endured.

You all know these traumas never go away.

There are still so many families desperately waiting to hear the fate of their loved ones, not knowing if they're alive or dead or hostages.

Infants in their mothers' arms, grandparents in wheelchairs, Holocaust survivors abducted and held hostage – hostages whom Hamas has now threatened to execute in violation of every code of human morality.

It's abhorrent.

The brutality of Hamas – this bloodthirstiness – brings to mind the worst – the worst rampages of ISIS.

This is terrorism.

But sadly, for the Jewish people, it's not new.

This attack has brought to the surface painful memories and the scars left by a millennia of antisemitism and genocide of the Jewish people.

So, in this moment, we must be crystal clear: We stand with Israel. We stand with Israel. And we will make sure Israel has what it needs to take care of its citizens, defend itself, and respond to this attack.

There is no justification for terrorism. There is no excuse.

Hamas does not stand for the Palestinian people's right to dignity and self-determination. Its stated purpose is the annihilation of the State of Israel and the murder of Jewish people.

They use Palestinian civilians as human shields.

Hamas offers nothing but terror and bloodshed with no regard to who pays the price.

The loss of innocent life is heartbreaking.

Like every nation in the world, Israel has the right to respond – indeed has a duty to respond – to these vicious attacks.

I just got off the phone with – the third call with Prime Minister Netanyahu. And I told him if the United States experienced what Israel is experiencing, our response would be swift, decisive, and overwhelming.

We also discussed how democracies like Israel and the United States are stronger and more secure when we act according to the rule of law. Terrorists purpo- purposefully target civilians, kill them. We uphold the laws of war – the law of war. It matters. There's a difference.

Today, Americans across the country are praying for all those families that have been ripped apart. A lot of us know how it feels. It leaves a black hole in your chest when you lose family, feeling like you're being sucked in. The anger, the pain, the sense of hopelessness. This is what they mean by a "human tragedy" – an atrocity on an appalling scale.

But we're going to s- – continue to stand united, supporting the people of Israel who are suffering unspeakable losses and opposing the hatred and violence of terrorism.

My team has been in near constant communication with our Israeli partners and partners all across the region and the world from the moment this crisis began.

We're surging additional military assistance, including ammunition and interceptors to replenish Iron Dome.

We're going to make sure that Israel does not run out of these critical assets to defend its cities and its citizens.

My administration has consulted closely with Congress throughout this crisis. And when Congress returns, we're going to ask them to take urgent action to fund the national security requirements of our critical partners.

This is not about party or politics. This is about the security of our world, the security of the United States of America.

We now know that American citizens are among those being held by Hamas.

I've directed my team to share intelligence and deploy additional experts from across the United States government to consult with and advise the Israeli counterparts on hostage recover- – recovery efforts, because as president I have no higher priority than the safety of Americans being held hostage around the world.

The United States has also enhanced our military force posture in the region to strengthen our deterrence.

The Department of Defense has moved the USS Gerald R. Ford

Carrier Strike Group to the Eastern Mediterranean and bolstered our fighter aircraft presence. And we stand ready to move in additional assets as needed.

Let me say again – to any country, any organization, anyone thinking of taking advantage of this situation, I have one word: Don't. Don't.

Our hearts may be broken, but our resolve is clear.

Yesterday, I also spoke with the leaders of France, Germany, Italy, and the UK to discuss the latest developments with our European allies and coordinate our united response. This comes on top of days of steady engagement with partners across the region.

We're also taking steps at home. In cities across the United States of America, police departments have stepped up security around centers for – of Jewish life. And the Department of Homeland Security and the Federal Bureau of Investigation are working closely with state and local law enforcement and Jewish community partners to identify and disrupt any domestic threat that could emerge in connection with these horrific attacks.

This is a moment for the United States to come together, to grieve with those who are mourning.

Let's be real clear: There is no place for hate in America – not against Jews, not against Muslims, not against anybody. We reject – we reject – what we reject is terrorism. We condemn the indiscriminate evil, just as we've always done.

That's what America stands for.

You know, just over 50 years ago – I was thinking about it this morning, talking with the Secretary of State, the Vice President in my office and – over 50 years ago, as a young senator, I visited Israel for the first time, as a newly elected senator. And I had a long, long trip – or meeting with Golda Meir in her office just before the Yom Kippur War. And I guess she could see the consternation on my face as she described what was being faced – they were facing. We walked outside in that – that sort of hallway outside her office to have some photos. She looked at me and w- – all of a sudden and said, "Would you like to have a photograph?” And so, I got up and followed her out. We were standing there silent, looking at the press. She could tell, I guess, I was concerned. She leaned over and whispered to me – she said, “Don’t worry, Senator Biden. We have a secret weapon here in Israel” – my word this is what she said – “We have no place else to go.” “We have no place else to go.”

For 75 years, Israel has stood as the ultimate guarantor of security of Jewish people around the world so that the atrocities of the past could never happen again.

And let there be no doubt: The United States has Israel’s back. We will make sure the Jewish and democratic State of Israel can defend itself today, tomorrow, as we always have. It’s as simple as that.

These atrocities have been sickening.

We’re – we’re with Israel. Let’s make no mistake.

Thank you.

Constructing a narrative of good vs. evil

From the very beginning, Biden sets up a stark dichotomy between good and evil, framing the situation as a battle between these two forces. The phrase “pure, unadulterated evil” (line 3) is not just a description but a powerful discursive formulation that immediately positions Hamas as the embodiment of evil. This binary framing simplifies the complexity of the conflict, making it easier for the audience to understand what has been happening and take a definitive stance. In times of conflict, such clear-cut narratives are crucial for rallying public support, as they create a moral clarity that justifies subsequent actions.

The choice of words like “slaughtered,” “butchered,” and “massacred” (lines 9, 11, 14) further intensifies the portrayal of Hamas as the embodiment of evil. These terms are not neutral; they are emotionally charged and designed to elicit a visceral reaction from the audience. By using such graphic language, Biden not only highlights the brutality of the attacks but also dehumanizes the perpetrators, positioning them as monstrous figures who are beyond redemption. This strategic dehumanization serves to reinforce the moral divide between Hamas and the victims, thereby justifying the need for a strong, retaliatory response.

Moreover, by repeatedly emphasizing the innocence of the victims – children, parents, the elderly – Biden constructs a narrative where the victims are wholly blameless and undeserving of their fate. This innocence stands in stark contrast to the portrayed evil of Hamas, further entrenching the binary opposition between good and evil. Such a narrative simplifies the moral landscape, making it easier for the public to align with Biden's stance and support the proposed actions.

Evoking historical and cultural trauma

Biden's speech skilfully connects the present-day events to historical traumas experienced by the Jewish people, such as antisemitism, genocide, and the Holocaust (lines 34-37). By doing so, he situates the current attacks within a broader historical narrative of Jewish suffering and resilience. This strategy both evokes empathy and solidarity with Israel and frames the conflict as part of a long-standing struggle against existential threats to the Jewish people.

The mention of Holocaust survivors being abducted by Hamas (line 27) is a particularly powerful discursive move. It serves to draw a direct line between the atrocities of the Holocaust and the present actions of Hamas, reinforcing the idea that the Jewish people are once again facing an existential threat. This connection between past and present not only heightens the emotional impact of the speech but also legitimizes Israel's right to defend itself. It suggests that the failure to act would be tantamount to allowing history to repeat itself.

Furthermore, by referencing these historical traumas, Biden appeals to a collective memory that is deeply ingrained in the consciousness of not only the Jewish community but also the global audience. This collective memory is a powerful tool in political rhetoric, as it taps into shared experiences and emotions, making the current situation more relatable and urgent. By framing the current conflict as a continuation of this historical struggle, Biden strengthens the moral imperative to support Israel and take decisive action against Hamas.

Establishing moral boundaries and justifying action

Throughout his speech, Biden draws clear moral boundaries, categorizing Hamas as a "terrorist organization" whose actions are "abhorrent" and "bloodthirsty" (lines 30-33). This categorization is crucial in constructing a moral hierarchy where Hamas is positioned at the very bottom, as a universally recognized evil. By labelling Hamas as terrorists, Biden appeals to a global consensus that views terrorism as an indefensible act, thereby justifying the need for a strong and immediate response.

The assertion that "Israel has the right to respond" (line 50) frames Israel's military actions as both a moral imperative and a legal right. Biden strengthens this justification by drawing a parallel to how the United States would respond if faced with a similar situation: "Our response would be swift, decisive, and overwhelming" (lines 54-55). This comparison signals unwavering support for Israel while normalising the idea of military retaliation as a necessary and appropriate response to terrorism.

The use of rhetorical devices, such as repetition of phrases (line 38-39), serves to reinforce the moral clarity of the situation. These repetitions act as a discursive tool to eliminate any potential ambiguity or dissent, making it clear that there is only one morally acceptable stance. By drawing such definitive moral boundaries, Biden effectively precludes any alternative narratives that might question the legitimacy of Israel's response.

Mobilizing support and solidarity

In addition to condemning the attacks, Biden's speech serves as a call to action. He emphasizes the United States' commitment to providing military assistance to Israel, ensuring that it has the resources needed to defend itself (lines 73-80). This appeal is carefully crafted to resonate with both domestic and international audiences, positioning the United States as a leader in the global fight against terrorism.

The invocation of shared values, particularly the rule of law (lines 56-60), serves to align Israel's actions with those of the United States and other democracies. By framing the conflict within the context of democratic values and international law, Biden seeks to garner broader support from the international community. This framing also positions Israel as a state that upholds these values, in contrast to Hamas, which is portrayed as violating every code of human morality.

Biden also makes a direct appeal to unity by stating, "This is not about party or politics. This is about the security of our world, the security of the United States of America" (lines 81-82). This statement is a strategic move to depoliticize the issue and frame it as a matter of national and global security. By doing so, Biden aims to rally bipartisan support and present a united front, both domestically and internationally.

Personalizing the tragedy and building emotional resonance

Biden personalizes the tragedy by vividly describing the victims' experiences, such as families hiding in fear, parents sacrificing themselves to protect their children, and the anguish of those awaiting news of their loved ones (lines 17-25). This personalization makes the abstract concept of terrorism more tangible and relatable, thereby increasing the emotional impact of the speech.

The reference to his own experiences and expressed empathy (lines 61-66) further humanize Biden and allow him to connect with the audience on a personal level. By acknowledging the pain and grief felt by those affected, Biden positions himself not just as a leader but as a fellow mourner, sharing in the collective sorrow.

Reaffirming long-standing alliances

Finally, Biden reaffirms the United States' long-standing alliance with Israel (lines 137-143), emphasizing that this relationship is built on shared values and a commitment to ensuring the security of the Jewish people. The anecdote about his meeting with Golda Meir and her statement, "We have no place else to go" (lines 124-136), is a powerful reminder of Israel's historical significance as a safe haven for Jews. This story not only reinforces the moral imperative to support Israel but also serves to highlight Biden's personal connection to the country and its leaders. Finally, it reinforces the idea that Israel's survival is not just a geopolitical issue but a moral imperative rooted in the lessons of history.

By reaffirming the United States' support for Israel, Biden solidifies the alliance and sends a clear message to the international community that the US will continue to stand by its ally, regardless of the challenges ahead. This reassurance is crucial for maintaining global support and ensuring that Israel has the backing it needs to navigate the crisis.

Conclusion

President Biden's speech following the October 2023 terrorist attacks in Israel is a carefully crafted, important piece of political rhetoric that employs a wide range of discursive strategies to construct a narrative, evoke emotions, and mobilize support. Through the use of binary framing, historical references, moral boundary-setting, and emotional resonance, Biden effectively communicates the gravity of the situation and the necessity of a strong, united response.

This analysis illustrates how language is used not only to convey information but also to shape perceptions, influence public opinion, and legitimize political actions during times of crisis. By examining the discursive strategies employed in Biden's speech, we gain a deeper understanding of how political leaders use rhetoric to navigate complex situations, build consensus, and mobilize support in the face of adversity. In doing so, we see how discourse is not merely a reflection of reality but an active force in shaping it, with profound implications for both domestic and international politics.

Testimony of a hostage

The psychological impact of being taken hostage in conflict situations can be profound and enduring, often introduced as resulting in severe trauma that shapes the survivor's perception of the event and their subsequent coping mechanisms. However, as I have emphasised before, previous studies have shown that the majority of people do not develop lasting pathological reactions as a result of traumatic events. Understanding how individuals construct their traumatic experience and the events around it can help us understand why and how some manage to maintain their psychological equilibrium while others suffer from mental disorders. Furthermore, analysing the influential narratives of first-hand victims – those whose testimonies are likely to shape public appraisal of the conflict – can help use predict the trajectory of the conflict itself. The narrative of Mia Schem, a 21-year-old Israeli woman who was captured by Hamas militants during an attack on a music festival, provides a raw and vivid account of such an experience.

Schem's testimony not only highlights the physical dangers she faced but also reveals the intense psychological stress and fear that accompany such life-threatening situations. Her narrative offers valuable insight into the cognitive and emotional processes that occur during moments of extreme duress, including immediate responses to violence, the strategies employed to survive, and the pervasive fear of further harm.

In the extract below, Schem recounts the harrowing moments during her escape attempt, the subsequent injury she suffered, and her interactions with her captors. This account serves as a critical source for understanding the psychological dynamics at play in hostage situations and the ways in which individuals navigate such overwhelming experiences.

EXTRACT 7.5. TESTIMONY OF MIA SCHEM, 29 DECEMBER 2023, ISRAELI TV CHANNEL 13 NEWS. (I = INTERVIEWER, S = MIA SCHEM)

I: Uh, Mia, can you tell us about your experience
at the Nova festival?
S: I went with my best friend Elia to the Nova festival.
From the moment we arrived,
I, I had a sinking feeling – (.) I couldn't enjoy myself.
Then, out of nowhere, terrorists started shooting at us,
murdering people.
Elia and I were among the first to escape.
We got in the car, and under immense pressure, I drove.
I: What happened next?
S: Suddenly, Elia yelled, "Mia, they are shooting!"
I floored it to bypass them, but then (.) they shot
the tires, and the car swayed to the right and stopped.
A pick-up truck full of Hamas terrorists passed us.
One of the terrorists looked at me (.) and shot me
in the arm.
My arm got totally detached (.) and I lost a ton of blood.
I picked up my arm from the floor and held it (.) and
stayed on the floor.
I: That sounds terrifying. What did you do next?
S: There was shooting, cars swaying to the right, to the left,
screeching tires, and men and women screaming.
I waited for the massacre to end.
Then it suddenly went quiet.
I saw a terrorist approaching.

He saw Elia, pointed his weapon at her, and screamed,
"Get up."
He tied her arms and took her.
They were checking the dead, and whoever looked alive
got shot in the head.
I: So, you pretended to be dead?
S: Yes. (.)
Elia's car blew up.
It was burning.
I realized that the fire was closing in on me, the entire
area was on fire.
I looked for a way out, but there was no escape.
Then, suddenly, I saw the road, and there was some guy
walking around the burnt cars.
I yelled, "Help," and he said, "Come" (.) (in Arabic: "Taaly").
I didn't know if he was Israeli; I hoped he was.
He said, "Come" (Taaly).
It was a split-second decision – should I stay there and
burn to death (.) or go with him?
I thought to myself, I don't want to die; I want to live.
I: So you went with him?
S: Yes, I went with him.
He held my arm and then started to touch me –
touching my upper body [points to her chest].
I started screaming and getting hysterical.
He realized my arm was detached from my body.
I guess it startled him, so he paused for a second and
called to a car nearby to come and take me.
Another terrorist then pulled me into the car by my hair
and kept my head lowered the entire ride.
I arrived in Gaza.
I: What did you experience in Gaza?
S: There are no innocent civilians there.
Families live under Hamas.
From the moment those children are born, they are
brainwashed to believe that Israel is Palestine and that

they must hate Jews.
I began asking myself questions: Why am I in a family
home?
Why are there children here?
Why is there a woman here?
I: That must have been very confusing and frightening.
S: Yes.
There was a terrorist who was watching me 24/7,
who was raping me with his eyes… an evil stare.
I was afraid of being raped.
It was my biggest fear there.

Mia Schem's narrative offers a unique window into the psychological and discursive processes that unfold during and after a traumatic event. As a 21-year-old Israeli woman who survived an attack by Hamas militants and was subsequently taken hostage, her story encapsulates the terror, confusion, and resilience experienced in life-threatening situations. This analysis aims to dissect her narrative through the lens of discursive psychology, a field that examines how psychological phenomena are constructed through language (Edwards & Potter, 1992).

Trauma narratives, especially those arising from conflict zones, provide critical insights into how individuals make sense of their experiences and communicate them to others. Schem's account is not just a record of events but a carefully constructed narrative that reflects her identity, moral positioning, and the broader socio-political context. By analysing her use of language, we can better understand the cognitive and emotional strategies she employs to cope with her ordeal. Moreover, we see how these strategies are shaped by and contribute to her identity as a survivor.

Imagery and sensory details

Schem's narrative is replete with vivid imagery and sensory details that serve to immerse the listener in her experience. For example, when she describes the onset of the attack, she says, "Out of nowhere, terrorists started shooting at us, murdering people" (lines 6-7). This phrase immediately conveys the sudden and chaotic nature of the event. The choice of words like "murdering" instead of a more neutral term like "killing" adds an emotional charge to the narrative, emphasizing the brutality of the attackers.

According to Edwards and Potter (1992), such vivid descriptions function to construct a particular version of reality that is compelling and difficult to dispute. The imagery Schem uses is not merely descriptive but serves to position her audience within the event, eliciting a strong emotional response. This aligns with discursive psychology's understanding of how language constructs social reality by shaping perceptions and emotional responses (Edwards, 1997).

Moreover, the inclusion of sensory details – such as the sound of "screeching tires" (line 22), the visual of a "pick-up truck full of Hamas terrorists" (line 14), and the physical sensation of her arm being "totally detached" (line 17) – amplifies the narrative's emotional impact. These sensory details do more than just convey information; they create a lived experience for the listener, allowing them to vicariously experience the terror and urgency of the situation. This technique of invoking sensory experience is discussed by Gergen (1994), who highlights how narratives that engage the senses are more likely to resonate with audiences and leave a lasting impact.

In trauma narratives, the use of sensory details often serves to convey the intensity of the experience and the profound psychological impact it has on the survivor. The description of physical pain and visual horror not only communicates the severity of the event but also the emotional and psychological scars it leaves behind. As Riessman (1993) notes, the inclusion of such details in trauma narratives often serves to legitimize the speaker's suffering and establish their credibility as a witness to extreme events.

Construction of victimhood and agency

One of the most striking aspects of Schem's narrative is how she navigates the roles of victim and agent. While she is clearly a victim of the attack and subsequent captivity, her narrative also emphasizes moments of agency, where she takes decisive action to survive. For instance, after being shot and losing her arm, she recounts, "I picked up my arm from the floor and held it and stayed on the floor" (line 18-19). This act of self-preservation, even in the face of severe injury, positions her not just as a passive victim but as an active participant in her own survival.

This duality of victimhood and agency is a common theme in trauma narratives, where individuals often oscillate between these roles as they make sense of their experiences. According to Wetherell and Potter (1992), this discursive strategy allows individuals to construct a more complex and resilient identity, one that acknowledges the harm done to them while also asserting their capacity for action. By emphasizing her agency in critical moments, Schem resists a purely victimized identity and instead presents herself as a survivor who actively fought for her life.

Furthermore, the construction of agency in the face of victimhood can also be seen as a coping mechanism. By focusing on the actions she took to survive, Schem may be attempting to regain a sense of control over her narrative and, by extension, her life. This aligns with research by Herman (1997), who argues that survivors of trauma often reconstruct their narratives to emphasize their agency as a way of reclaiming power and autonomy.

However, it is also important to note that Schem's agency is constructed within the constraints of her situation. Her decisions, such as whether to stay in the burning car or go with the man she hoped was Israeli, are framed by the extreme danger she faces. This highlights the concept of *bounded agency*, where individuals' actions are shaped by the limitations imposed by their circumstances (Hitlin & Elder, 2007). In this context, Schem's agency is not absolute but is instead a negotiation within the confines of her traumatic environment.

Managing accountability and moral positioning

Mia Schem's narrative also involves careful management of accountability, both for herself and her captors. When she describes the moment a terrorist shoots her, she says, "One of the terrorists looked at me and shot me in the arm" (lines 15-16). This straightforward account places the responsibility squarely on the perpetrator, without embellishment or editorializing. By presenting the act in this manner, Schem discursively constructs the terrorist as morally culpable, emphasizing the unprovoked and brutal nature of the violence.

This technique of managing accountability is crucial in trauma narratives, as it allows the speaker to delineate moral boundaries and assign blame. According to Billig (1991), the way individuals talk about their experiences often reflects broader moral and ideological positions. In Schem's case, her narrative positions the terrorists as the clear aggressors, thereby reinforcing her identity as an innocent victim of their actions.

Moreover, Schem's reflections on the broader context of her captivity in Gaza – for instance, where she asserts, "There are no innocent civilians there... they are brainwashed to believe that Israel is Palestine and that they must hate Jews" (lines 58-62) – further cement her moral positioning. By attributing broad culpability to the Gazan population, she not only justifies her own actions and decisions during captivity but also aligns herself with a larger ideological framework that views the conflict in stark moral terms.

This kind of moral positioning is a common discursive strategy in conflict narratives, where speakers often seek to justify their actions and experiences by situating them within a broader moral and ideological context. As van Dijk (1998) notes, the construction of in-groups and out-groups in discourse often involves attributing negative characteristics to the 'Other' while emphasizing the righteousness of one's own group. In Schem's narrative, this is achieved through the depiction of the Gazan population as uniformly hostile and indoctrinated, which serves to reinforce her moral and ideological stance.

However, this broad *attribution of blame* can also be seen as a way of coping with the trauma of her experience. By constructing the 'Other' as entirely malevolent, Schem may be seeking to make sense of the violence she endured and to place it within a framework that allows her to maintain a coherent sense of self. This is consistent with findings by Staub (1999), who argues that individuals who have experienced extreme violence often construct narratives that simplify the moral landscape in order to preserve their psychological well-being.

The role of repetition and emphasis

Repetition is a key discursive device in Schem's narrative, used to emphasize critical aspects of her experience and to convey the psychological impact of the trauma. For instance, when she reflects on her decision to leave the burning car with the man she hoped was Israeli, she repeats the thought, "I don't want to die; I want to live" (line 45). This repetition serves not only to emphasize her survival instinct but also to provide insight into the internal struggle she faced in making this life-or-death decision.

The use of repetition in trauma narratives is often indicative of the persistence of certain thoughts or feelings, which can be reflective of the psychological impact of the traumatic event. As Riessman (1993) notes, repetition in narratives can serve to underline the significance of particular moments or decisions, making them central to the speaker's construction of their experience. In Schem's case, the repeated emphasis on her desire to live highlights the fundamental human drive for survival, even in the direst circumstances.

Repetition also functions as a rhetorical device, creating a rhythm in the narrative that mirrors the cyclical nature of traumatic memory. According to Caruth (1995), traumatic memories are often characterized by their repetition and intrusion into the survivor's consciousness, reflecting the unresolved nature of the trauma. By repeating key phrases, Schem's narrative conveys the urgency of her experience and also reflects the lingering impact of the trauma on her psyche.

Furthermore, the repetition of certain phrases and themes in Schem's narrative may serve a social function, reinforcing the listener's understanding of her ordeal and eliciting empathy. Tannen (1989) discusses how repetition in conversation can create a sense of cohesion and shared understanding between speaker and listener, which is particularly important in trauma narratives where the speaker seeks validation and support. In this way, repetition helps to bridge the gap between Schem's experience and the audience's ability to comprehend and empathize with her situation.

The use of direct speech and internal dialogue

Direct speech and *internal dialogue* are prominent features of Schem's narrative, providing a window into her thought processes and emotional state during the events. For example, when she recounts the moment a terrorist approached her and her friend Elia, she uses direct speech: "He saw Elia, pointed his weapon at her, and screamed, 'Get up.'" (lines 26-27). This use of direct speech dramatizes the narrative, bringing the audience into the immediacy of the moment and highlighting the power dynamics between the captor and the captive.

Direct speech in narratives often serves to bring the voices of others into the speaker's account, creating a multi-voiced narrative that reflects the complexity of the social interactions (Wooffitt, 1992). In Schem's case, the direct speech of the terrorists not only conveys their aggression and authority but also underscores her own vulnerability and fear. The shift between Schem's voice and the voices of the terrorists creates a dialogical tension that mirrors the power struggle inherent in the situation.

Internal dialogue, on the other hand, provides insight into Schem's internal conflict and decision-making process. For instance, when she reflects on her choice to leave the burning car, she recalls thinking, "Should I stay there and burn to death or go with him?" (lines 43-44). This internal dialogue reveals the split-second nature of her decision and the extreme fear that motivated her actions. According to Hermans (2001), internal dialogue is a key feature of the dialogical self, where individuals engage in an internal conversation with different aspects of their identity or situation. In trauma narratives, internal dialogue often reflects the struggle to make sense of a chaotic and threatening environment.

The use of internal dialogue in Schem's narrative also serves to humanize her experience, allowing the audience to connect with her thought processes and emotions on a deeper level. By articulating her internal conflict, Schem invites the listener to empathize with her situation and to understand the complexity of the decisions she faced. This aligns with Bamberg's (2004) discussion of how narrative identity is constructed through the interplay of internal and external voices, where the speaker's internal dialogue plays a crucial role in shaping their self-presentation.

Moreover, the use of direct speech and internal dialogue highlights the relational aspects of Schem's narrative, where her identity is constructed in relation to others – both her captors and herself. This *relational construction of identity* is a central concern of discursive psychology, which emphasizes how individuals negotiate their identities through interaction with others (Potter & Wetherell, 1987). In Schem's narrative, this is evident in the way she navigates her interactions with the terrorists, using direct speech to convey their dominance and her internal dialogue to express her resistance and will to survive.

The construction of the 'Other'

Schem's narrative also engages in the *discursive construction of the Other*, particularly in her portrayal of the Hamas terrorists and the broader Gazan population. Her statement that "There are no innocent civilians there... they are brainwashed to believe that Israel is Palestine and that they must hate Jews" (lines 58-62) reflects a clear demarcation between "us" and "them," where the Other is constructed as inherently hostile and morally inferior.

The construction of the Other is a common discursive strategy in conflict narratives, where speakers often delineate clear boundaries between their own group and the opposing group to justify actions and make sense of the conflict. According to van Dijk (1998), such constructions are often rooted in broader ideological frameworks that position the in-group as morally superior and the out-group as dangerous or evil. In Schem's narrative, this construction serves to reinforce her identity as a victim of an unjust and brutal enemy while also aligning her experience with a broader ideological stance that views the conflict in stark moral terms.

This discursive construction of the Other can also be seen as a coping mechanism, where Schem seeks to make sense of the violence she endured by attributing it to the inherent characteristics of the Other. By framing the Gazan population as uniformly hostile and indoctrinated, she creates a simplified moral landscape that allows her to rationalize her experience and maintain a coherent sense of self. This is consistent with Staub's (1999) findings that individuals who have experienced extreme violence often construct narratives that emphasize the evil of the perpetrator as a way of preserving their psychological well-being.

However, it is also important to consider the implications of such constructions for the broader socio-political context. The portrayal of the Other as entirely malevolent can contribute to the perpetuation of conflict by reinforcing negative stereotypes and deepening divisions between groups. According to Tajfel and Turner's (1986) social identity theory, such constructions can lead to increased in-group cohesion at the expense of intergroup understanding and reconciliation. In Schem's case, her narrative not only reflects her personal experience but also contributes to the broader discourse of conflict, where the Other is dehumanized and positioned as a perpetual enemy.

Conclusion

Mia Schem's narrative offers a powerful example of how language actively constructs reality, identity, and moral positioning in the context of trauma and conflict. Through the use of vivid imagery, the balancing of victimhood and agency, the management of accountability, repetition, direct speech, and the construction of the Other, Schem's account provides rich material for discursive analysis. These techniques not only reveal how she makes sense of her traumatic experience but also how she communicates this experience to an audience, inviting them to share in her reality.

This analysis demonstrates the complexity of trauma narratives and the multiple layers of meaning that can be constructed through language. By examining Schem's narrative through the lens of discursive psychology, we gain deeper insights into the cognitive and emotional processes underlying her responses to extreme stress, as well as the broader social and ideological frameworks that shape her account.

Future research could further explore the intersection of individual trauma narratives with collective discourses of conflict, examining how personal stories both contribute to and are shaped by broader socio-political narratives. Additionally, there is a need for more comparative studies that analyse how different groups construct their identities and experiences in conflict situations, which could provide valuable insights into the dynamics of intergroup relations and the possibilities for reconciliation.

References

Bamberg, M. (2004). *Narrative Discourse and Identities. Narratives in Action.* John Benjamins Publishing.
Billig, M. (1991). *Ideology and Opinions: Studies in Rhetorical Psychology.* Sage.
Billig, M. (1995). *Banal Nationalism.* Sage.
Billig, M. (1996). *Arguing and Thinking: A Rhetorical Approach to Social Psychology.* Cambridge University Press.
Caruth, C. (1995). *Trauma: Explorations in Memory.* Johns Hopkins Uni.
Chilton, P. (2004). *Analysing Political Discourse: Theory and Practice.*

Edwards, D. (1997). *Discourse and Cognition.* Sage.

Edwards, D., & Potter, J. (1992). *Discursive Psychology.* Sage.

Fairclough, N. (1992). *Discourse and Social Change.* Polity Press.

Fairclough, N. (2003). *Analysing Discourse: Textual Analysis for Social Research.*

Gergen, K. J. (1994). *Realities and Relationships: Soundings in Social Construction.* Harvard University Press.

Goffman, E. (1974). *Frame analysis: An essay on the organization of experience.* Cambridge, MA: Harvard University Press.

Herman, J. L. (1997). *Trauma and Recovery: The Aftermath of Violence – From Domestic Abuse to Political Terror.* Basic Books.

Hermans, H. J. M. (2001). The Dialogical Self: Toward a Theory of Personal and Cultural Positioning. *Culture & Psychology, 7*(3), 243-281.

Hitlin, S., & Elder, G. H. (2007). Time, Self, and the Curiously Abstract Concept of Agency. *Sociological Theory, 25*(2), 170-191.

Pomerantz, A. (1986). Extreme case formulations: A way of legitimizing claims. *Human Studies, 9*, 219-229.

Potter, J. (1996). *Representing Reality: Discourse, Rhetoric and Social Construction.* Sage.

Potter, J., & Wetherell, M. (1987). *Discourse and Social Psychology: Beyond Attitudes and Behaviour.* Sage.

Riessman, C. K. (1993). *Narrative Analysis.* Sage.

Sacks, H. (1992). *Lectures on Conversation.* Blackwell.

Staub, E. (1999). *The Roots of Evil: The Origins of Genocide and Other Group Violence.* Cambridge University Press.

Tajfel, H., & Turner, J.C. (1986). The Social Identity Theory of Intergroup Behavior. In S. Worchel & W. G. Austin (Eds.), *Psychology of Intergroup Relations.* Nelson-Hall.

Tannen, D. (1989) *Talking Voices : Repetition, Dialogue, and Imagery in Conversational Discourse.* Cambridge University Press.

van Dijk, T. A. (1998). *Ideology: A multidisciplinary approach.* London, Sage.

van Dijk, T. A. (2000). *Ideology and Discourse: A Multidisciplinary Introduction.* Pompeu Fabra University.

Wetherell, M., & Potter, J. (1988). Discourse analysis and the identification of interpretive repertoires. In C. Antaki (Ed.), *Analysing everyday explanation: A casebook of methods* (pp. 168-183). Newbury Park: Sage.

Wodak, R., & Meyer, M. (Eds.). (2009). *Methods of critical discourse analysis* (2nd ed.). London: Sage.

Wooffitt, R. (1992). *Telling tales of the unexpected: the organization of factual discourse.* Hempstead: Harvester Wheatsheaf.

Chapter 8

Summary and final thoughts

The power of rhetoric in war

One of the most striking findings of our analysis is the diversity of accounts presented by different speakers for the same events, often revealing deliberate narrative manipulation as well as the importance of rhetorical formulations in relation to war. Political leaders, in particular, presented conflicting versions of events, tailored to serve their strategic interests and conceal specific facts while highlighting others or focusing on historical events. Some of these accounts contained illogical notions and fabrications.

The 2006 Lebanon-Israel war was constructed differently by the different political figures. Hezbollah's leader, Hassan Nasrallah, presented the unprovoked attack his militia waged as a legitimate and necessary resistance against Israeli aggression, emphasizing the defence of Lebanese sovereignty. He refused to accept responsibility for igniting the 2006 war. He omitted the fact that he did not consult with the legitimate Lebanese government. Fast-forward to 2024, the same person was still in power repeating the same rhetoric to justify the same acts until his assassination by Israel. Other Lebanese leaders, such as Walid Jumblatt, portrayed the conflict as a proxy war, driven by the interests of foreign powers, with Hezbollah acting as their tool, without providing solution. The same position has been repeated by Jumblatt and various Lebanese politicians within the 2023-ongoing war. Conversely, the leaders of Israel, both in 2006 and in 2024, framed their extensive military operations as legitimate self-defence, portraying their actions as retaliatory responses to attacks.

These contradictory accounts demonstrate how the same event can be constructed in entirely different ways to serve specific political purposes. And most importantly, they show how the construction of a war while it is ongoing affects the prospect for peace.

In Iraq, similar discursive patterns emerged during the 2003 invasion/liberation and subsequent civil conflict. Various influential speakers within Iraq constructed narratives that justified their involvement in the violence by appealing to sectarian or nationalist identities. Leaders from different sectarian groups often presented themselves as defenders of their communities while claiming to be patriots, even as they engaged in violence that further deepened divisions within Iraqi society. These narratives were not just reflections of the leaders' perspectives but were also actively constructed to mobilize support and legitimize their actions.

The 2023-present Gaza War further illustrated the use of selective narratives by the different sides. Israeli and Palestinian leaders provided opposing accounts of the same events, each side portraying itself as the victim and the other as the aggressor. Israeli leaders justified their military actions as necessary responses to terrorist threats, while Palestinian leaders depicted the Israeli actions as unjustified aggression against a besieged population. These conflicting narratives were crucial in shaping how each population understood the conflict and justified continued hostilities.

The complex and multifunctional discourses

The analysis of the speeches of decision-makers and laypeople shows that the different participants have constructed the armed conflicts and their personal experiences in the form of complex, realistic, coherent, and multifunctional discourses with various effects. To understand the meaning of any significant speech, it is essential to analyse it as a whole and identify its main message, the speaker's identity, the context, the details used as facts, and the rationale behind the talk.

The analysed discourses are rational in the sense that within each of the different accounts there is a sound argument that offers an explanation of the discussed events. They are realistic in the sense that they attend to realities that had occurred in the outside world, present them in a factual way, and can be corroborated. In doing so, the participants present themselves as aware of the nature and the scale of the wars' destructive consequences, and thus do not appear to be in a state of denial or negligence. These constructions are coherent, as the different components within each account are compatible with one another and with the overarching rationale of the discourse.

Moreover, each speaker invokes theoretical motivational notions, mainly positive, incorporating them into his or her account alongside a specific cluster of detailed descriptions of the negative events, presenting a meaningful narrative. Each of these accounts performs several discursive actions simultaneously, in particular, presenting the speaker and their group in a positive light, maintaining interaction, rejecting the actions of a particular side, highlighting the negative effects of the war, and presenting positive aspects and prospects.

Additionally, every narrative promotes a distinct stance on the war. A good example is Biden's speech in response to the October 7th attacks which casts Hamas as an inherently evil adversary that must be stopped by force. By presenting the acts of killing and kidnapping children and women as inherent to Hamas's ideology, where the primary goal is the annihilation of Jews, Biden frames the conflict in starkly binary terms: an "us versus them" divide. It is crucial to note that this speech did not emerge in isolation but responded to real events witnessed globally.

Hamas's leader also constructs the war between Israel and Hamas in binary terms: a war between evil Israelis who want to destroy Muslims' holy sites and the good Muslims who are defending them. He frames the attacks as a noble defence, pointedly ignoring the crimes committed by Hamas members and Palestinian attackers from Gaza against civilians – with many crimes documented in live videos by the attackers themselves, posted on social media and circulated through Hamas-affiliated and sympathetic media channels. This selective portrayal mirrors patterns observed in the discourse of the Iraq and Lebanon wars, which I have analysed in this book. In these discourses, leaders constructed specific versions of history, selectively emphasizing events that support their positions while omitting those that contradict them. This deliberate framing deepens divisions, reinforces in-group loyalty, and justifies actions by casting them as morally indispensable.

As examined throughout this book, these rhetorical formulations demonstrate how influential figures use selective memory and predictions of future events as powerful tools to shape public perception. Some rely on abstract or historical claims that overlook the immediate, impactful realities experienced by their audiences, while others address specific on-the-ground details to bolster their stances. This strategic emphasis – or omission – of information is instrumental in drawing clear allegiances and creating an "us vs. them" divide.

Ultimately, these strategies reveal that war narratives do not merely recount events but actively construct identities, allegiances, and calls to action. Through calculated selection and omission, each narrative channels public sentiment, validates specific actions, and drives collective responses, underscoring the complex and manipulative power of rhetoric in past and present conflicts.

Beyond passive suffering: The agency of war victims

In this book, I have presented and analysed accounts from war victims, drawing on both interviews I conducted and available media interviews, all recorded during the conflict. For instance, Iraqi politician and MP Mithal al-Alousi spoke while the bodies of his sons, who had just been killed, lay nearby. I interviewed a Lebanese man who had lost his brother in a bombing and another who had lost his son. These speakers did not portray themselves as helpless victims, nor did they focus solely on their suffering or recount the details of what had happened. Instead, they articulated complex narratives that engaged with the future by interpreting the events they experienced, positioning themselves as active participants in these historical moments.

In their accounts, they integrated positive aspects of the war into their discourse, presenting themselves and their lost loved ones in a dignified and positive light. In Lebanon, many individuals who lost family members during the 2006 war expressed continued support for Hezbollah, framing their personal losses as sacrifices for the greater good of the community. This internalization of the war narrative is a powerful example of how collective identity and discursive construction can lead individuals to support continued violence, even at great personal cost. Similarly, in Iraq, laypeople who endured the invasion and civil conflict often echoed the sectarian rhetoric of their leaders, viewing the violence as a necessary part of their collective identity and struggle.

Also in the 2023 Gaza war, the narratives of laypeople who experienced the conflict first-hand reflected the discourses propagated by their leaders. Israeli civilians who lived under the threat of rocket attacks often justified the military's actions as necessary for their protection, even when those actions led to significant loss of life on both sides. Palestinian civilians, meanwhile, frequently expressed a sense of pride in their resilience and resistance, viewing their suffering as a necessary part of their collective struggle for liberation.

This type of trauma-discourse demands thorough investigation and should be examined within a broader context, as it sheds light on how people who suffer presents themselves, their suffering and their intentions. Understanding how people present themselves as resilient and willing to continue living, whether through repeating the same destructive patterns or through learning from mistakes of the past, can be key to understanding how to deal with traumatised people.

Each of the analysed discourses exhibits dual effects. On one hand, they contain positive self-presentations of the speaker and their group, detailed accounts of suffering, practical explanations of the events, and reasons to resist resignation. The speakers presented a cause and meaning for life. This can mitigate the overall negativity of the experience, shifting focus from the personal harms they endured to less damaging aspects of the situation. Such framing may contribute positively to general psychological well-being, helping individuals cope with these experiences and withstand overwhelming negative consequences (see Sheldon, Elliott, Kim, & Kasser, 2001; Tetlock & Manstead, 1985).

On the other hand, these accounts often validate and advance the position of one of the warring sides, directly or indirectly supporting their stance. Thus, I argue that such narratives can have destructive effects by rationalizing and endorsing the continuation of conflict.

This perspective provides a partial explanation for findings in the literature indicating that most people do not develop severe psychological disorders following war trauma (e.g., Hotopf et al., 2006; Thabet, Tawahina, Sarraj & Vostanis, 2008; Weine et al., 1995, 1998; Witmer & Culver, 2001). It also aligns with observations that, in many conflicts, individuals maintain their support for one of the sides despite the significant suffering inflicted upon them, thereby prolonging the conflict.

The presented analysis challenges traditional psychological frameworks that treat war and other complex adverse experiences as negative or predominantly negative, which have underpinned a substantial body of research (e.g., Begic &

Mcdonald, 2006; Ehlers, Mayou & Bryant, 1998; Muldoon & Downes, 2007; Thabet, Tawahina, Sarraj & Vostanis, 2008). Additionally, this book offers alternative explanations to studies suggesting that collective identity serves as a lens through which people interpret armed conflicts (e.g., Kellezi, Reicher & Cassidy, 2009). It also contrasts with research that assesses the experience of war as a potential source of personal growth or resilience (e.g., Boals & Schuettler, 2010; Bonanno, 2004, 2010; Wilson, 2006).

The construction and deployment of collective identity

Another significant finding from our analysis is the role of collective identity in shaping the understanding of these conflicts. Across all three case studies, political leaders and influential figures constructed and invoked collective identities to justify violence and garner support for their positions. In many instances, these identities were framed in ways that dehumanized the enemy and elevated the in-group as morally superior.

In Lebanon, Hezbollah's rhetoric during the 2006 war emphasized the collective identity of the Shia community and the broader Lebanese nation as being under existential threat from Israel. This collective identity was used to justify the war as a necessary defence of the community's survival. The same discursive strategies were observed in Iraq, where sectarian identities were emphasized and manipulated by leaders to justify violence against rival groups. Sunni and Shia leaders alike framed their actions as necessary to protect their respective communities from existential threats posed by the other side.

In the 2023 Gaza war, both Israeli and Palestinian leaders deployed collective identities to justify their actions. Israeli leaders framed their military operations as necessary to protect the Jewish state from external threats, while Palestinian leaders invoked the collective identity of the Palestinian people as victims of occupation, justifying resistance by any means necessary. These identities were actively constructed and reinforced through the narratives presented by leaders, often at the expense of dehumanizing the other side.

Contradictory views within the same accounts

Our analysis also uncovered how speakers, both political leaders and laypeople, sometimes presented contradictory views within the same accounts. These contradictions often reflected the complex and multifaceted nature of the conflicts themselves, as well as the discursive challenges involved in justifying actions that were, in many cases, deeply contentious.

For instance, in Lebanon, some political leaders would simultaneously acknowledge the destructive impact of the 2006 war on the Lebanese population while also justifying the conflict as necessary for the greater good. These contradictory statements reveal the tension between the desire to portray the war as a just cause and the reality of its devastating consequences (Norton, 2007). In Iraq, similar contradictions were observed in the narratives of those involved in the civil conflict. Leaders who had previously called for national unity would later justify sectarian violence as a necessary defence against existential threats, reflecting the deep divisions within the country and the conflicting pressures on these leaders.

The 2023 Gaza war provided further examples of such contradictions. Israeli leaders, for instance, often framed their military actions as efforts to avoid civilian casualties, even as those actions resulted in significant loss of life. Palestinian leaders, on the other hand, would condemn Israeli attacks while simultaneously justifying their own use of violence as a legitimate form of resistance. These contradictions highlight the complexities of war narratives and the challenges involved in maintaining a coherent justification for actions that are often morally and politically contentious.

Normalising the suffering of war

Another critical finding is how speakers reconstructed the deleterious effects of war as necessary or even beneficial, thereby justifying the continuation of conflict. This discursive strategy was particularly evident in the way political leaders and laypeople alike rationalized the suffering and destruction caused by war.

In Lebanon, Hezbollah and its supporters often portrayed the losses and devastation caused by the 2006 war as necessary sacrifices for the defence of Lebanon's sovereignty and dignity. The destruction was reframed as a testament to the resilience and heroism of the Lebanese people, rather than as a consequence of poor strategic decisions or unnecessary aggression (Norton, 2007). Similarly, in Iraq, the immense suffering caused by the civil conflict was often reframed by sectarian leaders as a necessary struggle for the future of their communities. The violence and destruction were depicted as unfortunate but essential steps toward achieving a just and secure future for their respective sects (Dodge, 2012).

In the Gaza conflict, both Israeli and Palestinian leaders used similar strategies. Israeli leaders often framed the destruction caused by their military operations as unfortunate but necessary to ensure the safety and security of the state. Palestinian leaders, particularly those affiliated with Hamas, portrayed the suffering of the Palestinian people as a necessary price for resistance and eventual liberation. In both cases, the devastating effects of the war were not denied but were instead reconstructed as necessary evils in the pursuit of a greater good (Shlaim, 2023).

Implications for conflict studies

The results of this study show that individuals who have personally suffered due to war may convey their experience in the form of complex accounts that contribute to the prolongation of the war, rather than calling for putting an end to it altogether. Several speakers reformulated the negative implications of the war into less repulsive depictions. They also tended to shift the focus from consequences of the war – of which they were witnesses and victims – to discussions of issues such as who was involved, why and how, producing accounts that blame a specific side but not the other(s). These accounts were designed to justify prolonging the conflicts.

Consequently, one practical way to campaign against wars in general is by highlighting the importance of examining discourses of war – both lay and political – as action-oriented constructions that can induce compound implications on several levels.

War persists, in part, because it is not universally viewed as wholly deleterious and ethically unjustifiable. Thus, researchers can contribute to the campaign against armed conflict through creating coherent discourses that challenge and counter the rhetorical formulations used to justify, warrant, or propagate the mass killing of others. Increasing the awareness of the negative effects of how notions such as dignity, national identity, religious identity, and patriotism are constructed and employed to foment divisions and legitimise war is an important means in the campaign against war.

Implications for psychotherapy

It has frequently been argued that the impact of psychological research on psychotherapy has been limited and that current models of psychotherapy do not adequately reflect the rapidly growing body of psychological research (Castonguay et al., 2010). Several researchers have complained that psychological studies in general fail to examine the fundamental questions of psychotherapy (Beutler, Williams, Wakefield & Entwistle, 1995; Elliott, 1983; Goldfried & Wolfe, 1996). The findings of this study can provide both theoretical and practical insights into one of the important, yet underexplored, questions related to psychotherapy, that is, how and why people convey extreme experiences within their talk. These findings align with a number of discursive studies that argue for incorporating theoretical understandings of discourse into psychotherapy (e.g. Fee, 2000; Gibson, 2011).

Launer (1999) notes that one of the predicaments of psychotherapy is the discrepancy between the patient's and the therapist's versions of the problem at stake. He indicates that patients usually present their complaints in the form of complex narratives that offer a specific version of reality, which may not be compatible with the therapist's less complex and more concise version. This study argues that to fully understand and explain the experience of war and loss, we need to appraise the involved individuals' accounts as complex, functional formations with multiple effects, rather than as accurate reflections of reality or the speaker's feelings. As demonstrated in the extracts above, participants - who were involved in war and have suffered due to it - have formulated narratives that integrate, attend to, and deal with a wide range of internal and external issues simultaneously. Some of these issues are theoretical, such as discussions of culpability and justification, while others are more practical, concerned with reflecting and presenting specific versions of reality and advancing certain stances. Each of these accounts must be approached as a cohesive whole.

Similarly, therapists working with patients who convey their complaints in the form of complex formations may need to analyse these accounts as holistic formations, recognising their action-orientation and the various effects they may produce (see Burr & Butt, 2000).

The issue of collective identity

In this book, I presented 36 extracts related to conflicts that took place in three different countries. The different speakers, whether decision-makers or lay people, presented the events from the prism of collective identity. If we look at how Joe Biden, Benjamin Netanyahu, and Hassan Nasrallah presented the ongoing conflict, we see that they started by designating the audience they are interested in addressing. They use the "we" and "I" to build bonds with the audience and invoke emotions and call for specific action.

The findings of this study are in line with SIT and SCT literature that argues that collective identity plays a crucial role in our understanding of who we are, who other people are, and the world. The various speakers, whether decision makers reading a scripted speech or participating in a TV interview or laypeople speaking their minds anonymously, constructed and deployed narratives based on "us" and "them". Hence, the nature of events, the fighting sides, the right course of action are interwoven with the speaker's collective identity.

Contribution to discursive methods

The findings of this book make several methodological contributions. Firstly, this study has shown that the Arab participants use discursive devices that have been identified and explained in Western studies, indicating that discursive analysis can be effectively applied in Arabic-speaking societies. This is consistent with previous research that argued for the universal nature of talk (e.g., Wong & Olsher, 2000).

Secondly, this research provides a strong argument for the use of interviews in data collection, in particular when examining laypeople's views on conflicts.

Thirdly, this book highlights the importance of analysing lay, as well as political, accounts of war within their context and in a comprehensive way. It demonstrates the importance of examining what people who have been in war say, how they present themselves, and what they frame as relevant and important notions in relation to the conflict. This challenges studies that assume victims of war view the situation in limited ways, thereby restricting their perceived options for dealing with it. For instance, several studies examining the effects of the Lebanese war on civilians started from the notion that the Lebanese viewed the war as an extreme and unique event. In contrast, as Potter and Wetherell (1987) argue, such an approach overlooks the fact that people can construct and compose the world in an infinite number of ways.

References

Begic, S. & McDonald, T. W. (2006). The psychological effects of exposure to wartime trauma in Bosnian residents and refugees: implications for treatment and service provision. *International Journal of Mental Health and Addiction, 4*(3), 319-329.

Beutler, L. E., Williams, R. E., Wakefield, P. J., & Entwistle, S. R. (1995). Bridging scientist and practitioner perspectives in clinical psychology. *American Psychologist, 50*(12), 984–994.

Boals, A., & Schuettler, D. (2010). Advancing our understanding of posttraumatic growth by considering event centrality. *Journal of Loss and Trauma, 15*(6), 518–533.

Bonanno, G. A. (2004). Loss, trauma, and human resilience: Have we underestimated the human capacity to thrive after extremely aversive events? *American Psychologist, 59*(1), 20–28.

Bonanno, G. A. (2010). *The other side of sadness: What the new science of bereavement tells us about life after loss.* New York, NY: Basic Books.

Burr, V., & Butt, T. (2000). Psychological distress and postmodern thought. In D. Fee (Ed.), *Pathology and the postmodern: Mental illness as discourse and experience* (pp. 187–202). London, England: Sage.

Castonguay, L. G., Boswell, J. F., Constantino, M. J., Goldfried, M. R., & Hill, C. E. (2010). Training implications of harmful effects of psychological treatments. *American Psychologist, 65*(1), 34–49.

Dodge, T. (2012). *Iraq: From war to a new authoritarianism.* New York, NY: Routledge.

Ehlers, A., Mayou, R. A., & Bryant, B. (1998). Psychological predictors of chronic posttraumatic stress disorder after motor vehicle accidents. *Journal of Abnormal Psychology, 107*(3), 508–519.

Elliott, R. (1983). Fitting process research to the practicing therapist. *Psychotherapy: Theory, Research & Practice, 20*(1), 47–55.

Fee, D. (Ed.). (2000). *Pathology and the postmodern: Mental illness as discourse and experience.* London, England: Sage.

Gibson, M. (2011). *Melancholia and moralism: Essays on AIDS and queer politics.* Minneapolis, MN: University of Minnesota Press.

Goldfried, M. R., & Wolfe, B. E. (1996). Psychotherapy practice and research: Repairing a strained alliance. *American Psychologist, 51*(10), 1007–1016.

Hotopf, M., Hull, L., Fear, N. T., Browne, T., Horn, O., Iversen, A., Jones,

M. , Murphy, D., Bland, D., Earnshaw, M., Greenberg, N., Hacker Hughes, J., Tate, A. R., Dandeker, C., Rona, R. & Wessely, S. (2006). The health of UK military personnel who deployed to the 2003 Iraq war: a cohort study. Lancet, 367(9524), 1731 –1741.

Kellezi, B., Reicher. D. & Cassidy, C. (2009). Surviving the Kosovo conflict: A study of social identity, appraisal of extreme events, and mental well-being. Applied Psychology; An international Review. *Special issue: Social Identity, Health and Well-being, 58*(1), 59-83.

Launer, J. (1999). *Narrative-based primary care: A practical guide.* Oxford, England: Radcliffe Medical Press.

Muldoon, O. T. & Downes, C. (2007). Social identification and post-traumatic stress symptoms in post-conflict Northern Ireland. *British Journal of Psychiatry, 191*(8), 146–149.

Norton, A. R. (2007). *Hezbollah: A Short History.* Princeton University Press.

Potter, J., & Wetherell, M. (1987). *Discourse and social psychology: Beyond attitudes and behaviour.* London: Sage.

Sheldon, K. M., Elliott, A. J., Kim, Y., & Kasser, T. (2001). What is satisfying about satisfying events? Testing 10 candidate psychological needs. *Journal of Personality and Social Psychology, 80*(2), 325–339.

Shlaim, A. (2023). *Three worlds: Memoirs of an Arab-Jew.* London: Oneworld Publications.

Tetlock, P. E., & Manstead, A. S. R. (1985). Impression management versus intrapsychic explanations in social psychology: A useful dichotomy? *Psychological Review, 92*(1), 59–77.

Thabet, A. A., Abu Tawahina, A., El Sarraj, E., & Vostanis, P. (2008). Exposure to war trauma and PTSD among parents and children in the Gaza strip. *European Child & Adolescent Psychiatry, 17*(4), 191-199.

Weine, S.M., Becker, D.F., McGlashan, T.H., Laub, D., Lazrove, S., Vojvoda, D. & Hyman, L. (1995). Psychiatric consequences of "ethnic cleansing": Clinical assessments and trauma testimonies of newly resettled Bosnian refugees. *American Journal of Psychiatry, 152*(4), 536-542.

Weine, S.M., Vojvoda, D., Becker, D.F., McGlashan, T.H., Hodzic, E., Laub, D., Hyman, L., Sawyer, M. & Lazrove, S. (1998). PTSD symptoms in Bosnian refugees one year after resettlement in the United States. *American Journal of Psychiatry, 155*(4), 562–64.

Wilson, J. P. (2006). *The posttraumatic self: Restoring meaning and wholeness to personality.* New York, NY: Routledge.

Witmer, T. A. & Culver, S. M. (2001). Trauma and resilience among Bosnian refugee families: A critical review of the literature. *Journal of Social Work Research and Evaluation, 2*(2), 173-187.

Wong, J., & Olsher, D. (2000). Reflections on talk as a universal tool: Comparative studies in conversational analysis. In A. Liddicoat & C. Crozet (Eds.), *Second language conversations* (pp. 111-129). London: Continuum.

www.ingramcontent.com/pod-product-compliance
Lightning Source LLC
Chambersburg PA
CBHW062050270326
41931CB00013B/3010

9781739308667